The Royal Navy since 1815

Related titles from Palgrave Macmillan

Christopher M. Bell, *The Royal Navy, Seapower and Strategy between the Wars*
James Levy, *The Royal Navy's Home Fleet in World War Two*
Joseph A. Maiolo, *The Royal Navy and Nazi Germany, 1933–39*

The Royal Navy since 1815

A New Short History

Eric J. Grove

First published 2005 by
PALGRAVE MACMILLAN
Houndmills, Basingstoke, Hampshire RG21 6XS and
175 Fifth Avenue, New York, N.Y. 10010
Companies and representatives throughout the world

PALGRAVE MACMILLAN is the global academic imprint of the Palgrave
Macmillan division of St. Martin's Press, LLC and of Palgrave Macmillan Ltd.
Macmillan® is a registered trademark in the United States, United Kingdom
and other countries. Palgrave is a registered trademark in the European
Union and other countries.

ISBN 0–333–72125–X hardback
ISBN 0–333–72126–8 paperback

This book is printed on paper suitable for recycling and made from fully
managed and sustained forest sources.

A catalogue record for this book is available from the British Library.

A catalog record for this book is available from the Library of Congress.

10   9   8   7   6   5   4   3   2   1
14   13 12 11 10 09 08 07 06 05

Printed in China

Contents

Acknowledgements

There has been no single-author general history of the modern Royal Navy written in recent years that has had the benefit of including the perspectives of the group of naval historians who have done much over the last quarter of a century to change our views of how and why British naval development took the form it did in the nineteenth and twentieth centuries. I set out in this book to synthesize their work to provide a relatively short narrative that, it is hoped, will provide an up-to-date summary of Royal Navy policy, structure, technical development and operations from the end of the Napoleonic Wars to the close of the eventful twentieth century.

Length has been a great problem and the social side of the service has had to be relatively neglected, although important personnel developments are necessarily included. Inevitably, the text reflects what I think interesting at any period and others might have emphasized different aspects. I have also chosen the interpretations which seemed most convincing at the time of writing; others are entitled to disagree. In these senses, this is both an original work and 'synthetic' in the best sense. It is essentially what I teach and I hope it will be helpful to all who study naval history and strategy professionally, educationally and out of private enthusiasm and interest.

As can be seen in the relatively small number of notes, this book owes everything to my long-standing friends in the naval historical field who have comprehensively rewritten the subject in recent times; notably Professors Andrew Lambert, Jon Sumida and Geoffrey Till, Drs Andrew Gordon and Nicholas Lambert and Commodore James Goldrick RAN. My own original research complements theirs to cover the whole period. I express my thanks to them and my other sources – especially to John F. Beeler, both for his books and for his helpful comments on the first draft, and the increasing numbers of excellent researchers following in our footsteps. None is responsible for the blemishes in what follows, all are responsible for what strengths readers may find in it.

I must also express my appreciation to my publishers who have been more than forbearing with the many delays forced upon an author beset with the pressures of modern academic life and family upheavals. I am also more than grateful to three dear ladies who played key roles. My first wife Elizabeth Grove in her new profession of editor did much to improve and shorten the manuscript and she also provided the index. My friend and former student Mrs Jean Rostollan did much to motivate me to begin writing in earnest. Most of all, my new wife Sarian inspired me to finish, as part of the positive transformation of my life that this remarkable lady has wrought since the summer of 2003. This book is dedicated to her.

Eric J. Grove

Centre for Security Studies
University of Hull

To Sarian

Foreword

Geoffrey Till

It is said that military history (including naval history, of course) has become the new 'gardening' – at least as far as British television is concerned. Every evening, it seems, we are treated to some new account of a major battle or campaign, some breathless archaeological dig, or a major investigation of the place of the Army, or the Navy or the Air Force in national development. The less personally acquainted the public are with the military life, the more interested they seem to be in it. This media interest is replicated in the universities as well. There are far more courses in naval history than there were back in the 1970s and 1980s when the subject seemed to be in the doldrums. At public records offices and other archive centres, one can hardly move for eager young historians researching new aspects of naval history or seeking material that challenges established wisdom. These exhilarating developments have resulted in a sea of books partly, but by no means exclusively, driven by an apparently insatiable appetite for anniversary books of past campaigns or major events.

This naval renaissance has resulted in what Eric Grove has aptly termed a new history and it has tended to focus on two things. The first is to explore the place of naval power in national development. The contemporary preoccupation with concepts of 'Empire' partly results from concerns about the role of the United States in the twenty-first century, and partly by the need to come to some conclusion about the legacy of empire in helping to explain current political troubles. This has encouraged investigation of the role of seapower in the establishment of empire, in the creation and defence of international trading systems and in the development of a country's sense of itself. From this perspective, naval history provides a major window into national and international life. It helps us understand a country's image of itself, of its role in the world; this kind of naval history is also essential for any understanding of how the world worked in the past, and how it might work in the future.

The second major focus of the new naval history (this time encouraged by modern concerns about the political, economic, social and moral implications of scientific and technological advance) has concentrated on the way in which navies have responded to new technology, and in the way in which that new technology has helped shape naval fortunes. Thirty or forty years ago, it was almost the established wisdom to argue that admirals were a conservative lot, completely out of tune with contemporary technological advances and incapable of seeing what it could mean for the future of their service. But over the last few decades, shoals of books have appeared that challenge this tired old 'blunted trident' thesis, with major re-evaluations of naval responses to the arrival of iron and steam, the submarine, the aircraft, and so on. All these re-interpretations have reinforced our need to think through what they mean for the way we try to understand how navies work, and what they do. This aspect of naval history also provides a fascinating case study of the much broader issue of the complex relationship between the human race and the technological advance it produces.

From all these perspectives we need a straightforward summarizing work of synthesis that explains in a manageable and accessible style where we are now after the first stage of this naval renaissance. And this, of course, is what Eric Grove aims to provide. The balanced account that follows incorporates the results of the latest thinking on innumerable issues confronting the Royal Navy since 1815. It will surely become the definitive introductory text for all courses in British naval history in universities and service colleges around the world. His review of the workings of British seapower will help naval practitioners and all those interested in their ways understand the past better, and in the longer term ensure that the renaissance in naval history (and perhaps in naval fortunes too?) continues deeper into the twenty-first century.

Dean of Academic Studies
King's College London at the Joint Services Command and Staff College

1 The Coming of Steam

When the Napoleonic Wars ended in 1815 the Royal Navy was supreme on the world's oceans. The established rival navies of mainland Europe had been comprehensively defeated and the upstart United States put in its place by an aggressive maritime campaign. Control of the seas remained vital for the maintenance of Britain's imperial position after her victory over Napoleon's Empire, and Britain's leaders had every intention of asserting it.[1] However, there was no intention of maintaining a wartime-sized fleet. The annual numbers of sailors and Royal Marines voted by Parliament were already massively and rapidly decreasing from over 140,000 in 1813 to only 19,000 in 1817 although numbers actually borne were almost 23,000.[2] The number of officers employed in 1817 was almost 600, a reduction to less than 25 per cent of the 1813 figure.[3] Ships in commission came down from a peak of 713 in 1814 to 121 in 1818.[4]

One reason for shortage of funds was Parliament's abolition of income tax, which severely strained government finances, given the demands of servicing the war-inflated National Debt.[5] In 1817 the Select Committee on Finance recommended annual Naval Estimates of no more than £6 million (against almost £23 million in 1815). The Admiralty was able to squeeze a little more out of the Government into the 1820s but the peacetime naval spending was reduced by more than half as a proportion of the total budget.[6]

In this atmosphere of stringency, the naval authorities strove to maintain a fleet that could both execute its enhanced peacetime commitments and provide a sufficiently dominant force to deter and defeat likely opponents. In 1817 Foreign Secretary Castlereagh pronounced a two-power standard of naval strength and the following year set the standard for the rest of the nineteenth century by stating

1

that a combination of France and Russia was the 'only one that can prove really formidable to the liberties of Europe'.[7]

Given the poor condition of wartime ships built out of inferior timber, only 79 line-of-battle ships were fit for service, against a target of 100. The situation with frigates was even worse, with only 78 ships ready for service against a requirement for 160. Policy makers had to balance the various financial and manpower demands of new construction, repair and the maintenance of a seagoing fleet of sufficient strength.[8]

The authorities who grappled with these difficulties were the Admiralty and the Navy Board: the former was in charge of policy and overall direction, the latter in charge of the administration and upkeep of the ships of the fleet. They occupied different buildings in London, the former in Whitehall, the latter in Somerset House. The Navy Board pre-dated the Admiralty as a committee formed by Henry VIII to control his growing 'Navy Royal' in the sixteenth century. The Lords Commissioners for the Execution of the Office of Lord High Admiral dated back to the Revolution Settlement of 1689, although there was a brief period when the Lord Admiral resumed his personal duties from 1702 to 1709. In 1815 the Board of Admiralty had just evolved into its 'modern' form, headed by a politician and with a senior professional officer serving as First Naval Lord (although the latter still had a party affiliation).

The First Lord from 1812 was the amiable, judicious, experienced and powerful Robert Dundas, Second Viscount Melville.[9] Melville held the political reins in the Navy until 1830, with only a short break when the Duke of Clarence (later King William IV) was appointed Lord Admiral in 1827–8. Melville's influence was profound, notably in the selection of Admiral Sir Thomas Byam Martin as Controller, the Head of the Navy Board. Martin exerted enormous influence on the size and state of the fleet until his removal in 1831.

Melville and Martin were not the only key figures of this period. A third was Sir Robert Seppings, a Surveyor of the Navy from 1813 to 1832. As an Assistant Surveyor he had developed a new system of framing ships diagonally that greatly increased their strength. He also introduced new bow and stern structures that not only increased structural strength but also reduced vulnerability to raking fire. His improvements were major advances in ship design and were part of the contemporary technological revolution. Seppings also introduced iron into the construction of ships, using iron diagonal frames in frigates and smaller ships to save on timber and to increase volume.

Seppings's design features were introduced both into new ships and older vessels that were given 'large repairs', i.e. were rebuilt. Byam Martin was an enthusiast for large and powerful ships. No more 74-gun two-deckers (which made up almost half the operational fleet of 14 ships of the line in commission in 1820) were ordered after 1817.[10] The new standard for ships of the line was the 84-gun two-decker and the 120-gun three-decker. Some larger frigates were built from new or converted from smaller ships of the line.[11] In 1820 there were three 58–60-gun frigates in commission plus 18 of 42–50 guns and 14 of 24–26 guns. Thirty of the standard new Leda-class frigates, with 38 guns (plus eight carronades), were launched between 1816 and 1830.[12] Of the 42 sloops in commission in 1820, 23 were the traditional 18-gun type.

In 1821, under constant economic pressure, the Admiralty decided that its original plans for a mobilized wartime fleet were too ambitious. Cuts in ship orders would allow cuts in the dockyard labour force that would in turn allow a larger peacetime commissioned fleet. By 1823 the estimates were reduced to only £5.4 million, although the number of men rose to 26,000.

Naval Estimates grew again to over £6 million in 1827 because of the first of the many nineteenth-century naval scares. Heavily armed French and American ships were causing concern and the armament of British ships of the line was enhanced with more 32-pounders. The first completely new postwar class of ships of the line, the 90-gun Nile class, was ordered. By April 1827 the number of ships of the line in commission had increased to 17, with a further 57 fit for service. More 74-guns were cut down to provide powerfully armed large frigates.

The increased Naval Estimates was also connected with the brief ascendancy of George Canning, the former Foreign Secretary, who combined the duties of Prime Minister and Chancellor of the Exchequer. Canning also temporarily abolished the Admiralty, making William, Duke of Clarence, Lord High Admiral. It was expected that the King's brother would be no more than a figurehead and his Council would carry out the duties of the Board of Admiralty as before but William seized his chance to spend money to improve the lot of naval personnel. Although Clarence outlasted Canning, the Duke of Wellington as Prime Minister restored both Melville and the Board of Admiralty in September 1828. The following year's Naval Estimates reverted back to below £6 million, a figure they would not reach again until 1842.

Given this level of financial stringency, it is surprising how quickly the Admiralty and Navy Board adopted the new technology of steam propulsion. It is too often quoted that Melville's Admiralty 'felt it their bounden duty to discourage to the utmost of their ability the employment of steam vessels'. This statement represents the opposite of the truth.[13] A Mechanist to the Navy Board, Simon Goodrich, had been appointed as early as 1814, but attempts in 1815 to build a steamer, *Congo*, to explore the river of that name, failed because the engines were too heavy. By 1819 steam vessels were beginning to tow sailing ships in and out of harbour and between ports. Rather than creating their own craft, the cash-strapped Navy Board commissioned the Post Office to build and operate a steamer for the Holyhead–Dublin run. Goodrich examined these vessels and in November 1821 *Comet* was laid down by the Admiralty at Deptford, for completion the following year. She was 115 feet long and had 80 hp engines. The larger *Lightning* followed in 1823. She was first used as a coastal tug but was soon used to support ships on operational deployments.[14]

The wind was being conquered. By the end of 1827 *Lightning* was joined by *Meteor* and *Echo* and the Lord High Admiral appointed an established crew under a Lieutenant RN to the three ships. Thus they appeared in the 1828 Navy List as HM Ships (*Comet* achieved this status in 1831). Each was armed with two small guns. By 1829 the Royal Navy possessed a total of eight paddle steamers and had under construction a much larger steam warship, *Dee*, ordered in 1827 as one of the last acts of Melville's Board of Admiralty. Steam greatly increased the power of the fleet to project power at close ranges. This littoral emphasis in naval operations was clearly shown in the immediate aftermath of the Napoleonic War, in the bombardment of Algiers.

In the summer of 1816 Lord Exmouth was put in command of five ships of the line, five frigates, three sloops, two brigs and four bomb vessels, *Beelzebub, Fury, Hecla* and *Infernal*, the latter fitted out as an explosion vessel.[15] The British gunners had been specially trained for accuracy, with gunnery practice twice daily and full broadsides fired by each ship twice a week.

The bombardment began at 15:00 on 27 August. Exmouth was able to anchor his flagship within 80 yards of the battery at the head of the harbour mole. At this range the hail of accurate fire from his 50-gun broadsides were able to sweep away the Algerines. *Impregnable*, whose armament had been enhanced with heavier guns, anchored at longer range, but was unable to overwhelm its target before suffering serious casualties. The bombardment was maintained for nine hours, the bigger ships being supported by the smaller craft. *Infernal* was also sent in and exploded, though not in the position planned. The Algerine pirates' ships were burnt and the Dey acquiesced to British terms by releasing Christian prisoners. Algiers was a transitional action: it demonstrated the developing potential of well-deployed and well-armed ships against shore batteries but it also showed that shore-mounted artillery remained a significant threat. There were 818 casualties, with 128 dead. As Lambert says: 'a 16% casualty rate made this as bloody a battle as any in the age of sail'.[16]

The Algerine Treaties were short-lived and, in early 1824, another bombardment was being prepared. The paddle steamer *Lightning* was sent out, which made what was probably the longest voyage yet made by a steamer.[17] The intention was for her to tow sailing ships into the best bombardment positions, but this was not required as the Dey submitted to British pressure without the need for a full-scale action. Nevertheless it was the first operational deployment by a Royal Navy steamer.

In 1825 Mehemet Ali, the French-backed autonomous Egyptian warlord, sent forces to assist the Turks against the Greeks who had been in revolt since 1821. Propelled by pro-Greek public opinion, the British, who were concerned that this situation must not provide an opportunity for Russian expansion, joined with the French and Russians in the Treaty of London in July 1827 and offered mediation. The Greeks accepted but Turkey did not. Instructions were sent to the naval commanders in the area to enter into friendly relations with the Greeks and 'to intercept any expedition by sea, of men, arms etc. destined against Greece and coming from either Turkey or from Africa in general'.[18]

The British naval commander in the Mediterranean was the aggressive Vice Admiral Sir Edward Codrington, 'Go it Ned', who had been repelled by Egyptian conduct in Greece and was in favour of 'strong coercion' of Turkey.[19] A Muslim fleet of about 100 vessels was amassed at Alexandria.[20] To pre-empt diplomatic pressure forcing him to climb down, Mehemet Ali began to send these ships to sea on 5 August. This was a timely precaution as, two days later, Codrington received orders to intercept the Ottoman fleet and to act under the authority of Stratford Canning, British Ambassador at Constantinople. Canning authorized the admiral to use force if necessary to enforce the armistice. The Ottomans eluded their pursuers and arrived at Navarino on 7–8 September. Codrington had only five ships but he was confident enough of their fighting abilities to threaten the Turkish admiral with his orders to prevent the Ottoman reinforcement of Greece. Any firing at British ships would be 'fatal to the Ottoman fleet'.[21] On 25 September a temporary truce was achieved.

Codrington ordered a concentration of Allied ships off Navarino on 10 October. The Allied fleet was composed of three British ships of the line, four frigates, a sloop, three brigs and a cutter; seven French ships and eight Russian.[22] Codrington flew his flag in the powerful 84-gun two-decker *Asia*, armed with two ranks of 32-pounders in the latest style, supplemented by thin-walled, short-barrelled 42-pounder carronades on the upper deck. The other two British ships of the line were 74s, HMS *Albion*, launched in 1802 and a veteran of Algiers, and HMS *Genoa*, taken over from the French while being built in Genoa in 1814. Their armament comprised 18- and 24-pounders.

The 42-gun frigate *Dartmouth* went into Navarino on 18 October and obtained good intelligence concerning the Ottoman dispositions. The latter had over 60 warships of all sizes, but only three ships of the line.[23] The Allies agreed to enter Navarino on the 19th to force a more co-operative attitude from the Ottomans. Winds were too light to allow entry on that day and there were no available steamers, although Codrington had asked for them. The operation was therefore delayed until 20 October.

As they arrived the lead British ships anchored. Tension was great and when the boat of a British frigate sent to remove a threatening fireship was fired upon, the shooting became general. *Asia* disabled the Turkish flagship and, after an abortive attempt to make a truce with the Egyptian flagship, engaged her next. *Asia*'s powerful armament tore huge holes in the Egyptian's side. The battle raged for the rest of the day but the superior fighting qualities of the Allied ships proved devastating. They were more heavily armed and better built and their gunners were more experienced. The Ottoman fleet was almost annihilated, many damaged vessels being blown up by their own crews. One of the ships of the line and the four Egyptian frigates were able eventually to return to Alexandria as part of 46 survivors, some of them heavily damaged, that arrived by the end of the year. Ottoman human casualties, however, were great: 6000–7000 (ten times those of the Allies).

This was a violent form of what a later age would call 'peace enforcement'. The international force, having released Turkish prisoners, turned its attention to the Greeks, threatening them with Navarino-type sanctions if they persisted in operations outside their recognized blockading areas. The fleet, however, had to lick its wounds and the British, followed by the Russians, retired to Malta. All three British ships of the line had to be sent home for repairs but Mehemet Ali had been overawed and told British representatives there would be no war or reprisals. The Turks were less happy and threatened war, which eventually broke out with Russia alone in April 1828.

At home, the government was embarrassed by the scale of Codrington's victory, and the coming to power of Wellington saw a shift of policy in a more pro-Turkish direction. His government's King's Speech at the opening of Parliament called the battle an 'untoward event' concerning 'an ancient ally'.[24] Codrington was left in limbo at Malta. Not until May was he allowed to follow up his victory and blockade Greek ports in Turkish or Egyptian hands. In July a direct blockade of Alexandria began. The previous month Codrington had learned that the Foreign Secretary had demanded his recall but he was determined to obtain Egyptian agreement to a withdrawal from Greece before returning home. Codrington went in person to Alexandria to confer with Mehemet Ali and in August

1828 an agreement was signed covering the withdrawal of Egyptian forces from Greece. The promise of Navarino had been fulfilled.

Wellington's attitude to Codrington reflected his general approach to foreign and defence policy. The Iron Duke believed that economic realities demanded a less forward foreign posture. His attempts to trim expenditure, however, were countered by Sir George Cockburn, the able First Naval Lord who took up office in 1828. Cockburn had, as Second Naval Lord, been a strong supporter of Codrington. Each of the admirals was as ruthless and aggressive as the other, Cockburn having been responsible for the burning of Washington. Quoting foreign naval strength, Cockburn was able to prevent the Government's Finance Committee cutting the Naval Estimates too far; sailors and marines actually borne remained above 31,000.[25]

The battlefleet was in quite good shape, with 71 ships in good order and 19 building, meeting the revised wartime establishment of 90 ships.[26] Byam Martin tried to get more money out of Melville, who, as part of a government being pressed for tax cuts, could not oblige. The situation got even worse in 1830 when a new and reforming Whig administration took over under Sir Edward Grey. The incoming Whigs were no friends of the existing naval establishment and the winds of reform were about to blow over the Royal Navy – with storm force.

In opposition the Whigs had been strong supporters of cuts in the Naval Estimates, not least Sir James Graham, who became First Lord on 25 November 1830. Prime Minister Grey, whose last government post had been First Lord in 1806, and whose opinions on the Navy Board and the dockyards had been negatively influenced by Lord St Vincent, heavily influenced Graham. The First Lord ordered cuts in the line-of-battleship programme and in the dockyard labour force. There was a strong political imperative to discredit the Navy Board. As Lambert says, 'First, it would reinforce the commitment to change that had been central to the Whigs' appeal to the radical elements; and second it would provide the financial savings needed to bribe the independent landowning members who were vital to the passage of the major item on the political agenda, the Bill to reform parliamentary representation.'[27]

The Whigs were also deeply suspicious of the Tory character of the existing naval administration, in an era when the concept of apolitical officials was not yet established. Both Martin and Cockburn were Tory MPs and, although Martin stayed in office as Controller and head of the Navy Board, Cockburn was replaced as First Naval Lord by Nelson's former flag captain Admiral Sir Thomas Hardy. The situation was untenable and, after Grey had informed the King that Graham and Hardy found it impossible to conduct business with Byam Martin, the latter was dismissed on 17 October 1831. His replacement was Admiral George Dundas.

The Admiralty was now firmly in control of the Navy Board, but Grey and Graham wanted more. In the Admiralty Act of 1832 the Navy Board was abolished and the Board of Admiralty took over the entire administration of the Navy. Five Principal Officers – the Surveyor, Accountant General, Storekeeper General, Controller of Victualling and Physician General – were created, each responsible to a member of the Board, who, in turn, reported to the First Lord, who was responsible to Parliament.[28] The historic Navy Board ceased to exist in June 1832.

This administrative earthquake saw the appointment of a new Surveyor, Sir William Symonds, on 9 June. Symonds was a controversial figure with strong ideas on warship design. As Lambert has pointed out, he was intended more as a policy director in the new organization, but he could not resist imposing his strong ideas and was allowed to do so by the Admiralty. Work on existing designs was thus suspended and new ships were laid down according to the new principles.

Construction of new vessels proceeded slowly, however, as the Whigs cut the Naval Estimates. By 1833 these were down to £4.8 million, and £4.7 million in 1834, just over 9 per cent of the total national budget.[29] Cuts were made in dockyard staff and those clerks who were not made redundant had their working hours increased; rations at sea were also reduced. The number of men actually borne was 28,000 in 1834.[30] The number of officers employed at this time was about a thousand.[31] In 1834 the Fleet was made up of 16 ships of the line, with 72 in Ordinary, 6 large frigates with 14 in Ordinary, 8 smaller frigates with 60 in Ordinary, 17 steamers and 140 other vessels.[32]

The need for operational deployments took resources away from new construction. The forward diplomacy of Palmerston, the Whig Foreign Secretary, required the backing of British naval power. A British squadron had long been in the Tagus off Lisbon. It supported Portuguese independence from Spain, Brazilian independence from Portugal, and influenced Portuguese politics.[33] Strength varied: three ships of the line and a frigate in 1824, two of each type in 1826. The need to maintain forward presence meant ships rarely went to sea (one ship of the line was at anchor for a year and a half!) and the force was ultimately strengthened to three ships of the line and three sloops to allow sea training to be given to crews without arousing Portuguese apprehensions. In 1831, with civil war raging ashore between the constitutionalist and absolutist factions, the squadron had to be reinforced still further using, among others, units from Codrington's Squadron of Evolution, formed to conduct trials on new hull forms. During another crisis in 1836, when the Portuguese Queen had to be rescued by British Marines from rebels, the Tagus Squadron was increased to six ships of the line and it continued to be significant until the 1850s.[34]

The threat of France dominating Belgium (which had successfully revolted against the Netherlands in 1830) was a strategic factor in the formation of the Squadron of Evolution in 1831. It was deployed off the Belgian coast to encourage a withdrawal of French forces sent to assist the Belgians against a Dutch invasion. Further naval deployments were carried out in the Downs to deter a Dutch counter-attack in October 1831.[35]

In order to pressure the Dutch into a settlement, a blockade of the Netherlands was instituted in 1832, in co-operation with the French. The ships were again largely from the Squadron of Evolution. In late 1832 Sir Pulteney Malcolm deployed five ships of the line, four frigates, seven sloops, a brig and two steamers (*Dee* and *Rhadamanthus*).[36] The blockade had only limited effect and was unpopular with trading interests at home but it did, together with French operations ashore, help achieve a modus vivendi between the Belgians and Dutch.

The combination of Portuguese and North Sea commitments stretched the operational fleet, as it was capable of only coping with two European crises at once.[37] The impossibility of making a show of strength in the Mediterranean contributed to Turkey falling under Russian influence as she sought protection in the aftermath of Mehemet Ali's expansion into Syria in 1832. Once the Belgian crisis began to fade, reinforcements began to be sent and, by the autumn, Malcolm (commanding in the Mediterranean once more) had six ships of the line and a supporting steamer. The Tagus Squadron was available for further reinforcement and, with the French fleet, his force was more than a match for the Russian Black Sea Fleet. The Ambassador at Constantinople was authorized to bring the Mediterranean Fleet through the Dardanelles, should Turkey request it. This show of coalition naval strength, combined with naval pressure on Mehemet Ali not to try for independence, had the required effect: Turkey began to move away from Russia.[38]

In 1834 Graham left office, closely followed by his mentor Grey. Graham was replaced by Lord Auckland and Grey by Lord Melbourne. The pressure for cuts in Estimates continued, however, and Sir Thomas Hardy could take no more. In August he resigned to take over Greenwich Hospital, being replaced, first by Admiral George Dundas, then, shortly afterwards, by Admiral Sir Charles Adam. Auckland laid down a new establishment. Graham had left 11 ships of the line in commission and 11 'advanced', more or less fitted out and ready for their crews. Much political capital had been made of these ships but they decayed at the same rate as ships in commission. Thirty-six other ships were deemed to be 'in good repair' and 30 in need of repair. Fifteen were being built or repaired, giving a total of 103 (not counting ships in harbour service). Auckland proposed a reduced establishment of 75 ships of the line (25 of each rate) and 25 fourth-rate large frigates (the promotion of the latter category to capital status being noteworthy). Of these, 50 would be afloat, 25 complete on the stocks and 25 framed and ready for completion.[39]

At the end of 1834 the Tories briefly returned to power under Sir Robert Peel. A minority Prime Minister, Peel continued the policy of economy, but further reductions would have caused problems. De Grey, the new First Lord, consulted the Foreign Secretary, the Duke of Wellington, on policy requirements and, although manpower was cut to 26,000, the Estimates were reduced only minimally, to £4.4 million.

The Whigs returned to power in April 1835. The Earl of Minto replaced Auckland with Sir Charles Adam as his First Naval Lord. A reluctant government granted them £4.7 million in 1836 and £4.9 million in 1837 and the number of men voted increased to 34,000.[40] In mid-1836 there were 20 ships of the line in commission (eight at home, three guardships, six in the Mediterranean and three at Lisbon). The King opposed reductions in this active force, indeed measures were taken to improve the readiness of the advanced ships in Ordinary, all of which reduced funds for Symonds's new ships. Minto and Adam preferred to rely on repairs to existing units.[41]

The first ship of the line to be built on Symondite principles was HMS *Vanguard*, laid down in May 1833. A sister, *Goliath*, had been ordered the same year but there was a gap until *Superb* was ordered in 1838. Symonds had been able to restart a third-rate *Boscawen* to his new design, as a 70-gun two-decker, in 1834 and a sister, *Cumberland*, followed about two years later, but neither of these ships were in the water until the following decade. Symonds kept up the pressure for new construction, but with little success when the Treasury was exhorting the Admiralty 'to take every step in their power to reduce the Public Expenditure in their Lordships' department, to the utmost possible extent which is practicable without detriment to H. M.'s service'.[42]

In these circumstances, it is a sign of clear perception of its utility that investment in steam continued as it did. Indeed, the atmosphere of economy probably helped steam, as commanders began to value armed steamers as being of equal value to large manpower-intensive sailing ships, for peacetime contingencies at least (despite the opinions of enthusiasts, a steamer of this period was no match for the broadsides of a well-handled contemporary sailing vessel). In 1833 Malcolm, in the Mediterranean, rated his armed steamer as 'more useful to him than another 74'.[43] In his arguments with Symonds later in the decade, Minto recommended transfer of personnel to more labour-intensive steamers.[44]

Some 15 steamers were completed for the Admiralty between 1830 and 1837, with two more purchased specially for the packet service to Corfu operated by the Royal Navy. The advent of steam to this latter task cut passage time by two-thirds.[45] Most steamships were kept in commission: in 1837, of the 24 such steamers available, only two were in Ordinary. Indeed, there were as many, if not more, steamers in commission as there were ships of the line. A much larger vessel, HMS *Gorgon*, was under construction; it was over half as big again as the largest existing RN steamer. By the 1830s some paddle steamers were mounting between three and six 32-pounders, size of gun making up for inability to mount a broadside.[46] In 1837 the number of Royal Navy steamers was greatly increased when the 34 Post Office packets were taken over after complaints about the quality of service. The five Channel and Irish Sea routes were passed to contractors between 1845 and 1854, but many of the former packet steamers remained in naval service, expanding the increasing steam flotilla.[47]

Along with the rise of steam propulsion, another major 1830s development was the improvement of naval gunnery. The establishment of HMS *Excellent*, moored in Fareham Creek as a gunnery school, was the work of the Melville Board, but the establishment had the support of its successors and was made permanent in 1832. Seaman Gunners were enlisted for five or seven years for additional pay, an important move away from the traditional system of employing men for the duration of ships' commissions. A first-class certificate from *Excellent* became a prerequisite for promotion to Seaman Gunner. In 1838 it was laid down that each class of ship should have a certain number of seaman gunners and gunners' mates, and that *Excellent* should set the standard of gunnery throughout the fleet. Advanced gunnery courses were provided for officers.[48] A gunnery school was also established at Plymouth in 1838.

It was not just the accuracy of the guns that improved. In 1838 it was decided that all ships of the line and frigates should be armed with uniform armaments of 32-pounders of various lengths, supplemented by a few 8-inch shell guns. The French put great store on these new weapons although they were inferior in range, accuracy and rate of fire to solid shot cannon; the Royal Navy saw them as being of limited utility, at best supplements to conventional armaments. The early spherical shells did not live up to their destructive promise and were a danger to the ships that carried them. Even the larger 10-inch shell guns were inferior to the standard 32-pounder in range and accuracy and, after trials, they were confined to paddle steamers where the large explosive shell made up somewhat for the lack of a broadside.[49]

The international situation deteriorated in the late 1830s. The French Navy improved as relations with Britain became more uneasy. In 1838 a reinforced British fleet was sent to mediate between France and Mexico and French challenges elsewhere led to other moves, notably the cession of New Zealand by the native population to the senior naval officer in Australian waters. But it was in the Eastern Mediterranean that the main crisis continued, with Mehemet Ali's ambitions threatening the Turkish Empire, and Russia only too ready to pick up the pieces. [50]

Against this darkening international scene, the Government's naval policy was subjected to increasing criticism. The critics argued that the fleet was too weak, especially in home waters. Indeed, the battlefleet had been reduced to only 77 units, with 12 beyond economic repair. Minto was alarmed and a considerable programme of new construction was begun to counter the quality of the latest foreign vessels. In 1839 three new ships of the line were launched and no less than six ordered. In 1840 another two were launched and six more ordered. The Estimates increased to £5.5 million in 1839 and they jumped to £6.2 million the following year, passing the 10 per cent mark again as a proportion of the total budget.[51] Numbers voted increased to almost 40,000.[52]

This created something of a manning crisis. Attempts had been made to reform the provision of naval personnel. The old wartime system of impressment was becoming less acceptable and, in 1835, a register of known seamen was drawn up to allow wartime conscription, if necessary, to be carried out on a more coherent basis. Service was limited to five years. Peacetime volunteers were now also expected to serve five-year terms, although this was far from standard. There was a growing core of more or less permanent seamen, former boys retained in 1815; gunners; and others with an eye on the pension available since the 1820s for those with more than 21 years' service.[53] But this was not enough to cope with peacetime crises.

Since 1835 the number of seamen and marines borne had lagged behind the number voted. In 1836 the shortfall had been over 3500, in 1837 almost 2900, in 1838 over 3100. Things improved in 1839, with a small surplus of 692 borne over the 34,165 voted, but it proved impossible to meet the new 1840 total. In any case, the votes reflected reduced peacetime complements. Shortage of seamen meant reduction in capability as numbers of ships in commission were traded against the fighting capacity of individual units. The available fleet was stretched taut with very few ships left operational in home waters despite an increase in the total number of Royal Navy ships in commission, from 176 in 1835 to 228 in 1839.[54]

Foremost among the threats was still Mehemet Ali in Egypt. The Egyptian warlord, backed by France, was trying to carve out a new Egyptian Empire. At a four-power convention in July 1840, Britain, Russia, Austria and Prussia decided that he should be ordered to withdraw from Northern Syria, Arabia and Crete, in return for which he would be recognized as hereditary Viceroy of Egypt and be allowed to continue to hold Acre and some other territories. If he refused he would be deposed by force. The large paddle steamer *Cyclops*, a later, larger sister of *Gorgon*, delivered the ultimatum to Alexandria on 9 August. France opposed these moves and began to prepare for war. Melbourne found the situation 'most disquieting', given the balance of power between the British and French Mediterranean fleets, especially as the latter might well be reinforced by Mehemet Ali's ships.[55]

The outlook in Sir Robert Stopford's Mediterranean fleet, which grew from 29 to 37 units in 1840 (making it the largest individual station), was not happy. Commanding officers worried about lack of men, but, in reality, the French threat was more apparent than real. They too were having difficulties manning their ships and the British had a much greater reserve.[56] Despite doubts about dividing his fleet, Stopford ordered Captain Sir Charles Napier to hoist a Commodore's pendant and take a squadron made up of four ships of the line, a frigate and the steamer *Gorgon* to Beirut.[57] There had been an anti-Mehemet rising there which it was hoped it might revive at the sight of Napier's squadron. Stopford remained off the Dardanelles.

When the ultimatum expired, a general blockade of Egypt and Syria was declared and Napier used *Gorgon*'s mobility to scout the coast for possible landing points. On 9 September Stopford arrived with the main fleet. Thirty-three ships were visible off Beirut. Napier, unwilling to serve under Stopford, asked to go ashore in command, as the troops' commander had been taken ill. Stopford was only too keen to agree. A force of Royal Marines and Turkish troops were put ashore with Napier, who was soon in command of a mixed force of British, Turks, Austrian marines and dissident locals. It was protected from attack by the guns of HMS *Revenge*, which dominated the road between it and Beirut. The fleet then bombarded Beirut and demolished its defences, but Napier was not yet ready to occupy it.

Coastal towns and fortifications fell to British ships and landing parties. Napier put himself in command of a joint attack on Sidon, to be carried out by the 84-gun *Thunderer*, no less than four paddle steamers, the brig *Wasp*, an Austrian frigate and a Turkish ship carrying between them 750 Royal marines, 100 Austrians and 500 Turks. The big paddlers, *Gorgon* and *Cyclops*, had been built with covered gun decks but only carried armament on the upper deck, leaving their large lower gun decks free for troops. *Stromboli*, built afterwards to a slightly smaller but basically similar pattern, did not have gun ports on this deck. They were, in effect, pioneer assault ships, capable of covering their landing parties with six heavy guns on their upper decks. With this force Sidon was bombarded and taken and the garrison captured.

Napier next defeated the Egyptians ashore at Boharsef, an engagement in which he showed considerable bravery. As Lambert said, his 'army of British and Austrian marines, rocket troops and Turkish soldiers had gained one of the Royal Navy's most interesting victories'.[58] Napier then reconnoitred the fortress city of Acre, which Stopford was ordered to attack. The fleet commander sailed from Beirut on 31 October with seven ships of the line. The four steamers, *Gorgon, Phoenix, Stromboli* and *Vesuvius*, preceded the fleet (moving slowly under light airs) and summoned the Egyptians to surrender. The frigates *Pique* and *Talbot* surveyed the shoals and laid navigational buoys, at which the Egyptians, mistaking them for anchor buoys, aimed their guns. Stopford planned to use the steamers to tow his ships into position but the wind was sufficient on the day (3 November,) and the role of the steamers was changed to mobile shell firers and, in *Phoenix*'s case, command ship.

The ships anchored much closer to the walls than the Egyptians expected and, at 800–900 yards, the fire of their *Excellent*-trained gunners was devastating. The 104-gun flagship *Princess Charlotte* had been almost completely rearmed with 32-pounders, albeit mainly of the shorter models, as she was a relatively old and small ship. These proved highly effective, however, as did those of the other ships of the line. There was some confusion about the final deployment, which led to recriminations after the battle, but it only took about three hours for virtually every gun on the western face of the fort to be disabled. The southern attack was at even closer range, 500–600 yards, at which even carronades were effective.

The Egyptian fire was inaccurate, being aimed at the buoys and not the ships, and only one shot hit a carronade in the 72-gun HMS *Edinburgh*, killing four. At 16.20 the main magazine ashore blew up, hit by a shell, either from *Gorgon* or the 72-gun *Benbow*. Over a thousand men, 25 per cent of the garrison, were killed and resistance weakened. The guns on the southern face in action were quickly disabled and firing ceased at 17.00. Stopford ordered a general cease-fire at 17.50.

Some of the ships had their rigging badly damaged and had to be towed away, but damage to hulls was slight and the entire fleet lost only 18 killed and 41 wounded. The ships had fired some 48,000 rounds. The demoralized Egyptians evacuated the city and were replaced by troops landed by the fleet, reinforced by those from Beirut.

Stopford sent Napier in the 84-gun *Powerful* to Alexandria, which had been blockaded by a small squadron while the fighting went on in the Levant. Napier, without authorization, entered into negotiation with Mehemet Ali through the good offices of Captain Sir Thomas Mansell of HMS *Rodney*. Mansell knew the Egyptian leader and eventually Napier went ashore in the steamer *Medea* to conclude an agreement. Mehemet Ali agreed to evacuate Syria and restore the Ottoman fleet in return for becoming hereditary governor of Egypt. The four-power terms had been accepted and Palmerston, a political ally of Napier's, welcomed the result. The irrepressible Napier wrote a little prematurely, and disingenuously, to the Admiralty: 'I do not know whether I have done right in settling the Eastern question...'[59]

Palmerston certainly saw the wider implications of the triumph at Acre, the last engagement thought worthy of record when the gunroom at the new Royal Naval College at Dartmouth was built over half a century later. He saw it as:

an event of immense political importance as regards the interests of England [sic] not only in connection with the Turkish question, but in relation to every other question which we may have to discuss with other powers. Every country that has towns within cannon shot of deep water will remember the operations of the British fleet off the Coast of Syria in September, October and November 1840 whenever such country has any differences with us.[60]

Pax Britannica had indeed been consecrated.

British sea power was also being applied in the Far East. In 1837 the Chinese Imperial government imposed strict measures to stamp out the trade in opium, which balanced the East India Company's trade in tea and which provided a significant part of the revenues of the government of India. In 1839 the situation had become serious and there was a clash between the 28-gun frigate *Volage*, the 18-gun sloop *Hyacinth*, and a fleet of war junks. In 1840 British forces were built up under Commodore Sir Gordon Bremer. The 72-gun liner *Blenheim* came from the Cape, along with 42-gun frigate *Blonde*, 20-gun corvette *Nimrod* and 18-gun sloop *Pylades*. The 26-gun frigates *Calliope* and *Samarang* came from the West Coast of South America. There were also transports containing troops and a number of steamers, both of the East India Company and the Indian Government's Bengal Marine, as well as the experimental iron-hulled paddler *Nemesis*, 'a privately promoted mercenary without status as a ship of war'.[61]

Chusan was occupied after a brief action. Skirmishing continued until the end of 1840 as negotiations with the Chinese were carried out, but at the beginning of 1841 it was decided to attack the forts in the approach to Canton. *Nemesis* particularly distinguished herself in this action, which forced the Chinese to sign a convention resuming trade and also ceding Hong Kong, which had become a base for British merchants. The British evacuated Chusan but the Chinese were only playing for time. A naval demonstration achieved another truce but fighting quickly began again and troops were landed. They soon commanded Canton. But, controversially, the British forces were withdrawn in return for an indemnity and a resumption of trade.

Palmerston was unhappy with this course of events and ordered a more forward policy. Rear Admiral Sir William Parker, appointed Commander of the East Indies and China Station, arrived by steamer in August 1841. Under his command, Amoy, Chusan, Chinhae and Ningpo were taken in amphibious operations. In March 1842 the Chinese counterattacked and Parker's ships supported the defence. A Naval Brigade was part of a landed force that defeated a Chinese army but it was thought that only an advance up the Yangtze would finally bring China to terms. British ships appeared off Nanking in early August. Troops were landed and bombardment threatened and on the 29th a major treaty was signed aboard the 72-gun liner HMS *Cornwallis*. The Treaty of Nanking gave Britain an indemnity, access to Canton, Amoy, Foochow, Ningpo and Shanghai and perpetual ownership of Hong Kong. There was little China could do against the firepower of British warships, coupled with the mobility of the new steamers. Palmerston's claim could be expanded to anyone within cannon-shot of deep or shallow water. With steam propulsion, rivers as well as littorals gave British sea power access. This was Pax Britannica indeed.

2 The Steam Battlefleet

Peel's Tories formed a new administration in 1841; Graham was
Home Secretary and Lord Haddington First Lord. The latter was
not a major figure and his appointment was a sign that the Prime
Minister would take a personal interest in naval policy. Cockburn,
a friend of Peel's, became First Naval Lord. Peel unlocked the long-
term resources of the country for the Navy by reintroducing
income tax. Despite continued overall budget deficits and against
a background of tension with both France and the United States,
the Naval Estimates were further increased. They went up from
£6.8 million in 1841 to £7 million in 1842, and after a dip rose
again to £7.9 million by 1846, almost 12 per cent of the total
budget.[1] The number of men borne was never below 38,000 from
1841 to 1846.[2]

The increased resources went on an active fleet of smaller vessels
and cost-effective steamers rather than the battlefleet, the size of
which remained limited, much to the chagrin of the Prime Minister
who, in 1844, was moved to remark: 'six millions of money and only
seven of the line'.[3] New ship construction proceeded only slowly.
The need to season wood meant it was unwise to build wooden ships
in under three or four years, but *Goliath*, second of Symonds's 80-gun
Vanguard class of second-rates, took eight years from keel laying to
launch, in 1842. Her sister, *Mars*, launched in 1848 at Chatham,
took a year longer. There were also significant delays between
ordering and keel laying. Symonds's 110-gun first-rate *Queen* was
launched in 1839, 12 years after being ordered and six after keel laying.
The second of class, *Windsor Castle*, had been ordered in 1833 but
not laid down until 1844. Twelve new ships of the line were ordered
between 1840 and 1843.[4]

Cockburn disliked Symonds professionally and politically and turned to other designs: the controversial Surveyor found himself progressively marginalized. The 80-gun *Cressy*, ordered in 1842, was designed by Read, Chatfield and Creuze of the School of Nautical Architecture and the new 120-gun first-rate *Royal Albert* laid down in 1844 was designed by Oliver Lang, Master Shipwright at Portsmouth Dockyard.

Symonds's ships made poor gun platforms but his fast, smaller ships were a success in one of the Royal Navy's major contemporary duties, the suppression of the slave trade. Britain had abolished the slave trade in 1807 and in 1824 it was declared to be piracy. By 1826 agreement had been obtained from Spain, France, Portugal and Brazil to ban the trade; nevertheless it continued. British ships bore the brunt of countering it, mixing philanthropy with self-interest, for slavery gave some commercial advantages to those who continued to practise it.[5]

The duty was quite asset-intensive. The number of sloops and brigs on the Cape and West Africa Station (created in 1832) grew from five in 1833 to 18 in 1839. The stations were altered the following year: the Cape and Brazils now deployed 18 sloops and brigs and West Africa 12.[6]

The work was eventful. In 1835 the brigantine HMS *Buzzard* (10 guns) had captured a Spanish slave brig *Formidable*, losing two men; 500 of the 707 liberated slaves were put ashore at Sierra Leone. The same year the 5-gun schooner HMS *Skipjack* captured the well-armed slaver *Martha*. The action lasted seven and a half hours and almost 450 slaves were liberated.[7] The total of slaves landed alive that year was 6899 from a dozen ships captured.[8] In 1837 the 18-gun sloop *Scout* took a Portuguese ship with 576 slaves on board.[9] The total number of slaves liberated in the year of Queen Victoria's accession was 8652, a peak total, from 29 ships. In 1844 some 52 slave ships were captured with 3219 slaves.[10]

Another duty that took resources was surveying and exploration. The number of ships engaged on such duties doubled to 26 between the 1830s and the 1840s.[11] This reflected the influence of Sir Alfred Beaufort (of windspeed scale fame) who, between 1829 and 1855, was Hydrographer of the Admiralty. Two bomb vessels, *Erebus* and

Terror, were fitted out under Captain James Clark Ross to explore the Antarctic and, after they had penetrated the ice pack, land was duly found in 1841 and named Victoria Land after the new Queen. Ross remained on task until 1843, and his success encouraged an attempt to find the North West Passage, again using *Erebus* and *Terror*, this time modified with auxiliary steam heating and propulsion, under the command of Captain Sir John Franklin. The polar ice pack proved impenetrable for the ships and the entire expedition succumbed to cold and illness.

In 1844 the smaller steamers became sloops in three classes, with *Gorgon* and her derivatives in the largest category.[12] The larger *Cyclops* spawned a generation of second-class steam frigates, eight of which had been commissioned by 1847.[13] Such ships offered cost-effective increment of capability to the fleet and their capacity to tow more heavily armed sailing ships made them significant force multipliers. Ship's engineers also grew in status. They had been given warrant rank in 1836 and, in 1847, the first two ranks of engineers, Inspectors of Machinery Afloat and Chief Engineers, were given wardroom status.[14]

The largest steamers of this period were the new generation of faster and more heavily armed first-class paddle frigates. The first was a conversion from a Leda class 38-gun frigate launched in 1829, HMS *Penelope*. Work began in 1842 and she was commissioned in 1843 with ten 8-inch shell guns on the main deck and two 42-pounder pivot guns and ten 42-pounder carronades on the upper deck. This was both a testament to the differences in armament demanded by paddles and the speed of dockyard work when priority was given. More conversions were considered but the next two ships were new built; the rather unsatisfactory *Retribution* and the magnificent 3189-ton four-funnelled HMS *Terrible*, commissioned in 1845 with a main armament of 16 of the heaviest available guns.[15]

Technical progress took two still newer lines in the 1840s. Iron seemed attractive as a constructional medium as it allowed more carrying capacity for a given displacement. It had three major disadvantages, however: a tendency to suffer brittle failures, given contemporary iron-making techniques; serious fouling at sea as copper bottoms could not be used because of electrolysis; and compass errors because of the magnetism of the hull. As D. K. Brown has astutely argued, these disadvantages were less marked in riverine operations in hot climates as wrought iron is less likely to fail if warm.[16] It was no coincidence that the first iron fighting ships for the Royal Navy, indeed the first iron warships to serve in any major navy, were paddle gunboats for service on the River Niger, ordered in 1840. The Royal Navy's first iron seagoing warships, the paddle sloop *Trident* and paddle frigate *Birkenhead*, were launched in 1845. With the Royal Dockyards congested, the Admiralty was being forced to build cruising vessels in private yards and the latters' abilities with wood were not trusted after bad experiences in the Napoleonic War. More iron ships were ordered but it was a false start.

Combat experience seemed to argue against iron. In 1845 an Anglo-French force intervened in Uruguay to back the government against rebels supported by Argentina. It led to operations on the Parana River Passage by a squadron that included three paddle steamers, *Gorgon, Firebrand* and the French *Fulton*, plus four British and four French sailing vessels. The stronghold at Obligado was destroyed after a sharp action, despite the doubts of the British government. Movement on the river continued to be opposed and reinforcements were sent, including the famous wooden paddle sloop *Alecto* (see below) and the new iron sloops *Harpy* and *Lizard*. Passing the Argentine guns, HMS *Lizard* was riddled for two hours and suffered some limited damage.[17] This was seized upon by the opponents of iron at home.

The tide was turning against iron ships in London. In 1846 the iron tender *Ruby* was shot to pieces at HMS *Excellent*, leading its commanding officer, Henry Ducie Chads, to state that iron ships were unfit for war purposes. The Whigs opposed iron ships, as did Symonds. The whole argument became politicized and with the arrival of a Whig government in July 1846 it was not surprising that iron as a primary construction medium for new warships was abandoned. *Birkenhead* was put into reserve and the construction of four more iron frigates was suspended.

A more immediately important technology was the screw propeller. Without this, steam could never be more than an auxiliary to the main fighting fleet. The latter depended on the broadside for the deployment of its massive and increasing firepower and broadsides were incompatible with paddle boxes. There were also worries about the vulnerability of paddles and their associated machinery, mounted high in the ship. An American inventor, John Ericsson, demonstrated a screw launch to the Admiralty in 1837. The Admiralty barge, containing the First Naval Lord, Sir Charles Adam, Beaufort and Symonds, was towed by Ericsson's craft on the Thames. The British officials were suspicious of the steering performance of the complex Ericsson screw, placed right at the rear of his vessel – and put off by Ericsson's manner.[18] A simpler screw with better steering potential was available in the form of Francis Petit Smith's design, already patented in 1836 and known to the Admiralty when they rejected Ericsson's device. Petit Smith got backing and set up the Screw Propeller Company to build a demonstrator vessel, the *Archimedes*, shown off to an Admiralty party including Symonds in October 1839. Although deficient in speed compared to a paddler, its military advantages were obvious.[19] The great engineer Isambard Kingdom Brunel, designer of the screw passenger vessel *Great Britain*, was appointed as a consultant for the adoption of the screw, and his position survived the change of administration in 1841. HMS *Rattler*, a screw sloop, was built to compare with similar paddle steamers and she underwent trials in mid-1843. A small additional trials vessel, *Dwarf*, was also purchased.

Rattler was not an optimal screw warship; indeed her engines were mounted like those of a paddle steamer to obtain the fairest test results. She is best known for her trials with her paddle half-sister *Alecto* in 1845 (culminating in the famous tug of war). But Lambert and Brown are united in their view that this was just a public relations exercise – at most a proving of propeller design – and the utility of the screw had been fully accepted beforehand.[20] The later trials of the sloops *Niger* (screw) and *Basilisk* (paddle) also proved little.[21]

In 1844 tension with France grew as French writings about the potential of steam to undermine traditional British supremacy combined with French expansionism in North Africa and the Pacific.[22] Fears grew as to the state of harbour defences against a *coup de main* with steamers. The result was an attempt to give some ships limited auxiliary power combined with maximum fighting power, to allow them to move anywhere quickly to protect vulnerable ports in the Solent, Medway, Plymouth and Pembroke. Thus were born the blockships, the Royal Navy's first steam line of battleships.[23] Four 72-gun liners were chosen, *Ajax, Blenheim, Edinburgh* and *Hogue*, and two 44-gun frigates, *Horatio* and *Seahorse*. The former were given 450 hp engines and the latter 350 hp machinery. The larger ships were given a powerful armament of 28 32-pounders on the gun deck, 26 8-inch shell guns on the main deck and six heavy guns on the upper deck – they were highly capable warships. The four iron frigates under construction were also to be screw-propelled and six wooden screw frigates were ordered.

In early 1846 the political crisis brought about by the repeal of the Corn Laws forced a Cabinet reconstruction. Lord Ellenborough, a politician with a reputation for dynamism and rapid decision, briefly became First Lord. Ellenborough wanted greater efficiency in ship construction and formed a Committee of Reference on Shipbuilding to reduce Symonds's waning power still further. He also proposed reform in the administration of the Dockyards. On the operational front, America as well as France was threatening. Ellenborough formed a special squadron of about 20 ships, under Rear Admiral Sir William Parker, in which steamers were in equal proportion to sailing ships 'for the purpose of ascertaining in what matter the two arms can best be made to assist each other in war'.[24]

In mid-1846 the Whigs returned to office under Lord John Russell. Lord Auckland became First Lord and Sir Charles Adam returned as First Naval Lord. This effective combination defended the Naval Estimates, which stayed at around the £8 million mark from 1846 to 1848 with 44,000–45,000 men borne.[25] After its success in Parker's squadron, the balanced steam and sail fleet became the essence of main fleet deployments as the battlefleet was mobilized more often than at any time since 1815. In the Mediterranean in 1847 were nine sailing ships of the line, each paired with a steamer; the latter were to tow the sailing ships when necessary as well as use their mobility to support more heavily armed liners in action. The 110-gun *Queen* was in the Tagus with two steamers, while available for home waters were four 120 s and an 84, each with an attached steamer. The only other liner in full commission was the 80 *Collingwood*, on the East Indies and China Station.[26]

Auckland continued his predecessor's reform policy. Symonds was finally induced to resign, being replaced by Sir Baldwin Walker with expanded powers, and the Committee of Reference became the Council of Science. In 1848 Auckland produced a new Establishment to provide a battlefleet of 50 first- and second-rates afloat, 15 building and 15 in frame ready for immediate construction. Third-rates were to be phased out as line-of-battle ships. To support this, Walker submitted a detailed programme of construction and repair.[27] He also predicted the rapid adoption of the screw propeller.

France had laid down a first steam liner, *Le Napoléon*, the previous year. A British steam liner, the appropriately named HMS *James Watt*, was designed the same year but not begun due to lack of dockyard space and the need to collect timber. It was the availability of timber for one of the 1843 liners not yet begun, *Agamemnon*, that led to the first steamship of the line ordered as such to receive that name. *Agamemnon* was reordered on 25 August 1849 and launched three years later. She was completed as a 91-gun ship, as was *James Watt*, launched eight months later. Work on sailing ships was stopped in 1849 and conversion of ships laid down as sailing vessels began, the first being the 70-gun *Sans Pareil* taken over at the beginning of the year and completed in 1851.

Two sets of trials in 1850 set the scene for the naval developments of the decade. The first confirmed the importance of the screw. A squadron was sent to the Tagus, under Commodore William Fanshawe Martin. It contained three of the six new wooden screw frigates and the latter impressed Martin, who reported back to the Admiralty on the utility of the sailing warship with auxiliary screw propulsion. Only lack of coal and unreliability of machinery prevented the steamers relying on their screws for primary power.[28] Iron, however, was still unwelcome. A series of further trials at *Excellent* begun in 1849 went on into 1851. Chads concluded that the effects of shot on contemporary iron were such that it was not a proper construction medium for warships and that such effects could not be avoided. *Birkenhead* was converted into a troopship (coming to a sad and famous end in 1852), as were three of the suspended iron screw frigates, the fourth being sold.

There was pressure for retrenchment in 1848, resisted by Auckland, who became ill and died. His successor at the beginning of 1849, Sir Francis Baring, was able to resist the worst of this pressure for cuts, the Estimates falling to just over £7 million in 1849 to £6.5 million in 1851. Numbers of men were reduced only slightly, to 39,000.[29] The steam liner programme continued, but relatively slowly. Baring, advised by Walker, realized that in a technologically dynamic environment contemporary ships would rapidly become obsolete. Only a minimum programme to meet the French threat should therefore be built, Britain's superior industrial base being relied upon to cope with emergencies, as required.

A 101-gun two-decker, *St Jean d'Acre*, was laid down in 1851, using existing materials and engines. The following year at Pembroke the three-decker, *Windsor Castle*, was cut in half, extended, engines fitted and launched on 14 September, the day of the Duke of Wellington's death. She was commissioned as the 131-gun steam liner *Duke of Wellington*. Another three-decker, the 121-gun *Royal Albert*, was selected for conversion at the beginning of 1852 and Walker earmarked two incomplete two-decker 90s, *Algiers* and *Hannibal*, for similar work.

Such was the programme inherited by Lord Derby's new Tory administration, formed after Russell's parliamentary defeat in February 1852. The new First Lord was the Duke of Northumberland, but within a year Lord Aberdeen's Whig–Peelite coalition came to power and Graham returned as First Lord. Pressure for cuts in expenditure was mitigated by the threat of war and invasion raised by the new French leader, Louis Napoleon. In 1852 Parliament voted to increase the numbers of men in the fleet from 39,000 to 45,500, the largest post-1815 figure yet, and by 1853 the Estimates stood at £7.2 million, naval expenditure being 10.5 per cent of the total national budget.[30]

The need to man the navy at an increased level caused a fundamental change in the 1850s: the creation of continuous service. In 1846 a first step towards this had been made: it was arranged that men from just-decommissioned vessels could leave their effects in the dockyards while they went on paid leave of up to six weeks, after which they would return to join a ship fitting out for service.[31] Attempts were also made to recruit reserves and a small force of 'Dockyard Riggers' was created in 1848 to add to the Coast Guard.

In July 1852 Northumberland appointed a Committee on Manning that reported the following year. Its recommendations, that after July 1853 all boy entrants would be engaged for a ten-year stint of continuous and general service from age 18, were accepted by the Graham Board and embodied in an Order in Council of April 1853. Transfer to the new conditions of service by older ratings was encouraged. Men who accepted long-term service were offered a pension after 20 years. New rates of Leading Seaman, Captain of Guns and Chief Petty Officer were instituted, with higher rates of pay.[32] This was little short of a revolution.

The crisis also forced a further build-up of the battlefleet. Walker balanced the conversion of seasoned hulls with new construction. Conversions began in late 1852 on the three ships he had already earmarked plus the 91-gun *Caesar, Nile, Orion* and *Princess Royal*, 80-gun *Cressy, Majestic* and the old *Royal George* (docked for repair and emerging as a none too satisfactory 120-gun steam liner). The following year, conversion of the 131-gun *Marlborough* and 91-gun *Exmouth* began. Three new ships were started, the 91-gun *Edgar* and *Repulse*, and the 101-gun *Conqueror*. Lambert calls this 'the first major construction programme for forty years' which 'marked the decision to build a steam battlefleet, rather than a sailing fleet with a leavening of steamers'.[33]

In 1853, as the latest crisis with France faded away, another and more serious one loomed with Russia. The Russians wished to use the question of access to the Christian holy places in Palestine to give them a vehicle for continuous intervention in Ottoman affairs. The Cabinet decided to support Turkey and deter Russia by sending to Besika Bay the Mediterranean Fleet; six liners, a large frigate and ten steamers commanded by Vice Admiral Sir James Dundas. Strength in home waters was increased by bringing home the experimental squadron from the Tagus and strongly reinforcing it into a powerful Western Squadron. A Royal Review was staged at Spithead on 18 August and the ships returned to Portugal via Ireland. This force,

11 sailing liners, three steam liners, a blockship, and 15 other steamers, 'served as a strategic reserve, as a squadron of evolution and as the nucleus of a Baltic Fleet if one were required'.[34]

All this was carried out against the background of a Russian invasion of Turkish-controlled Romania and a Turkish declaration of war. Dundas had been joined by a more powerful French fleet, and units of the two navies advanced through the Dardanelles to protect Constantinople. In November the Russians scored a crushing victory over a much inferior Turkish squadron off Sinope. This galvanized public opinion in Britain, and the British and French fleets entered the Black Sea to prevent further Russian attacks. By this time the Mediterranean Fleet had been reinforced by the steam liners *Agamemnon* and *Sans Pareil*, in part to balance the three steamships of the line of the French fleet but also to give operational advantages, such as providing support for smaller steamers in forward operations. The paddle frigate *Retribution* was sent to Sevastopol to warn that any Russian warships which did not return to port would be attacked. On 27 February the British and French governments gave the Russians an ultimatum to evacuate the Turkish Danube provinces. The Russians refused to comply and the allied fleets moved off the Bulgarian coast. On 27 March 1854 Britain and France formally declared war on Russia, and a Treaty of Alliance was concluded between Britain, France and Turkey.

The first operations were carried out against Odessa, the forts of which had fired on the boat of the paddle frigate *Furious* when she was evacuating the British Consul under flag of truce. An allied bombarding force largely made up of paddle frigates was deployed. A red-hot shot from HMS *Furious* blew up a Russian magazine and considerable devastation was caused to military installations.[35]

In May the allied fleet appeared off Sevastopol. Operations undertaken with steamers, including *Agamemnon*, on the eastern shores of the Black Sea saw the loss of the paddle frigate *Tiger* after she went aground off Odessa.[36] An Anglo-French army disembarked at Gallipoli and a blockade of the mouths of the Danube was initiated at the beginning of June. The army was then moved forward to Varna as paddle frigates watched Sevastopol. The allied ships identified 12 Russian sailing liners, four sailing frigates and two steam frigates, but the Russians had no intention of making a major sortie against the overwhelming qualitative strength of the allies with their vast superiority in steamers.

The movement to Varna caused a Russian withdrawal from the adjacent territory. Influenced heavily by Graham, the allies decided, at the end of June, to attack Sevastopol to destroy the Russian Fleet at source.[37] This doctrine reflected contemporary British thinking which, since about 1840, had emphasized capitalizing upon the greater power of contemporary naval forces against the shore to prevent an enemy utilizing bases to embark an invading army. Cherbourg had been the target originally but now, rather ironically, the idea was turned against a Russian Black Sea naval base, with France as an ally.[38] The destruction of the Russian fleet would remove much of the threat to Turkey. Orders to take Sevastopol were received by a doubtful Dundas on 6 July 1854.

The operation was delayed by sickness and only got underway at the end of August. The risk was taken of using French ships of the line to carry troops. This reduced the strength of the covering squadron and Dundas worried that the temporarily superior Russians might sally forth to take advantage of allied vulnerability. In fact the Russians did nothing and the allied army of 22,000 British and 25,000 French was put ashore at Eupatoria. The whole army deployed 128 guns, the armament of a single line of battleship.

As the allied armies advanced on the base, the Russians blocked it with five ships of the line and two frigates and used their guns and crews ashore. The rest of the Russian fleet was drawn up as best it could to cover the harbour. The demise of the Russian fleet as a mobile force plus the inadequacy of the ground forces as a siege train, led Dundas to form a Naval Brigade of about 4,500 seamen and Royal Marines with 140 of the fleet's heaviest guns. This more than doubled the striking power of the allied ground forces, albeit at the cost of a third of Dundas's crews and half his ammunition. Two of the three new gun vessels just sent out from Britain were disarmed for this purpose.

A joint attack on Sevastopol was planned for 17 October and there was debate in the allied naval command as to the ships' contribution. The French commander was more optimistic than Dundas about the value of a bombardment from the sea, even though it could be no more than a diversion from the attack by the army. Eight British sailing liners were engaged, the screw liners *Agamemnon* and *Sans Pareil* and the large sailing frigate *Arethusa*. Five steamers, including the remaining gun vessel, *Lynx*, acted as a mobile inshore bombardment force while the other steamers brought the sailing ships into position, some lashed to the latter's disengaged port sides.[39] Firing did not begin until 13.30 and it took about an hour for all ships to be engaged. Fort Constantine's magazine was set off by a shell from the paddle frigate *Terrible* and some 1100 Russians were killed or injured but the port's defences were still firing effectively as the allied fleet withdrew. The Russians were able to inflict some damage, although, considering they fired 16,000 rounds, it was limited. Shells and red-hot shot caused two sailing liners and *Arethusa* to retire. The 90-gun *Rodney* went aground but was successfully refloated by her attendant *Spiteful*, helped by *Lynx*.

The engagement showed both the strengths and the weaknesses of contemporary fleets and forts. At ranges of about a mile neither could inflict decisive damage on the other, although the activities of the inshore steamers, largely immune to guns that could not depress far enough to engage them, showed the way forward.

In the fighting around Sevastopol the Naval Brigade, further reinforced after the bombardment, proved vital. It particularly distinguished itself in the Battles of Balaclava and Inkerman, a number of the new Victoria Crosses being won.

The land actions around Sevastopol helped give the Russian War its more familiar name of the 'Crimean War' but this is highly misleading. The Baltic was seen by the allies as the important front, where it was necessary not only to contain Russia's greatest naval force but also where pressure could be brought to bear on areas of even greater sensitivity to the Tsar than the Crimea. As the crisis developed in early 1854, the timing of the war ultimatum was set in order that an allied squadron might reach and attack the Russian naval base at Reval, at the entrance to the Gulf of Finland. In February Graham began to mobilize a North Sea Fleet and the Cabinet appointed as its commander the aggressive Vice Admiral Sir Charles Napier. To man the force the Dockyard Riggers and

members of the Coast Guard were called out, although they were far
from adequate in quality or quantity. Nevertheless, on 10 March,
Napier led his fleet out from Spithead. It was very much a steam
fleet, comprising four screw liners and four 60-gun blockships, three
paddle frigates and four screw frigates. They were joined in the
Channel that evening by another steam liner and the steam sloop
Hecla, which had left Hull on 19 February on an intelligence-gathering
mission to the Baltic. The fleet was instructed to proceed to Vinga
Sound, outside the Kattegat, prevent the Russian fleet leaving the
Baltic, and offer British protection to the Swedes and Danes.[40]
On 23 March the fleet moved through the straits to Kiel, being joined
by two sailing liners and their accompanying paddlers. Napier
decided that the best base from which to cover both the Belts and
the Sound was Kjoge Bay, near Copenhagen, where he arrived on
1 April. Three days later news of the declaration of war was received.
Napier sent a typical signal to the fleet to stiffen his rather dubious
ships' companies: 'Lads, war is declared with a numerous and bold
enemy. Should they meet us and offer battle, you know how to
dispose of them. Should they remain in port, we must try and get at
them. Success depends on the quickness and precision of your firing.
Also, lads, sharpen your cutlasses, and the day is your own'.[41]

Three more British steam liners and four sailing liners further
reinforced the fleet. These included the 70-gun *Boscawen*, diverted
from being flagship of the North American Station, and its predecessor,
HMS *Cumberland*, sent straight to the Baltic on her return across the
Atlantic. Understandably, the crew was described as 'mutinous'.[42]
Napier's first task was to work up his hastily collected fleet into an
operational force.

In the first instance his orders limited him to defence and reconnaissance. Napier was not to engage on any 'desperate venture'. He
sailed on 12 April to take up position to begin blockade operations.
Bad weather created problems but raids were mounted and a paddle
steamer squadron, under Rear Admiral James Hanway Plumridge,
penetrated the Gulf of Bothnia.

By June an impressive allied fleet had been gathered in Baro
Sound. It included 14 British screw liners and blockships, six sailing
liners, two paddle frigates, four paddle sloops, two survey ships

(including the original steamer *Lightning*) and a hospital paddler. The French provided nine ships of the line, six large sailing frigates, a paddle frigate, a screw corvette, a screw sloop and two paddle sloops.[43] This did not include steamers deployed forward. When, later in the month, Plumridge rejoined the flag to confer with Napier, he left Captain William Hall (known as 'Nemesis Hall' for his activities in the famous China Wars iron steamer of that name) in the survey sloop *Hecla* to attack Bomarsund in the Aland Islands. *Hecla* led the larger paddle frigates *Odin* and *Valorous* in an attack on the evening of 21–22 June. Some limited damage was inflicted on the fort but the action is best remembered for the earliest deed of valour for which a Victoria Cross was awarded, when Mate Charles Lucas threw a shell with its fuse burning overboard.[44] Napier was annoyed that the operation had exceeded orders and achieved little at the cost of useful ammunition.[45]

The fleet moved forward towards the Gulf of Finland and a small paddle steamer squadron was sent, under Captain Bartholomew James Sulivan in the survey sloop *Lightning*, to reconnoitre Kronstadt. He reported that the Russian fleet looked 'rather slummy in their appearance; and as they cannot evidently make up more than seventeen or eighteen of the line it is impossible for them to come out. Our English screw ships alone could destroy them'.[46] An attack on Kronstadt was, however, considered impossible without a specialist assault flotilla.

It was decided instead to lay siege to Bomarsund and a French army was embarked at Calais in 14 British ships (half of them partially disarmed RN vessels), which sailed on 22 July. Before the troops arrived, the units of the fleet moved on the Aland islands, while a powerful force was left watching the Gulf of Finland. Gunnery specialist Rear Admiral Chads was placed in command of an attack force composed of the four 60-gun blockships and the 34-gun screw frigate *Amphion*. The early paddle steamers *Lightning* and *Alban* were in navigational support, Sulivan in the former leading the squadron through the narrow Ango Channel into Lumpar Bay south of Bomarsund on 28 July.[47] Troops were landed on 9 August as well as naval guns. The pioneer first-class paddle frigate *Penelope* was sent in to explore the effectiveness of the Russian defences but went aground, only being refloated with considerable difficulty. On 15 August a landed naval battery of 32-pounders firing 18 rounds per hour demolished part of Fort Nottich, which capitulated. A similarly deployed 10-inch shell gun from HMS *Blenheim* plus the allied ships offshore bombarded the main fort and the demoralized Russians surrendered.

There was talk of taking on Sveaborg in the Gulf of Finland but the French were on their way home and Napier knew he could not rely on his fleet as it stood to take on the Russian base. The main body of the fleet withdrew to Kiel in late October and Napier arrived at Spithead in mid-November. On the 22nd he was ordered by Graham to strike his flag. Unrealistic public expectations had been built up by the press and a scapegoat was required. Graham blamed Napier and this led to a long personal controversy between the two men. Napier entered Parliament and never served at sea again; Sir Charles Wood replaced Graham in March 1855. Graham's departure was a result of the major political crisis in January that resulted from dissatisfaction with the conduct of the war. A motion of censure was passed and the government was reconstructed, with Palmerston as Prime Minister. Wood, the new First Lord, was a competent enough man but his arrival, coupled with Palmerston's elevation, reduced 'the political weight and independence of the Admiralty'.[48]

Napier had been right to doubt the viability of normal warships with deep draughts and short-range guns against powerful forts. The war saw the mass production of large numbers of specialist coast attack craft. The first six Arrow class 'gun vessels' had not made much impact in 1854. Only one (see above) had been used at Sevastapol and Napier used his, HMS *Wrangler*, as a despatch vessel.[49] A class of six smaller, shallower draught 100 ft. Gleaner class 'gunboats', each armed with two 68-pounder rifled muzzle-loading Lancaster shell guns, was ordered in 1854, followed in October by 20 slightly larger Dappers. Graham also ordered the building of 54 vessels carrying 13-inch mortars. To provide larger assault ships, the conversion began of five more 60-gun blockships, using similar machinery to the gunboats. Perhaps the most interesting ships of this October programme, however, were five armoured batteries, of French conception, armed with fourteen 68-pounders and fitted with

3.5–4 inch armour over wooden bulwarks. They were specialist shore bombardment vessels and could only make 5.5 knots.[50]

In the Black Sea the new British commander was the previous second in command, Sir Edmund Lyons. Although critical of his intellectual capacity, Lambert describes him as 'active and forceful... with a willingness to take responsibility'.[51] The fleet improved both in morale and equipment. In January Lyons received two more steam liners, the 91-gun *Princess Royal* and 101-gun *St Jean d'Acre*, to add to *Royal Albert, Agamemnon, Hannibal* and *Algiers*. The never satisfactory *Sans Pareil* was sent home, along with some of the sailing liners whose crews were needed to man more suitable ships fitting out at home. The lightly armed paddle frigates *Sampson* and *Retribution* were replaced by the more powerful *Leopard, Odin* and *Valorous* and the 24-gun screw frigate *Dauntless*. The six Arrow class 160 ft. gun vessels were concentrated in the theatre, together with two iron paddle gun vessels purchased from Prussia, HMS *Weser* and HMS *Recruit*. By June 1855 six new small gunboats and an equal number of mortar vessels were also deployed.

In February 1855 the blockade of Russian ports was renewed and the Straits of Kerch were blocked by steamers. The Sea of Azov now became a focus of the maritime offensive. The Russian armies depended on the food-growing areas surrounding it and, as troops became available, it was decided to capture Kerch and destroy the Russians' supplies. This expedition was carried out by an allied army of over 15,000 men and a fleet that included all six of Lyons's steam liners and 27 other British steamers, including a light squadron, commanded by the C.-in-C.'s son Captain Edmund Lyons in the screw corvette *Miranda*. It contained a mix of screw and paddle sloops, the six Arrows and *Recruit*. Kerch fell easily and the light squadron proceeded into the Sea of Azov, reinforced by four French vessels. There it destroyed food supplies sufficient to feed 100,000 men for four months and sank 250 Russian vessels. Lyons was reinforced by two small steamers and launches armed with howitzers and rockets to penetrate into the Don estuary, where more damage was done. The allies now dominated the coast; no supplies could reach the Russian army from the Don basin by water; the forces at Sevastopol were doomed.

In June Captain Lyons handed command over to Captain Sherrard Osborn, in the paddle sloop *Vesuvius*. Early the following month Osborn received the six new gunboats, with orders to clear the Azov littoral of fisheries, mills and stores surplus to local requirements. Osborn also continued the destruction of Russian shipping. Only the icing-up of the Straits forced the squadron to withdraw at end of the year. One gunboat, *Jasper*, was lost when she ran ashore and had to be burnt after her crew had been taken off.

The main fleet continued to bombard Sevastopol, giving what support it could to the army. In these operations Captain Lyons was killed, which affected his father deeply. The new mortar vessels were employed in the final fighting for the city, which fell in September. Admiral Lyons then lost his sailing liners, which were dispatched to the Mediterranean and Bosporus. It was decided to turn the remaining fleet on Kinburn, the fortress of which protected the navigation of the Rivers Bug and Dnepr. The French argued that its conquest would block communications between Kherson, Nikolayev and Odessa and perhaps force the Russian evacuation of the Crimea. The British were less sanguine, but had no better idea for a continued offensive in the theatre.[52]

An army of 9000 men was embarked in October. The fleet consisted of some 90 units, including ten allied steam liners and the first three French armoured batteries. The similar British vessels were not yet ready, Graham's lingering suspicion of iron delaying their construction. Much of Osborn's Azov force was temporarily recalled for this operation as it contained the specialist gunboats. The troops were landed south of the fort and gunboats moved inside the spit upon which the fortress lay. On the 17th the bombardment of the defences began, led by the mortar and gun boats. The French armoured batteries then moved in and bore much of the brunt of the action. They anchored about 1000 yards from the fort and delivered about 3000 rounds that set the installation on fire and began to demolish its walls. The ships were repeatedly hit but to little effect. The screw liner *Hannibal* then took up position 600 yards off the end of the spit, silencing the battery there and allowing an allied force of paddle frigates and sloops to move inside. The rest of the steam liners opened fire on the western side, *Agamemnon* firing 500 rounds in 45 minutes. The Russians were overwhelmed by the hail of shot shell and mortar bombs and they surrendered. This crushing example of the power projection capacity of a modern fleet was the last major event of the Black Sea war. The taking of Sevastapol and the fleet contained therein meant that the original allied objective of the war had been achieved. Whether the Russians would accept defeat, however, depended on the events in the Baltic.

The previous administration had planned a major Baltic campaign for 1855. A fleet entirely of steamers was to be sent, under the former Second Naval Lord, Rear Admiral the Hon. Richard Saunders Dundas. Lambert considers that he lacked decision and resolve but is fairer in regard to him as 'a capable administrator, fluent in French' (crucial for combined operations with them) 'and an excellent seaman'.[53] The new First Lord sent Dundas with limited aims: 'He was to cooperate with Allies, keep up a strict blockade, carry out minor attacks to tie down Russian troops, examine the major arsenals and report on Bomarsund.'[54]

The fleet set sail at the end of March, entering the Gulf of Finland on 25 May. The specialist bombardment vessels were delayed by shortage of men but reconnaissance of Kronstadt and other harassing operations were carried out, despite the threat from primitive mines. On 27 June Dundas's options widened at last with the arrival of his assault flotilla and it was decided to make an attack upon Sveaborg, close to modern Helsinki. This was partly a rehearsal for a later attack on Kronstadt, and partly an attempt to be seen to be doing something. The attack was carried out by 16 British gunboats and a similar number of British mortar vessels, plus five of each type provided by France. The allies also deployed three new blockships, *Cornwallis, Hastings* and *Pembroke*, the screw liners *Duke of Wellington, Exmouth* and *Edinburgh*, and three French screw liners. The mortar vessels were drawn up in an arc at a range of 3300 yards, supported by three British paddle frigates and one screw frigate. As usual, Sulivan's preliminary reconnaissance had played a decisive role in these dispositions.

The bombardment began on the morning of 9 August. The gunboats circled in front of the mortar vessels and diversionary attacks were carried out on the flanks. Rockets from ships' boats carried the bombardment into the first night. Trouble was experienced with the tendency of the mortars to crack but serious fires and explosions were soon seen ashore and the bombardment was kept up throughout the second night. The British mortar vessels alone fired 3141 bombs, the French almost as many. The results were good, about 75 per cent of the Russian arsenal being destroyed. Sveaborg could no longer be used as a base. Lambert concludes that 'Sveaborg made the best use of available light forces, achieving a useful result at very small cost'.[55]

Kronstadt was the major prize, however, and a critical pressure point on Russia. Unfortunately the fleet was not yet strong enough to attempt it, although the blockade continued. Much was expected the next year, especially following the success of Kinburn. The Russians also thought Kronstadt, and thus St Petersburg, was vulnerable. For 1856 the British were planning to attack Kronstadt with a Baltic fleet more than twice the size of that of the previous year, no less than 225 ships, including 18 steam liners, 100 gunboats, 46 mortar vessels and two floating batteries.

The pressure worked. Russia accepted allied terms that she should evacuate occupied territories and that the territorial integrity of the Ottoman Empire should be respected. The Black Sea was declared a neutral zone and the Aland Islands were not to be fortified. The signing of the Treaty of Paris was marked by a huge Review at Spithead, in April 1856, when the 'Great Armament' was displayed in all its glory. Some 240 vessels were arrayed for Queen Victoria, including 24 steam liners, 19 screw frigates and corvettes, 18 paddle frigates and corvettes and four armoured batteries. There were 120 gun vessels and gunboats, no less than 93 of the Albacore class, 20 of the Cheerful class and 12 of the Clown class having been ordered during the war. There were 50 mortar vessels and mortar floats, two ammunition ships, a hospital ship and a floating foundry (proved necessary to mend the mortars at Sveaborg). The gunboat flotilla made an 'attack' on Southsea Castle. The lesson was clear. The Royal Navy could now project effective and destructive power from the sea when and where it wished. No potential enemy coast or naval base – French, Russian or American – was safe.

3 The Ironclad Age

As Prime Minister Palmerston memorably put it, Britain had no eternal friends or enemies, only interests, and the end of the war with Russia allowed the country to concentrate once more on her erstwhile ally but most formidable potential enemy, France. Seven new liners, including the 121-gun *Victoria* and *Howe*, had been ordered during the war and three more in 1856–7 but new ship construction was delayed by the postwar contraction of the dockyards and the amount of repair work necessary. It was also felt prudent to keep up with the French and Americans in frigates, the latter threat in particular causing the laying down of six very large frigates of larger tonnage than contemporary liners. The last two, the huge *Mersey* and *Orlando*, laid down at the end of 1856, mounted 40 of the heaviest guns available: 10-inch shell guns and 68-pounders. They were formidable fast capital ships but proved too large for wooden construction and were very short lived.

In 1858 Lord Derby became Prime Minister, with Sir John Pakington as First Lord. The same year the French began to apply their new ironclad armour technology to seagoing warships with the laying down of three new 36-gun vessels, *Gloire, Invincible* and *Normandie*. Walker, the Surveyor, did not think they had yet made the steam liner obsolete and his advice to the Parliamentary Committee, set up by Lord Derby in late 1858 to examine the increase in the Naval Estimates, led to Britain maintaining her existing programme of liner conversions to maintain battlefleet superiority. Palmerston supported this policy of a two-power standard when he returned to office in June 1859, his administration laying down seven Bulwark class liners to join the ten (including two 121-gun ships) ordered during or just after the war.

Despite his doubts, Walker had recommended to Pakington that an answer be provided for the *Gloire* in kind:

Although I have frequently stated that it is not in the interests of Great Britain – possessing as she does so large a navy – to adopt any important change in the construction of ships of war which might have the effect of rendering necessary the introduction of a new class of very costly vessels, until such a course is forced upon her by the adoption by foreign powers of formidable ships of a novel character requiring similar ships to cope with them, yet it then becomes a matter not only of expediency, but of absolute necessity . . . This time has arrived.[1]

Walker did not see the answer as being an ironclad ship of the line but an ironclad version of the Mersey-type frigate that could smash the slower *Gloire* and allow the steam liners to engage their French equivalents. In July 1858, therefore, a large screw armoured frigate was ordered. Its designer, Chief Constructor Isaac Watts, had to use iron construction to give the necessary size, strength and speed, although the armour would be wooden-backed. Thus were born HMS *Warrior* and HMS *Black Prince*, the mightiest ships of their day. *Warrior* was laid down on 25 May 1859 and her sister in October. They were commissioned in October 1861 and September 1862 respectively. They had 4.5-inch armoured belts with 18-inch wooden backing and were armed with a main battery of ten of the new 110-pounder Armstrong rifled breech loaders and twenty-eight 68-pounder smooth bores. These guns could fire solid, explosive and incendiary shot, including the newly developed molten metal rounds. Nothing could reflect better Britain's clear industrial superiority. *Warrior* was so far in advance of her contemporaries that she would have been in no danger from any combination of wooden ships, and would have had little trouble with *Gloire*. The French ship had a badly cramped gun deck battery, over-large gunports and less effective guns.[2] Quality cost money, however, and, to economize, two similar but smaller ironclads, *Defence* and *Resistance*, were laid down in 1859 and launched in 1861; they were, in part, intended for use as rams. Two more small, but slightly faster, 'iron cased frigates', *Hector* and *Valiant*, were laid down in 1861, together with an improved Warrior, *Achilles*.

Palmerston's First Lord, the Duke of Somerset, was open to pressure from colleagues and advisers. The Prime Minister both influenced him to continue with wooden walls a little longer than was probably advisable and obtained his acquiescence in the 'Palmerston's Folly' forts built to defend the naval ports from an army landed by surprise by steamships. Rear Admiral Lord Clarence Paget, First Secretary of the Admiralty, turned the First Lord against Walker, who finally resigned in February 1861 from the newly renamed post of Controller. Paget also advised the building of the smaller ironclads. Walker was succeeded by Rear Admiral Sir Robert Spencer Robinson. The new Controller was difficult and unpopular but was intelligent, dynamic and progressive and more wholeheartedly pro-ironclad than Walker.

Another major influence on policy was the Chancellor of the Exchequer, William Ewart Gladstone. He opposed expenditure on wooden ships and timber, although perhaps as much from motives of economy as of technological conviction. The Naval Lords were pressing for 20 more armour-plated ships to match French developments. Ten more Provence class ironclads had been ordered in addition to the six already under construction. In April 1861 a vote in the House of Commons called for the end of the construction of further wooden ships of the line (the last one, the 91-gun *Defiance*, had been launched the previous month). The Treasury obtained a reduction in the Admiralty's ambitions by more than half but a start in the new programme was made by taking the steam liner *Royal Oak* on the stocks for conversion to a *Gloire*-type ironclad. Alarming news of the French programme, however, led the Board to conclude that 'only the most vigorous and energetic measures will prevent the Command of the Channel at an early date falling into the hands of the French Emperor'.[3] Robinson was anxious not to offend Gladstone, and limited the immediate programme to armouring four more incomplete liners, *Caledonia, Ocean, Prince Consort* and *Royal Alfred*. The Board was also worried about building further Warriors until the type had proved itself, but in August 1861 three more large iron-built ships were ordered: *Minotaur, Agincourt* and *Northumberland*. This would give 15 ironclads to match the 16 generally inferior French vessels. More liners were also earmarked for conversion, once new designs had been proved.

The Admiralty was also being troubled by the enthusiastic Russian War hero Captain Cowper Coles, who had built an armed raft which was used effectively in the Sea of Azov. He had developed the idea of a rotating armoured turret, the development of which received some subsidy from the Admiralty. But Coles's plans for turret ships were found to be impractical for seagoing men-of-war by the Board's professional advisers.[4] Coles, however, obtained the strong support of the Prince Consort and much of the press. His turret was completed and subjected to trials that it passed successfully, leading to demands to build a turret ship. *Royal Sovereign*, one of the earmarked wooden liners, was chosen for conversion. In 1862 she was cut down to the lower deck, upon which were mounted one twin and three single turrets mounting 150-pounder smooth bores (later replaced by 10-inch muzzle-loading rifles). She was a powerful ship and a useful addition to the ironclad fleet for littoral operations such as an attack on Cherbourg but, with no rig and low freeboard, was in no sense a seagoing warship. Neither was the smaller, new-built turret ship, loyally called *Prince Albert*, which was laid down at the same time and completed in 1866. She was also a low freeboard vessel, armed with four turrets each mounting a 10-inch gun.

In 1861 Somerset accepted the proposals of Edward Reed, Secretary of the Institution of Naval Architects, to build smaller wooden ironclad ships in the sloop and corvette category. The continued use of wood was attractive to use up stocks of seasoned timber. In 1862 conversion began of the sloop *Research* and the corvette *Favourite*, while the ironclad sloop *Enterprise* was laid down new the same year. The sloops seem to have been primarily intended for use as rams with the main fleets while the corvette went to the North America and West Indies Station on commissioning in 1866. None was very successful but they helped prove Reed's concept of concentrating armour of increased thickness in a centre battery containing a smaller number of heavier guns, which could also be moved to face fore and aft ports via embrasures cut in the side. Reed was appointed Chief Constructor from 1863. His centre-battery ironclad ram, HMS *Pallas*, laid down in October 1863 and again built of wood, was a base for a larger 300 ft. all-iron frigate built on the same lines. HMS *Bellerophon*, laid down in December 1863 and completed in 1866, carried ten 9-inch muzzle-loading rifles in a centre battery behind 6-inch armour with 10-inch wood backing. She was in every way a first-class ship and no more broadside ironclads were laid down after two large wooden ships, *Lord Clyde* and *Lord Warden*, in 1863. Four of the converted liners were commissioned as broadside ships in 1863–4 but *Royal Alfred* was delayed and completed to the new centre-battery layout, as were two other earmarked liners, *Zealous* and *Repulse* (the latter commissioned in 1870 as the last wooden major unit in the Royal Navy).

This was still an exploratory period in warship design and in 1865 a new centre-battery armoured corvette of moderate dimensions was laid down. *Penelope* was a shallow-draught vessel possibly primarily intended for littoral operations in the Baltic.[5] The following year a larger variant of *Bellerophon* was begun, the well-named HMS *Hercules*, armed with 10-inch muzzle-loading rifles and with armour half as thick again as her predecessor.

As these new developments took place at home, the work of the fleet overseas continued. The Far East was a major focus, the experience and equipment of the Russian War proving useful in the littoral operations that occurred after the seizure of the British-flagged merchantman *Arrow* on 8 October 1856. The war-experienced Rear Admiral Sir Michael Seymour, in the sailing 84-gun *Calcutta*, with steamers and ships' boats and their crews, took retaliatory and coercive action. The following year Seymour was reinforced by a flotilla of the new gunboats whose presence enabled successful operations against junks moored close to Canton. The victory could not be followed through because of the Indian Mutiny but at the end of 1857 an Anglo-French force including a Naval Brigade of 1500 men finally occupied Canton. The Chinese proved obdurate and on 20 May almost a dozen British and French gun vessels and gunboats bombarded the Taku forts at the entrance to Peiho river both accurately and destructively. The Chinese abandoned the forts and, led by the gun vessel HMS *Cormorant*, the allies broke the boom on the river. The flotilla then moved on Tientsin, which commanded Chinese communications with central and southern China. The Chinese had little alternative but to sign a treaty that conceded all allied demands.

The Chinese, however, refused to ratify the agreement and in 1859 more coercion was necessary. The experienced Seymour was replaced by Rear Admiral James Hope, who, in June, again led a force to the mouth of the Peiho to obtain passage to Peking, by force if necessary. The Chinese had blocked the entrance to the river and Hope thought he could carry the position with his two gun vessels and nine gunboats – but he sailed into a trap. His flagship, the gunboat *Plover*, was so badly damaged she had to be lashed to the side of the larger gun vessel *Cormorant*, to which a wounded Hope transferred his flag. *Kestrel* was sunk and three more gunboats went aground, one to prevent her sinking. With the forts apparently silent, about 350 Royal Marines plus a few sailors went ashore, but the landing parties sank into the mud, suffered heavily from Chinese fire and had to withdraw. Eighty-nine personnel were killed and 345 wounded in 'the Royal Navy's only significant defeat in the nineteenth Century'.[6] *Cormorant* and *Plover* were both lost, as was the gunboat *Lee*, but *Kestrel* was raised and two other grounded gunboats were floated off.[7]

In 1860 a large Anglo-French army was sent out to avenge this defeat, war being formally declared on China. Troops were landed and the entrance to the river cleared. Supported by Hope's flotilla on the river, the allies advanced on Tientsin. Then, supported by ships' boats carrying the siege train and stores, the army advanced to Peking. The Chinese were forced to sign another treaty, giving foreign access to Chinese ports and the capital. The British also gained Kowloon to add to Hong Kong, and British gunboats began their task of policing Chinese rivers.

Japan also felt the power of the Royal Navy in an engagement that had much technical significance. After the American trade treaty with Japan was signed in 1854, anti-Western feeling was strong and in 1862 a British merchant was murdered. Retribution was demanded. If the Japanese authorities refused, 'the Admiral commanding British forces in these seas will adopt such coercive measures, increasing in their severity, as he may deem expedient to obtain the required satisfaction'.[8] This was Vice Admiral A. L. Kuper, C.-in-C. of the East Indies and China Station. He flew his flag in the 35-gun screw frigate *Euryalus*, with a screw corvette, screw sloop, paddle sloop, two gun vessels and gunboat *Havock* under command. Off Kagoshima three Japanese-owned steamers were captured and destroyed when Japanese forts opened fire, to some effect, with 13 men being killed and 50 wounded. Despite deteriorating weather, Kuper returned their fire and considerable damage was caused ashore. Five more Japanese vessels were destroyed before the storm forced the British to withdraw.[9]

Problems were experienced with the Armstrong breechloaders during this engagement. There were 28 accidents from 365 firings. Vent pieces were blown out, firing was delayed, the path of shells was unpredictable and the shells were unreliable. Most of the problems were with the big 110-pounders and it was decided to withdraw them from service and adopt more reliable heavy muzzle-loading rifles.[10]

The Armstrongs were still in service, however, the following year when war between Japanese factions allowed more action against anti-Western forces. In September 1864 Admiral Kuper led a more powerful international force to penetrate the Straits of Shimonoseki. He still flew his flag in *Euryalus*, but now he also had the 78-gun liner *Conqueror* carrying a battalion of Royal Marines and two 110-pounder Armstrongs on her upper deck. These were used at long range, with more defects becoming apparent. After the bombardment, landing parties occupied the defending forts and destroyed them, some guns being brought off. Sailors and marines did considerable fighting ashore. The Japanese agreed to open the strait and, after another naval demonstration off Osaka, the Japanese ratified the treaties with the Western powers.[11]

The American Civil War and the forcible removal by the Union navy of Confederate emissaries from the British ship *Trent* in October 1861 led to crisis with the USA. This necessitated the strengthening of the North America and West Indies Station, which was reinforced to nine liners with two large and five smaller frigates in 1862. The fleet was concentrated at Bermuda. As the chances of intervention on behalf of the Confederacy receded, the fleet was run down to one liner and five frigates. The first four ironclads were, however, based in the Tagus to reinforce station commander Rear Admiral Sir Alexander Milne if the situation deteriorated. These would have been much more than a match for the coastal ironclads of the Union navy.[12] The American Civil War also saw a windfall in the shape of two turret rams being built for the Confederacy by Lairds; they were taken over and commissioned as *Scorpion* and *Wivern*. They spent most of their lives as harbour defence ships on the America and West Indies and China Stations respectively.

After the Russian War, in the context of the perceived crisis with France, the size of the Royal Navy increased and the amounts voted went up accordingly. The numbers of sailors and marines voted increased from 55,700 in 1857 to 84,100 in 1860, although the numbers were down again, to 69,000, by 1865. The Estimates came down to less than £10 million after the war (14 per cent of the total budget in 1858) but increased again to £12.6 million in 1861 (over 18 per cent). They then came down again to £10.4 million in 1865 (16 per cent of the budget).[13]

In this period the lower deck made the transition to long-term service. In 1857 the Admiralty weeded out less suitable personnel as part of a cull of seamen in home waters. This had negative effects in giving the Admiralty a bad reputation as a long-term employer.[14] Nevertheless, by 1858 two out of three sailors were on long-term engagements and, by 1865, nine out of ten.[15] The year 1857 also saw the adoption of standardized ratings' uniforms.[16] After the difficulties of the Russian War, attempts were also made to improve the reserve situation. In 1856 the Coast Guard was transferred from the Customs Board to the Admiralty and restricted to younger men with fleet experience. Guardships were provided at ports to provide training but Coast Guard numbers remained limited.

In 1858, following pressure from several quarters, including the royal couple, a Royal Commission on Manning was set up, which reported the following year. Its aim was to allow the peacetime fleet to increase from 151 to 370 units in the event of an emergency. This required an increase in seamen from 47,000 to 100,000, of whom up to 40,000 would be seamen and 20,000 gunners. The Commission recommended the creation of a proper Royal Naval Reserve (RNR), recruited from experienced merchant seamen who would undertake part-time naval training in return for a retaining stipend. At first the take-up was very low, but the crisis with the USA was of considerable assistance in gaining recruits and the RNR, created in August 1859, had 12,000 enrolled by 1862, and 17,000 by 1865.[17] In the meantime, though, the increase in numbers required by the French war scare had to rely on older methods. A bounty was offered, a traditional device not used against Russia. The men thus raised were often of dubious quality but their impact on the professionalization of the long-term men on the lower deck was limited.

One reason for this was that the Commission recommended measures to improve training of the long-service ratings. It recommended training ships, both static hulks and a flotilla of brigs. The sailing liner *Illustrious* had become a training establishment for boy seamen in 1854 and she was joined by *Implacable* in Plymouth in 1855. The experiment, though highly successful, was short-lived as *Implacable* was soon closed and *Illustrious* was converted into an officer cadet training establishment in 1857. For the first time, new-entry officers, previously largely (and since 1837 completely) entered straight into ships, were to undertake a formal training course. At the beginning of 1859 *Illustrious* was replaced at Portsmouth by the larger sailing liner HMS *Britannia*, which, after a brief, uncomfortable sojourn at Portland, arrived at Dartmouth – a suitably remote anchorage to reassure Victorian parents – in 1863.

In accordance with the Manning Commission's recommendations, static training ships for ratings were re-established. In 1860 *Implacable* was reopened at Devonport and the following year *Boscawen* was established in Southampton Water. *St Vincent* opened at Portsmouth in 1862 and *Ganges* at Falmouth in 1866. Training brigs gave sail experience. Other recommendations of the Commission were free uniforms for continuous-service entrants, free bedding and feeding utensils for recruits, an improved scale of victualling and improved pay for gunners.[18]

By the mid-1860s, therefore, the modernization of the Navy had proceeded apace. Officers and men were part of a professional, uniformed service. They were serving in a fleet whose cutting edge was provided by powerful armoured vessels. The wooden sailing battlefleet, built in such quantity since the late 1850s, was obsolete. In 1864 the Controller recommended the retention of only eight wooden liners as a home reserve, to be used as guardships. A similar number continued to serve on foreign stations as there were as yet no suitable ironclads to replace them. Almost the entire operational fleet was steam powered. The Navy could not pause for breath, however: yet more technological developments were on the way.

In 1866 the defection of some Government supporters over parliamentary reform caused a brief return of the Tories, in a minority government under Lord Derby. Disraeli was Chancellor and Pakington again First Lord. Disraeli was very critical of the Admiralty, writing to the Prime Minister in extreme terms about its maladministration and waste.[19] Pakington responded with equally extreme claims as to the poor state of the fleet and the need to maintain, if not increase, the Estimates. Naval Lords who were MPs threatened resignation and, despite the Chancellor's efforts, the estimates for 1867–8 saw an increase of over half a million pounds to about £11 million. In early 1867 ministerial reshuffling saw a new First Lord, Henry Corry, a naval administrator of some experience. Much to Disraeli's disgust, Corry was able to defend the Estimates the following year, although the Chancellor was able to prevent a second major increase in expenditure. The French threat was again stressed, to ensure an adequate ironclad programme. In 1867–8 six 6000–7000 ton centre-battery ironclads were laid down, primarily for foreign stations, as was a full-sized improved Hercules, HMS *Sultan*.

The arrival of the distant station ironclads allowed the last wooden capital ships to be withdrawn. HMS *Rodney*, the last in commission, returned home from the China Station to pay-off in 1870. The previous year five steam liners had taken part in the cruise of the Reserve Fleet, the last time a non-armoured British wooden battle line would be seen. There were now enough ironclads to cope with a French threat that was, the politically motivated cries of the Admiralty notwithstanding, declining.[20] Despite the good performance of the Austrian two-decker *Kaiser* in action at Lissa in 1866, wooden line-of-battle ships seemed obsolete in an era of rapid technological change. It was neither cost-effective nor politically acceptable to maintain the wooden battlefleet, although existing vessels had many more years' service ahead of them as static hulks.

The controversy over seagoing turret ships took much attention. The Derby government had inherited one and began another. Captain Coles had kept up his pressure for turret ships and in 1865 a Committee had been set up to investigate the practicability of such vessels. It reported that a turret ship had many advantages but that it was difficult to combine turrets with the freeboard needed to provide a true seagoing capability with sails.[21] It was decided, therefore, to build a trial ship; the result was HMS *Monarch*, laid down at the beginning of June 1866, shortly before the change of government. *Monarch* had a high freeboard and two centrally mounted turrets, each with two 12-inch muzzle-loading rifles. She was as satisfactory as any fully rigged turret ship could be and was a minor triumph for her doubtful designer, Reed, who thought the concept of the fully rigged turret ship flawed.

Coles was far from satisfied and, even before *Monarch* had been laid down, his public criticisms had led to his being sacked from his position as consultant to the Admiralty. Backed by public and press opinion, he was soon reappointed and allowed to build, in co-operation with Lairds of Birkenhead, a seagoing turret ironclad of his own design. Reed and Robinson were both sceptical of the low freeboard proposed but Pakington, conscious of the political support for Coles, approved of the design 'on the entire responsibility' of the designer and Lairds.[22] Robinson and Reed effectively washed their hands of the affair, perhaps somewhat irresponsibly. HMS *Captain* was laid down in January 1867.

A little less controversially, turrets were applied to five smaller mastless ironclads laid down in 1867–8. Three were coast defence ships for colonial use; a fourth, *Glatton*, was a coast attack monitor; and the fifth, *Hotspur*, a fleet ram. Ramming had been apparently vindicated at the 1866 Battle of Lissa, between the Austrians and the Italians. Given the inability of the guns of the period to penetrate or even hit moving armoured targets, the unrealistically high hopes put into ramming were were understandable.[23] Ram bows became standard in most warships, not just specialist 'rams'.

The Tory Government's building programme was impressive, no less than 13 ironclads being authorized. Indeed its failure to control the Admiralty contributed to the defeat of the Conservatives in the election of 1868 and the return to office of the Liberals under Gladstone. The Prime Minister appointed Hugh Childers as his First Lord. Childers has been a figure of considerable controversy, subjected at the time – and since – to denunciation as ignorant, doctrinaire, brusque, offensive and unwilling to listen to advice.[24] However a more balanced view is now possible thanks in large part to the work of John F. Beeler.[25] Childers was certainly not ignorant of the Navy. He had served as Civil Lord during the latter years of the Somerset administration and since 1866 he had been on close terms of friendship with the Controller, Spencer Robinson. Childers was chosen to pursue a Gladstonian policy of retrenchment and financial prudence. He, and many others, thought this could only be carried out by a programme of radical administrative reform.

Childers changed the way the Admiralty conducted its business. The Board was reduced in size by two Naval Lords and the duties of its members were altered. The First Naval Lord lost his control of *matériel* and the dockyards to Robinson, who became 'Third Lord and Controller'. The First Naval Lord, assisted by a Junior Naval Lord, picked up all business connected with manning, operations and deployment. Childers' old post was strengthened as 'Financial Secretary'. These three officials were now department heads responsible to the First Lord, who held meetings with relevant Board members in his room as required. The Board as a whole met only rarely and briefly, 33 times in 1870 as opposed to 249 occasions four years before. Childers also introduced a scheme to retire flag officers by age. Unfortunately this led to a break with the difficult Spencer Robinson, who became a focus of discontent. This led in turn to tensions with Reed, who resigned in July 1870 to join Whitworths, the arms manufacturer.

Childers inherited HMS *Captain* as she was approaching completion. He was an enthusiast for the more radical ship, despite increasing professional doubts about her design. *Captain*'s freeboard was less even than that designed, just over 6.5 feet, and this for a ship with a heavy sail plan. As a sign of his confidence, Childers put his second son, a Midshipman, on board. In 1870 she went to sea with Admiral Sir Alexander Milne's Channel Fleet. Coles was on board to observe his triumph. On the night of 6 September 1870, under sail in heavy winds, HMS *Captain* capsized and sank with the loss of all but 17 of her ship's company of 490. Coles and Midshipman Childers were among those lost.

At the Court of Enquiry, Reed give the misleading impression that the ship had been sent to sea despite clear warnings that it was unsafe.[26] The Court concluded 'that the *Captain* was built in deference to public opinion expressed in Parliament and through other channels, and in opposition to the views and opinions of the Controller and his department and ... the evidence all tends to show that they generally disapproved of her construction'.[27] Childers tried to defend himself, arguing in a minute published in December that he blamed the Controller for not warning him of any misgivings about *Captain*'s safety. Childers was already a sick man and the pressure led to a complete nervous breakdown and an offer of resignation. Gladstone refused it and ordered a rest, making his First Lord's prospects better by dismissing Robinson. Childers' health problems persisted, however, and at the beginning of March Gladstone decided he could no longer continue in office.

The much-maligned man left a mixed legacy. He succeded in cutting the estimates quite significantly, to less than £10 million, less than 14 per cent of the national budget.[28] The dockyards at Deptford and Woolwich were closed in 1869. Part of the logic of this was, however, to release funds for new construction as three new ironclads were authorized that year. They were radical ships, seagoing variants of the three colonial monitors. Reed had explained the conception of the new larger ships in a memorandum in March 1869. The Admiralty's object, he wrote, had been 'to produce a warship of great offensive and defensive powers well adapted for naval warfare in Europe. The capability of the ship to cross the Atlantic has also been considered; but the primary object, and that in view of which the qualities of the design have been regulated, is that of fitness for engaging the enemy's ships and squadrons in the British channel, the Mediterranean, and other European seas'.[29]

The first two of the new and revolutionary ships, *Devastation* and *Thunderer*, were laid down in 1869 and a slightly larger third, *Fury*, in 1870. They carried twin 12-inch muzzle-loading rifles in turrets fore and aft and had armoured belts a foot thick, backed by up to a foot and a half of wooden backing. The first two were launched in 1871 but not completed for some time, to await the findings of a 'Committee on Designs of Ships of War', set up in the immediate aftermath of the *Captain* disaster.

Childers' reforms required a powerful First Lord and his illness allowed the new system to degenerate into apparent chaos and paralysis. Favourable press commentary gave way to serious criticism. The new First Lord was George Goschen, a man of no naval experience but very conscious of the need to restore public confidence in the service. He proceeded cautiously and not until March 1872 did he propose changes.[30] The Board was reformed with three Naval Lords jointly responsible for policy, although the First Naval Lord remained the First Lord's principal professional adviser. The Controller left the Board as an officer under the First Lord (with a Deputy Controller to superintend dockyards) and a Naval Secretary was created to oversee personnel. The Financial Secretary became a Parliamentary Secretary, and effectively a deputy First Lord, while the Civil Lord, previously his assistant, took over specifically financial issues. The Board was to meet again as a whole to decide policy collectively.

Attention now turned to the report of the Committee on Designs. The evidence of the witnesses examined by the Committee demonstrated both the advanced nature of Admiralty thinking and the way in which the Navy thought about naval war. As Captain Sherard Osborn put it, 'the probabilities are, that the day for fleet actions on the high seas has gone by; and that fleets will in future be used at strategical points upon their own or their enemies' coasts'.[31] This work emphasized operations against shore fortifications. The new low-freeboard seagoing turret ships lent themselves to such operations in support of more specialist coast attack vessels (disguised for political reasons as 'coast defence ships'). The scare in 1870 caused by the Franco-Prussian War allowed four such small double-turreted monitors of the Cyclops class to be laid down.

With both economy (the Estimates were only 9.5 million in 1872–3, 13.5 per cent of total budget[32]) and technological uncertainty acting as a brake on construction, progress with the new turret ships was not rapid. *Devastation* was commissioned after thorough tests in 1873, but *Thunderer* only proceeded slowly. On the advice of the Committee, *Fury* was redesigned with improved protection (14-inch armour), armament (12.5-inch guns) and stability. She also had the extra range conferred by the Committee's recommended compound engines: 5700 miles at 10 knots as against 4700 in *Devastation* and *Thunderer*. Reed's successor, Nathaniel Barnaby, said that, as modified, the renamed HMS *Dreadnought* was 'as efficient an engine of war for naval actions in the Channel, Mediterranean or Black Seas as can be contrived in the present state of knowledge'.[33] Work began again on her in 1872.

Goschen did not follow the Committee's recommendations slavishly. It had come out against the continuance of sails for cruising, but the fleet still needed such vessels to maintain a truly global capability, especially as rival powers were still building such ships. More centre-battery ships were therefore laid down in 1873; *Alexandra*, a fine unit with two 11-inch and ten 10-inch muzzle-loading rifles (MLRs) in a two-deck battery, and *Temeraire*, which mounted two of her four 11-inch MLRs in barbettes fore and aft, as well as two more 11-inch and four 10-inch in the centre battery. A smaller masted ironclad, HMS *Shannon*, was also laid down in 1873. It was seen as a necessary counter to similar small French and Russian ironclads, especially on foreign stations where larger first-class ships would be uneconomical. *Shannon* was armed with 10-inch and 9-inch MLRs and had 6–9-inch armour with a foot of wooden backing.

The early 1870s saw a race in gun size between Britain and Italy for their new first-class ironclads. Both powers were planning ships with the largest guns centrally mounted on turrets placed on top of a short, very heavily armoured citadel. Pushed by the British announcement that their new ship *Inflexible* would mount 60-ton guns, the Italians decided to give their two new Duilios weapons of similar size. This caused the Admiralty to increase *Inflexible*'s armament to 81-tonners of 16.25-inch calibre. The Italians then ordered huge Armstrong 100-ton 17.7-inch guns for their ships but the Admiralty, after some debate, decided to stay with the 16.25s because of limitations of space. The huge muzzle-loading rifles loaded through hatches outside the turrets, to which the weapons had to be returned after every shot, and had a rate of fire of one round every eleven minutes. *Inflexible*, a super-ironclad of 12,000 tons, with two feet of armour, was laid down on 24 February 1874.

Static underwater explosive charges, 'torpedoes', (i.e. what would now be called mines) had been used against the Royal Navy in the Russian War. Attempts to deliver them on spars from small craft were practical but dangerous and an automobile torpedo had obvious advantages. It was developed by Bolton-born émigré engineer

Robert Whitehead, at his works in Fiume. The first prototype was built in 1866 but was erratic in depth-keeping. This was solved by Whitehead's secret depth-control mechanism and by 1868 he was displaying 14-inch and 16-inch compressed air-powered torpedoes with speeds of about 6 knots and an effective range of a few hundred yards. The First Lord, Corry, stated that 'the professed performance of the torpedo is so marvellous that one could hardly believe it'.[34] The Royal Navy soon showed interest and a committee of gunnery officers from the Mediterranean Fleet observed trials at Fiume in the autumn of 1869. Their report led to Whitehead being invited to Britain, with his new devices. As D. K. Brown has put it, this was yet 'another demonstration of the nineteenth century Admiralty's readiness to consider and adopt novel technology'.[35] Whitehead gave a convincing demonstration, and two examples of each size of weapon were purchased for trials for the paddle sloop *Oberon* in September and October 1870. Ranges and speeds of 600 yards at 7 knots were obtained. The old wooden corvette *Aigle* was sunk by a 16-inch torpedo at almost 135 yards. The Admiralty duly bought Whitehead's secret and the manufacturing rights for £15,000, beginning production at the Royal Laboratory at Woolwich Arsenal in 1872.

The same year a committee was formed to consider the best means of delivery of the new weapon, whose most effective combination of speed and range was 200 yards at 9 knots. A hit was devastating, but with a torpedo speed slower than that of a contemporary warship, such a success would only be practical against a stationary target, either disabled or at anchor. The Committee proposed four forms of deployment. Normal surface warships could be fitted with launching carriages. Ships' boats could be fitted with dropping gear for Whiteheads and equipment for spar torpedoes. Specialist torpedo launches could be built for deployment in larger ships and larger purpose-built torpedo vessels could be constructed. The first of the latter was HMS *Vesuvius*, laid down at Pembroke in March 1873 and commissioned the following year. Ninety feet long, she was built for stealth; she had a submerged bow torpedo tube and could carry ten 16-inch Whiteheads. She was meant for attacks in harbours at night and her maximum speed was just under 10 knots. Given the slow speed of the Whiteheads themselves, surprise would be vital in a torpedo attack. It is surprising that so much attention and enthusiasm was given to the torpedo, a weapon of such dubious fighting value – one that would not sink an armoured warship for another 20 years.[36]

The strength of the overseas stations was a matter of dispute, the supporters of economy, notably both Disraeli and Gladstone, railing against large numbers of vessels spread about the globe. As Gladstone wrote to Goschen in 1871:

That for which I have been disposed to contend is that we are to have a powerful fleet in and near our home waters, and that outside of this nothing is to be maintained except for well defined and approved purposes of actual service, and in quantities of force properly adjusted; and not under the notion that there are to be fleets in the various quarters of the world when a difficulty arises with a foreign country, or an offence to our own ships then and there to deal with it with a strong hand.[37]

Unfortunately the 'well defined and approved purposes of actual service' required significant overseas flotillas to support foreign and imperial policy and maintain good order at sea. The numbers of ships on foreign stations were however reduced, from 145 in 1865 to 100 in 1871, the largest individual station being China, with 23, half of them gun vessels and gunboats.[38]

Forty-four of the 100 combatant ships on foreign stations in 1871 were gun vessels and gunboats. New construction of these invaluable little vessels was required because of the rapid deterioration of the war-built units. Eleven 755-ton Plover class wooden gun vessels were launched in 1867–8 with a twelfth in 1871. No less than 18 shallow-draught 600-ton composite gun vessels of the Beacon class were also launched in 1867–8, using the engines of the older but rotten Russian War vessels. Compound engines were used in the 430-ton Ariel class composite gunboats, nine of which were launched in 1871–3 and the four improved Beacons of the Frolic class were launched in 1872. The shallower-draught vessels in particular lent themselves to coastal attack in major conflict as well as to imperial riverine work.

A new type of specialist shallow-draught gunboat also appeared in 1870 for littoral duties, the so-called 'flat-irons' – short tubby vessels of about 250 tons mounting a 10-inch muzzle-loading rifle. After two prototypes were launched in 1867 and 1870, a production batch of 20 Ant class were launched between 1870 and 1874. To get these vessels built, their coast defence function was emphasized to obtain the funds from worried parliamentarians; but their real purpose was more aggressive: Cherbourg or Kronstadt. They could be deployed strategically by being fitted with temporary keels and their construction allowed the larger contemporary compound-engined gunboats and gun vessels to be used for deeper-draught seagoing constabulary and presence duties.

Larger cruisers were also needed on the foreign stations. In 1871 there were nine steam frigates, a dozen corvettes and 18 sloops deployed overseas.[39] The frigates were still almost all wooden, but in 1866 a new type of large unarmoured iron frigate had been laid down. In a reversal of the practice with capital ships, these vessels were clad with wood, which allowed coppering to deal with tropical marine growth. Three were built, *Inconstant* and *Shah*, together with a slightly smaller *Raleigh*, and they proved useful foreign station ships; their wartime role was to deal with American commerce raiders. Fifteen wooden screw corvettes (1500–2000 tons) were launched between 1867 and 1874, two slightly larger examples with provision for troop carrying (one of them the last ship built in Woolwich dockyard) and three iron corvettes of over 3000 tons. Wood was retained as the construction medium for new sloops: six 1600-ton examples of which were launched in 1865–6 (the Amazon class) and six 940-tonners (the Fantome class) in 1873–4.

The cruisers and gunboats were kept busy policing the seas all over the world and supporting British interests afloat and ashore. The China Station remained active. Between 1861 and 1869 12 gunboats and two gun vessels captured 46 pirate craft.[40] In August 1868, in a dispute about missionaries, the imposing station flagship – the steam wooden liner *Rodney* – was sent up the Yangtze to assist in obtaining British demands. This was one of the last operational deployments of such a ship.

An interesting and little-known naval operation took place closer to home off Spain in 1873, when the dissolution of the Spanish state caused the seizure of Cartagena and most of the Spanish fleet by a dissident group, the 'Intransigentes'. The new Spanish republican government declared the ships to be pirates. The British built up a squadron off the Spanish coast and worked in co-operation with the newly unified German government. The British force included the broadside ironclad *Lord Warden*, the centre-battery ironclads *Swiftsure, Triumph* and *Invincible*, and the centre-battery corvette *Pallas*. Two rebel ironclads were captured and handed over to the Madrid government and Valencia was protected from rebel bombardment.[41]

In 1873 war also broke out in the Gold Coast between the Ashanti and the British-protected peoples of the coast. Men were landed from the available British warships to help defend the coastal settlements. Small naval gun and rocket boats from the larger vessels supported operations against rebel sympathizers in Elmina on the coast. Commodore John Commerell VC was sent to take charge and reinforce operations, but in his initial moves there was trouble with dissident locals and casualties ensued, including the Commodore, who was wounded and had to quit the station. A naval brigade operating ashore played a key role in securing Elmina and forcing the Ashantis to retreat. The brigade remained even when more troops arrived and took part in the victorious advance that culminated in the burning of Kumasi in February 1874.[42] The ship of the line HMS *Victor Emmanuel* was deployed as a depot ship and won the last battle honour bestowed on a 'wooden wall'. She subsequently went on to Hong Kong, where she became receiving ship until 1898.[43]

February 1874 also saw a change of government in Britain. The Conservatives under Disraeli won the general election with a clear majority. The new Prime Minister was a traditional opponent of naval expenditure and the prospects for the Admiralty were not good. Oscar Parkes called the subsequent period the 'Dark Ages of the Victorian Navy'.[44] It was indeed a time of limited expenditure, but no more limited than in previous years. Indeed, the Disraeli Government saw a slight increase in the Naval Estimates. The last Gladstone Estimates had totalled £9.9 million; the first Disraeli Estimates were £10.3 million and expenditure in 1874–5 was 14.4 per cent of the total budget.[45] The Prime Minister had hoped that his choice of First Lord, the portly Ward Hunt, was a man after his own heart and 'that there would be no repetition of the continual demands for increased funding that had marred the three previous Conservative administrations'.[46] Hunt was described to the Queen by the Prime Minister as 'having the sagacity of an elephant as well as its form' – he had to have a semicircular piece cut out of the Admiralty Boardroom table to take his ample girth.[47] The First Lord was so comfortable in his new environment that he went native. He accepted an alarmist assessment prepared by Sir Alexander Milne, the First Naval Lord, and the other Naval Lords, arguing that the fleet as it stood was inadequate for war. Hunt argued in the House of Commons that he wished to possess a fleet of 'real and effective ships and not dummies'.[48] A minor naval scare was created, although Hunt was made to look a little silly by the very limited increases in expenditure he was allowed by the Prime Minister and the Treasury. The following year the First Lord returned to the fray, arguing to the Prime Minister that the Royal Navy only had 30 of the 32 ironclads needed, and, of those, fewer than 20 were ready for immediate service. He wished to increase the dockyard labour force, increase pay for warrant officers to stimulate improvement and spend more on torpedo warfare.[49] He duly obtained an increase to £10.8 million.

Hunt continued his campaign for the next year. A Memorandum on HM Fleet was prepared by Milne, in which he and his colleagues made serious complaints about the state of the fleet, especially in unarmoured vessels. The 'alarmist' tone, which may have been sincerely meant but which was objectively somewhat unrealistic given the contemporary naval balance, did the trick financially; the Estimates for 1875–6 totalled £10.9 million, despite the darkening economic position as the Victorian 'Great Depression' began to bite.[50] The upward trend continued into 1876–7, with the Estimates exceeding £11 million (£11.3 million) for the first time since 1868–9. Income tax had to be increased back to the level the Government had inherited. In preparing the Estimates for 1877–8, Hunt was able to claim that the state of the fleet was now such that a reduction in the Estimates was possible, to just less than £11 million. These were the last that the rotund Hunt prepared. His health was failing and he died at the end of July 1877.[51] It cannot have helped Hunt's condition to have waged such an indefatigable – and largely successful – campaign on behalf of his department. In the circumstances, Parkes's criticism of the minister as 'our most ineffective naval administrator' seems particularly unjust.

During Hunt's period of office, the ships laid down in the previous administration were brought to completion. *Thunderer* was commissioned in 1877, as were the centre-battery ships *Alexandra* and *Temeraire* (the latter only a month after Hunt's death.). All four Cyclops class coast-attack monitors were also in service by the end of May 1877. *Shannon* was close to commissioning and *Dreadnought* and *Inflexible* had been launched. The latter was delayed by a public attack on her design by Reed that led to the creation of a Committee to investigate.[52] Two larger versions of *Shannon, Nelson* and *Northampton* were laid down in late 1874 and launched in 1876. Although much criticized in later years, at the time these were regarded as highly desirable flagships for foreign stations, where their enhanced mobility – compared with previous ironclads – was at a premium.[53] Two new smaller and more economical 12.5-inch gun versions of *Inflexible, Agamemnon* and *Ajax* were laid down in 1876. They were primarily intended for coastal operations both offensive and defensive and had a shallow draught that reduced their handling characteristics.[54]

Armoured ships, however, were not the main issue of the Sea Lords' complaints. It was the state of the unarmoured fleet that caused most concern. A new class of six corvettes, the 2120-ton Emeralds, was launched in 1875–7, as were three 4000-ton Bacchante-class corvettes. Construction also began in 1876 of the first six of a new class of 2380-ton corvettes of the Comus class. All these ships had compound engines for long range under power (all were also fully rigged) but their speed was limited to around 13 knots for the smaller ships and no more than 15 for the larger. A revolutionary new type of all-steel cruiser was, however, under development. Two all-steel 3730-ton high-speed 'despatch vessels' were laid down at Pembroke in November 1875 and March 1876. In 1879 *Iris* and *Mercury* turned out to be the fastest ships of their day, the latter making 18.57 knots on trials. They were unarmoured but heavily subdivided for protection and were armed as corvettes with ten 64-pounder muzzle-loading rifles. They set new design standards and these two ships can rightly be called the first modern cruisers. The Hunt cruiser programme was completed by a new class of five

1130-ton sloops of the Osprey class. New classes of gun vessel, gunboat and flat-iron gunboat were also begun, no less than 27 such vessels being launched by 1877.

Hunt had defended his estimates with specific reference to the need to invest in torpedo warfare and in 1876 he allowed Thornycroft, the builder of steam launches, to build a similar vessel for torpedo attack. Thus was born *Lightning*, Torpedo Boat (TB) No. 1, a 32.5-ton vessel capable of 19 knots and carrying twin 14-inch torpedoes in frames amidships for lowering into the water. On completion in 1877, she was sent to the torpedo school, HMS *Vernon*, to develop tactics for such vessels and techniques for countering them. In the year of *Lightning*'s completion *The Times* mused that six such vessels built for an 'expense quite trifling compared to great ships of war' might be more of a threat to first-class ironclads than the new Italian Duilios.[55]

Hunt's tenure of office seems less a 'dark age' than a time of healthy naval policy. The number of ships on overseas stations came down slightly, from 100 in 1871 to 98 in 1876, but the units that were deployed abroad were efficient enough.[56] In 1874–5 Captain G. L. Sulivan was appointed to the steam liner HMS *London*. Sent to Zanzibar to act as an anti-slavery headquarters ship, she utilized small steam craft to capture 39 slaving dhows between October 1874 and April 1876.[57] Sulivan also assisted the Sultan of Zanzibar in 1875 in reasserting his authority over Mombasa after a five-hour bombardment by gun vessels supported by smaller craft.[58]

In 1875 a punitive expedition was sent up the River Congo in retaliation for attacks on a British merchant schooner. In a classic example of gunboat diplomacy, the corvettes *Active* and *Encounter*, the paddle sloop *Spiteful*, and the gunboats *Merlin, Foam* and *Ariel* proceeded upriver under the command of Commodore Sir William Hewett and attacked and destroyed villages suspected of being implicated in the piracy.[59]

A more famous engagement took place on 29 May 1877 off the western coast of South America, between the rebel Peruvian ironclad *Huascar*, declared a pirate by its government, and the frigate HMS *Shah* (flagship of the British C.-in-C. Pacific, Rear Admiral A. F. R. De Horsey), accompanied by the corvette *Amethyst*. Amethyst's 64-pounders were of little use against the turret ship's armour but *Shah* had more success with her 9-inch and 7-inch RMLs. *Huascar* tried to ram *Shah* but was driven off. A torpedo fired by *Shah* – the first ever fired in anger by the Royal Navy – was easily avoided. The action showed above all the difficulty ships of this period had in inflicting damage on each other; *Huascar* scored no hits on the two British hulls at all. She was hit about 70 times but only lost one killed and three wounded. An attempt to sink her by a boat raid miscarried, but the hapless rebel ship was later surrendered to the legitimate government.[60]

The unfortunate Hunt's successor, appointed on 14 August 1877, was W. H. Smith, grandson of the founder of the famous chain of newsagents. Smith had entered Parliament in 1868 and had been given the post of Secretary of the Treasury after the 1874 election victory. He had no naval background – indeed he was the model for Gilbert and Sullivan's Sir Joseph Porter KCB in *HMS Pinafore* – but was an able enough administrator. Disraeli hoped he would maintain his Treasury instincts but the situation was not appropriate. Naval expenditure for 1878–9 would rise to almost £12 million; the reason was a war crisis.

Russia's victory over the Turks in the war of 1877–8 was marked by the Treaty of San Stefano in March 1878, which mapped out a 'big Bulgaria', potentially under strong Russian influence, that would give Russia access to the Aegean. The question of Russian access through the Dardanelles was left to bilateral Turkish–Russian – rather than international – agreement. Britain could not accept this settlement and war threatened. Even before San Stefano in January 1878, after the fall of Plevna, a vote of credit of £1.4 million had been added to the Naval Estimates to purchase for the Admiralty ironclads under construction in Britain for Turkey and Brazil. This had been mooted since 1875 and was now carried out to demonstrate British resolve to contain Russian ambitions. Two, *Belleisle* and *Orion*, were armoured centre-battery rams being built at Samuda's yard at Poplar; the third was a Reed centre-battery masted ironclad *Superb*, building at Thames Iron Works, all for Turkey; the fourth, the masted Reed turret ship *Neptune*, building at Dudgeons at Milwall, was for Brazil. Of these, only *Belleisle* was available for immediate service; the others were commissioned between 1880 and 1882.

As the crisis deepened in 1876, the C.-in-C. Mediterranean, Vice Admiral Sir James Drummond, concentrated his fleet at Besika Bay near the mouth of the Dardanelles. There were ten ironclads in the Mediterranean, including *Pallas* and *Research*, the flagship being *Hercules*. In early 1877 Drummond was succeeded by Vice Admiral Sir Geoffrey Phipps Hornby. In the words of Clowes, Phipps Hornby, a former Second Sea Lord, had

established for himself a reputation scarcely second to that of any British naval officer then living. He was a great student of professional history; he had a wonderfully clear head, and a scientific mind; he was a natural diplomatist, and an unrivalled tactician; and, to a singular independence and uprightness of character, he added a mastery of technical detail, and a familiarity with contemporary thought and progress that were unusual in those days among officers of his standing.[61]

Phipps Hornby joined the fleet at Malta in *Alexandra* on 17 May 1877 and took it once more to Besika Bay, where it remained until December, when it went to Vourla Bay at the entrance to the Gulf of Smyrna. As the Russians advanced, Phipps Hornby received orders to pass through the Dardanelles to Constantinople, but these were soon countermanded and then altered to a move into the Sea of Marmora. Phipps Hornby had six ironclads, the centre-battery ships *Alexandra, Swiftsure* and *Sultan*, the centre-battery/barbette ship *Temeraire* and the broadside ironclads *Agincourt* and *Achilles*. *Agincourt* and *Swiftsure* were left at Gallipoli and Phipps Hornby arrived off Constantinople with the others on 15 February 1878. This acted as significant diplomatic support to the Turks. As Disraeli limbered up to confront Russia, *Devastation* replaced *Sultan* and the Channel Squadron, under Vice Admiral Lord John Hay, was sent to Suda Bay in Crete. Hay then moved to occupy Cyprus.[62]

To replace the Channel Squadron at home, a Particular Service Squadron was formed from the Reserve Fleet, under Admiral Sir Astley Cooper Key. This was composed of the centre-battery ironclad *Hercules* (flag), turret ship *Thunderer*, broadside ironclads *Warrior, Hector, Valiant, Resistance* and *Lord Warden*, the armoured corvette *Penelope*, the turret coast-attack ships *Prince Albert, Glatton, Cyclops,*

Hecate, Gorgon and *Hydra*, the new unarmoured corvette *Boadacea*, the flat-iron gunboats *Blazer, Bustard, Tay* and *Tweed* and the paddle despatch vessel *Lively*.[63] This was a heterogeneous group but it posed a significant coast-attack threat in European waters and was a not inconsiderable bargaining chip in Disraeli's negotiations. The Prime Minister's diplomatic success was mainly a result of his willingness to deploy the considerable striking power of the contemporary Royal Navy in support of diplomacy. With the Russians safely withdrawing, Phipps Hornby came back through the Dardanelles in March 1879.

The time of the Russian war scare saw a considerable enhancement in the Royal Navy's torpedo capabilities. Eleven more Thornycroft torpedo boats were built in 1878–9, with seven more boats built by other builders for comparison. Thornycroft also built 11 small 60.5-ton second-class torpedo boats for use on larger ships' davits. A floating base for these smaller boats was also procured: the converted merchantman HMS *Hecla*, launched as a 'torpedo depot ship and floating factory' in 1878. She acted as mobile headquarters for torpedo and mine warfare in the Mediterranean, as well as a means of striking at enemy ships in harbour. The most spectacular torpedo development was, however, an attempt to combine the torpedo with a major 2640-ton unit, a fast (18 knot), low ram-type vessel with an armoured deck and armed with five 18-inch underwater torpedo tubes, one at the bow and two on each beam. She was intended as a main fighting unit to sink ships disabled after the first mêlée of an action at sea or to break into an enemy port and attack vessels there.[64] *Polyphemus*, as she was named, was laid down at Chatham in September 1878 and commissioned in 1882. She was an innovative vessel, although soon to be made obsolete by the development of quick-firing artillery.

Cooper Key became First Naval Lord in 1879. Beeler characterizes him as a 'cautious and conservative man, traits that would have served him well in more stable circumstances, but which were detrimental in times of great upheaval'.[65] Key's appointment was an attempt to head off attempts by Phipps Hornby and others to strengthen the professional staff at the Admiralty. Hornby had made his appointment as First Naval Lord conditional on such reforms. Key, despite his Liberal sympathies, was willing to serve under Smith – a First Lord often preoccupied with general political duties – and

he had no problems in continuing when Gladstone swept to power
in 1880.

The criticisms of Key and the contemporary Admiralty are over-
stated. Progress in technology was made and a prudent conservatism
was a useful counter to the overenthusiasm for innovation that would
soon do much to destroy French sea power. As Director of Naval
Ordnance in 1868, Key had overruled the Ordnance Select Committee that had recommended readoption of breechloaders. The
Committee was vague in its reasoning. Key and other British
gunnery officers had pointed to specifics, the higher muzzle velocity
of British muzzle-loaders, their greater strength and reliability.[66]
Improvements in breech-loading technology, combined with the
new, slower-burning powders needing longer barrels, changed the
situation in the 1870s. In 1878 Sir William Armstrong informed
the Admiralty of the potential of his new breech-loading artillery.
There was some discussion of mounting the new guns in *Ajax* and
Agamemnon, but the then First and Second Naval Lords, Sir George
Wellesley and Sir Arthur Hood, were unenthusiastic.[67]

The situation was changed by a serious accident in HMS *Thunderer*
in January 1879, caused by double-loading one of her muzzle-loading turret guns. An Ordnance Committee was appointed to consider
the adoption of breechloaders. The Admiralty tried to rush its fences
by independently calling on the War Office (still responsible for the
procurement of artillery) to build Armstrong breechloaders for the
next ironclads. The Ordnance Committee recommended guns
designed by the Royal Gun Factory at Woolwich and the latter were
eventually adopted, rather against the will of the Admiralty, which
was increasingly chafing at War Office control of naval guns. The
three ironclads laid down in 1879, two enlarged, 9420-ton versions
of the Agamemnons, *Colossus* and *Majestic* (later renamed *Edinburgh*),
and the smaller 6200-ton *Conqueror* turret ram were all to be armed
with 12-inch breechloaders. Advantage was also taken of the new
guns to design a ship using barbettes rather than turrets. Key did
not like the open mountings on top of the armoured towers but
Smith was convinced of the cost advantages and authorized the
experimental barbette ram, HMS *Collingwood*. Breech loading was
now generally adopted; 20-pounders had already been used as

anti-torpedo boat armament and medium-calibre 6-inch, 5-inch and 4-inch breechloaders were now also brought into service. Six-inch breechloaders were fitted to the new ironclads to supplement the slow-firing big guns and to inflict damage on the unprotected areas of enemy ships. The Agamemnons had two, the Colossus class five, *Conqueror* four and *Collingwood* six.

Gladstone's First Lord was Thomas George Baring, Earl of Northbrook, who was somewhat preoccupied as 'Gladstone's colonial trouble-shooter'.[68] His financial background was again designed to limit the Estimates. Northbrook was indeed able to keep annual naval outlays below £11 million in the early 1880s. The lowest year was 1882–3, £10.5 million, less than 12 per cent of total budget, but no lower than the previous administration's levels in absolute terms.[69] Ships on foreign stations remained at about the hundred mark and ironclad construction proceeded relatively slowly.

The much-delayed *Inflexible* was finally commissioned, complete with new electric light installation, in 1881. The Agamemnons followed in 1883, but their two larger sisters did not appear until 1886–7. *Collingwood* was laid down in July 1880 but again was not completed until 1887. The *Collingwood* concept was, however, expanded into a full class of barbette ships, of the Admiral class, stimulated by concern over French building programmes. *Anson, Camperdown, Howe, Rodney* and *Benbow* were all laid down in 1882–3. The first four were armed with four 13.5-inch breechloaders, the last with two huge 16.25-inch weapons. They also carried three 6-inch breechloaders on each beam. Their design seems to represent the beginnings of the return to emphasis on ship fighting ship at sea. Barnaby, their designer, thought that contemporary French ships seemed to be 'designed to appearance with a view to heavy fighting in the Mediterranean, the Channel and the Baltic, than for purely coastal work'.[70] Two new second-class armour-plated steel barbette ships, *Imperiuse* and *Warspite*, for foreign stations, were also laid down in 1881. They were armed with four 9.2-inch breechloaders and ten 6-inch, and were completed in 1886 and 1888 respectively.

Construction of non-armoured vessels also continued. The new steel cruisers, based on the Isis-class despatch vessels, were developed and put into production in the shape of four 4300-ton Leanders, laid down in 1880–1, and four slightly smaller but more heavily armed Merseys, laid down in 1883–4. These had an armoured protected deck that, in the Merseys, extended the full length of the ship. Six more traditional 1420-ton Satellite-class large sloops (later rated corvettes) were laid down in 1880–1 (and another in 1883). Two fine 2770-ton corvettes, *Calypso* and *Calliope*, were also laid down in 1881. *Calliope* is famous as the only warship to survive the Samoan hurricane in 1889. All these ships were armed with the new medium-calibre breechloaders. In 1880–4 nine new sloops were launched, along with four composite gun vessels and over a dozen new composite gunboats. The torpedo flotilla was also enhanced, with an improved class of 56 ft. second-class boats built by Whites for use from larger ships; these replaced the earlier second-class boat and became the prototype for a new class of general-purpose steam picket boat.

In 1882 occurred what Laid Clowes called 'the most serious naval operation in which British men of war were engaged in the last quarter of the nineteenth century'[71]: the bombardment of Alexandria. Brigadier Arabi Pasha had seized power in May 1882, in a coup intended to liberate Egypt from Anglo-French power. An international squadron assembled off Alexandria, where riots took place in June that drove out most of the foreign residents, some of whom took refuge on the warships. The forts defending the port were strengthened by Arabi's troops while the Anglo-French coalition was rocked by France's unwillingness to associate too closely with what many Republicans saw as a popular revolt. The responsibility thus fell on the British and on Admiral Sir Frederick Seymour's Mediterranean Fleet. This consisted of the centre-battery ironclads *Alexandra, Invincible, Sultan* and *Superb*, the centre-battery/barbette ship *Temeraire*, the centre-battery corvette *Penelope* from the home reserve, the pioneer turret ship *Monarch*, and the newly commissioned giant turret ship *Inflexible*. In support were three gun vessels, *Beacon, Bittern* and *Condor*, two smaller gunboats, *Cygnet* and *Decoy*, the paddle despatch vessel *Helicon* with the torpedo depot ship *Hecla* acting as an ammunition supply vessel in the absence of targets for her torpedo boats.

On 10 July Seymour insisted that the Egyptians evacuate their defences and disarm, on pain of bombardment the following day. This caused a final evacuation of foreigners in non-British warships and a British liner. The C.-in-C. transferred his flag to *Invincible*, whose shallow draught enabled her to operate in the harbour itself. Seymour had little fear of the defences, which were of antiquated construction and mainly armed with old smooth-bore guns: there were only 44 rifled pieces available to the Egyptians, less than half the British total. Seymour planned to take *Invincible* and *Penelope* inside the harbour itself, with *Monarch* placed inshore to the westward beyond the breakwater. *Inflexible* was to stand off the breakwater to support the inshore squadron and engage the Ras el Tin forts as required. The other ironclads were to engage the Ras el Tin and other batteries on the Arsenal peninsula to the east of the harbour – although in the event *Temeraire* supported *Monarch*. Led by Lord Charles Beresford's *Condor*, the smaller vessels engaged the Marabout forts to the west, earning *Condor*'s commanding officer a 'well done' from the C.-in-C.

Firing began at 0700 and lasted ten and a half hours. Seymour was hindered by having to use armour-piercing shells with a small bursting charge or common shell with defective fuses. It was estimated that about half the rounds fired did not explode, exploded prematurely or broke up on impact. *Inflexible*, commanded by Captain John Fisher, managed to fire her giant muzzle-loaders 208 times and her shooting was judged to be good. She was damaged by the blast of her own guns and by several hits. Other ships hit were *Alexandra, Sultan, Invincible, Superb* and *Penelope*, but their armour proved effective in preventing serious damage. Only five men were killed and 28 wounded while silencing the forts and inflicting about 550 casualties (about 150 killed), 25 per cent of the total defending force.[72]

On the following day Seymour was reinforced by the broadside ironclad *Achilles* from the Channel Squadron and the Egyptians hoisted a flag of truce after a few more rounds from *Inflexible* and *Temeraire*. The Egyptians proved reluctant to surrender but by the 13th, after *Helicon* had evacuated 150 more refugees, the defences had been abandoned and Seymour landed sailors and marines under Captain Fisher to help maintain order. On the 17th more of the Channel Squadron arrived, the broadside ironclads *Agincourt* and *Northumberland* with the troopship *Tamar*, and began to land reinforcements. Fisher organized an improvised armoured train that proved useful for reconnaissance.

Rear Admiral N. Hewett, C.-in-C. East Indies, landed marines at Suez on 2 August; at the other end of the Canal on the 20th, *Monarch* landed marines to occupy Port Said. The ram *Orion* and the corvette *Carysfort* supported the taking of Ismalia by a naval landing force and soon the Suez Canal was in British hands. A Naval Brigade took part in the battle of Tel el Kebir on 13 September, which defeated Arabi Pasha's forces and confirmed British power in Egypt. This necessitated operations against the Mahdi, the religious leader in the Sudan in revolt against the Egyptian government. In these operations, naval personnel distinguished themselves ashore, notably Captain Arthur Knyvet Wilson of *Hecla*, which had been ordered through the canal to give support to Hewett's landing forces at Suakin. Wilson won the VC at the battle of El Teb.

The operations in Egypt marked the last classical nineteenth-century bombardment. Despite Clowes's comment that Alexandria had not been a 'very brilliant or dangerous exploit', it had been successful and was another demonstration of the capability of a strong contemporary fleet against inferior defences.[73] Ships could still defeat forts. Even the critical Parkes admits that, 'The Egyptian war showed the navy to advantage, and both the bombardment of Alexandria and the Nile operations reacted to our national prestige at the expense of France. Naval power had been exercised to safeguard British interests when another nation equally threatened had preferred to climb down, and the man in the street was in good conceit with the Fleet.'[74]

The naval policy makers of the 1860s and 1870s had been vindicated. There had been no 'dark ages'. Yet times were changing. The promise, if not the performance, of new technology implied that fighting at sea, rather than from it, would preoccupy naval planners more than it had done in the previous decades. Doubts were being expressed both in private and in public about the adequacy of the Royal Navy to engage in such operations. The stage was being set for a redefinition of both the nature and the size of the fleet.

4 The Two-power Standard

In September 1879, after the Russian War scare, the Carnarvon Commission had been appointed to investigate imperial defence. It recommended that the defence of the Empire 'should be based on command of the sea rather than on large garrisons and fortifications' and 'that the strength of the Royal Navy should be increased with as little delay as possible'.[1] Although the Reports of the Commission were kept confidential, as the Gladstone Government worried about excessive pressure on the Estimates, the major new ship-building programme described at the end of the previous chapter was already in train. A sister turret ram to *Conqueror, Hero*, was laid down in 1884, making a total of 12 new ironclads under construction that year.

Also, because of the Commission, a Foreign Intelligence Department in the Admiralty was established at the end of 1882. Other changes in Admiralty structure occurred that year. The Naval Lords were increased from three to four once again, with the Controller rejoining the Board. To balance naval and civilian membership an additional Civil Lord was created to act as Deputy Controller.[2]

French ironclad programmes in the late 1870s and early 1880s were considerable and worrying. The margin of British superiority seemed slim and caused pressure for new construction and flurries in the press in 1882–4. The Admiralty was more confident. At the end of 1884 the First Naval Lord estimated that he had 27 ironclads in commission against France's 11; within a month there could be 13 more against only one French.[3] Happily for the Admiralty, French naval politics confirmed British superiority. The influence of the Jeune Ecole and its enthusiasm for torpedo warfare and commerce raiding contributed to many of their proposed armoured ships being seriously delayed or abandoned. No new French battleships were laid down between 1883 and 1889.

The ideas of the Jeune Ecole had their echoes in Britain. In July 1884 Northbrook confided to the House of Lords that even if his department had unlimited money it would not know how to spend it. Developments in both artillery and torpedoes made it 'most imprudent greatly to increase the number of these enormous machines'.[4] These views reflected those of Key and the professional members of the Board, who were impressed by the potential of torpedo attack, especially on ships at anchor. The First Naval Lord also thought that a large sum for new building would only encourage foreign construction. The Estimates for 1884–5 were, however, the largest since 1878–9, £11.2 million, 12.9 per cent of national expenditure.[5]

The trend in naval expenditure would soon turn rapidly upwards. In the autumn of 1884 the *Pall Mall Gazette* published a series of articles entitled 'The Truth about the Navy', based on information provided by Captain Jackie Fisher, by now commanding HMS *Excellent*, and Reginald Brett (later Lord Esher), private secretary to the Secretary of State for War. These very successfully focused attention upon the alleged deficiencies of the fleet in ships, equipment, organization and personnel. Cooper Key and the Board, who had plans for further new construction, exploited the agitation.

An extra £3.1 million was eventually obtained for a new construction programme over the next five years. This 'Northbrook Programme' included two new turret ships armed with twin 16.25-inch guns, *Victoria* and *Sans Pareil*. These were effectively enlarged Conquerors, designed more for coast attack than seaborne engagements. For trade-protection work, a new class of 5000-ton belted cruisers, the Orlando class, was ordered, armed with two 9.2-inch and ten 6-inch breechloaders. Five were laid down in 1885. To provide a fleet torpedo craft for both offensive and defensive operations, two small Scout class torpedo cruisers were laid down in 1884. These were now put into production as six units of the Archer class. The recently stimulated navalist lobby considered this flurry of new activity insufficient. Unjustly, Cooper Key was blamed for the lack of a more ambitious programme but he had achieved approximately what he had realistically expected.

The international situation now helped the navalists. In 1884 Russian expansionism caused concern. In March the Russians defeated the Afghans and the British made clear their determination to oppose their moves. The main counter was a Particular Service Squadron, formed under Phipps Hornby, as a Baltic Expeditionary Fleet for littoral operations in that theatre. It comprised 13 armour-plated ships, the broadside ironclads *Minotaur, Agincourt* and *Lord Warden*, the centre-battery ships *Hercules, Sultan, Iron Duke, Shannon* and *Repulse*, the turret ships *Ajax* and *Devastation*, the turret rams *Hotspur* and *Rupert* and the corvette *Penelope*. The torpedo ram *Polyphemus* and the depot ship *Hecla* provided alternative approaches to torpedo warfare, plus a mixed bag of eight cruisers, including an armed merchantman, and a flotilla of flat-iron gunboats. Sixteen torpedo boats were also allocated to the squadron. With conciliatory noises coming from St Petersburg, the Squadron carried out exercises that emphasized offensive and defensive torpedo warfare. *Polyphemus* achieved fame by breaking into Berehaven by smashing the boom, a clear demonstration of the continued emphasis on offensive littoral operations.[6]

The Russian War scare led to an enhancement of torpedo capabilities. Over 50 large torpedo boats were built as possible 'catchers' for enemy torpedo boats. Four 550-ton torpedo gunboats of the Rattlesnake class were also laid down. Heavily armed with both guns and torpedoes, they were designed to make 19.5 knots, as fast as many torpedo boats at the time. Two more Archer-class torpedo cruisers brought the class to eight.

As the war scare dissipated in 1885, the issue of Ireland divided Gladstone's Cabinet, which was defeated in the House on 8 June. Lord Salisbury formed an interim administration with Lord George Hamilton as First Lord. Hamilton wanted to make significant changes in both the Admiralty and the Dockyards. As a first step, he sacked Key as First Naval Lord and replaced him with Sir Arthur Hood. Barnaby also tendered his resignation as Chief Constructor, tired of the constant bickering of his brother-in-law Reed. Hood recommended the appointment of William White, who became Director of Naval Construction in October and Assistant Controller in December.

Against this background, the Board was discussing two more armour-plated ships. Over Barnaby's opposition, the Northbrook Board had recommended twin-turret ships, which appealed to Hood, who exerted his influence to obtain a modified version of *Dreadnought* with breech-loading guns and an armoured secondary battery. Like *Victoria* and *Sans Pareil*, the new armour-plated turret ships, *Nile* and *Trafalgar*, were to have the latest triple-expansion engines, giving them ranges of 6500 to 7000 miles at 10 knots, compared to 5700 miles in *Dreadnought*. The new engines had an even more marked effect on the Orlandos, two more of which were ordered for laying down in early 1886. These ships had a range of 8000 miles at 10 knots. The days of sail power were passing.

Gladstone, helped by the revised franchise of 1884, won the December 1885 election, and the Marquis of Ripon became First Lord in the Liberal Government that assumed office in February 1886. It confirmed plans for new armoured ships, although when he moved the 1886 Estimates, the Parliamentary Secretary John Hibbert asserted: 'I may safely say that these two large ironclads will probably be the last ironclads of this type that will ever be built in this or any other country.'[7] He did not remain in office long enough to judge the veracity of his prophecy, for the Government soon fell on the old hurdle of Irish Home Rule. Hamilton returned as First Lord in Lord Salisbury's Government in August 1886, staying in post until 1892. During this change of governments, Lord John Hay replaced Hood, who returned with the Conservatives, and this was the last time that a First Naval Lord's appointment was politically based. Hood was both temperamentally and politically conservative but careful and hard working.

Hamilton was able to complete the reorganization and re-equipment of the dockyards. This, combined with a desire to limit service Estimates, generated doubts over the utility of large armour-plated ships and White's desire to review their design prevented the laying down of any ironclads in 1887 and 1888. The existing ships under construction were anyway being delayed because of problems in manufacturing their heavy breech-loading guns at Woolwich, and, in the case of the 16.25-inch weapons for *Benbow*, *Victoria* and *Sans Pareil*, at Armstrongs. *Benbow*, *Rodney* and *Collingwood* were commissioned in 1888, *Anson, Camperdown* and *Howe* in 1889, *Victoria* and *Trafalgar* in 1890 and *Sans Pareil* and *Nile* in 1891. By the time they came into service they had been reclassified as 'battleships', a name officially adopted in October 1887.[8] This reflected the growing maturity of the ocean-going battlefleet, now abandoning sail power, and making the transition back to engaging its enemies at, rather than from, the sea. During the war scare of 1888, the Duke of Edinburgh, commanding in the Mediterranean, was told not to attack Toulon as he wished. Instead, if it came to war, the fleets were to engage the French at sea.[9]

The biggest ships laid down in the late 1880s were 'cruisers', as the smaller rates were officially reclassified in 1887. Two were innovative 9150-ton first-class ships with a protected deck, *Blake* and *Blenheim*. There were also five small and rather unsuccessful second-class ships of the Medea class. Six small third-class cruisers were laid down in 1888–9, four for distant stations and two faster variants for the fleet. As a result of the Imperial Defence Act of 1887, a belated response to the Carnarvon Commission, five larger Pelorus-class third-class cruisers were built for imperial station duties. The same period saw the completion of four composite and two steel sloops, as well as the laying down of 13 torpedo gunboats of the Sharpshooter class, two for the Indian Marine and two for the Australia Station, paid for by the Imperial Defence Act. The perceived supremacy of the torpedo was further confirmed by the laying down in 1888 of a 6600-ton torpedo boat carrier built on protected cruiser lines. Armed with 4.7-inch guns and capable of 20 knots, HMS *Vulcan* could double as a cruiser but her main armament comprised six new 16.5-ton Yarrow second-class torpedo boats, each of which could carry two 14-inch torpedoes.

The Junior Naval Lord on the Hamilton Board was Lord Charles Beresford, the hero of Alexandria, who had confirmed his reputation by his activities both ashore and in improvised river steamers against the Dervishes in the Sudan in 1885. He circulated a memorandum calling for a strengthening of the existing intelligence organization to operate as a war staff. Their Lordships were unimpressed by what they regarded as an impertinence, but Beresford nevertheless approached the Prime Minister with his proposals. This led to the conversion of the Foreign Intelligence Department into a larger Naval Intelligence Division (NID) but, although it contained a small Mobilization Division, its powers remained limited.[10]

In 1887 the Golden Jubilee of Queen Victoria saw a Review at Spithead. Ships of myriad shapes and sizes made a fascinating spectacle, after over a quarter of a century of breakneck technological development. Some contemporaries were less than impressed by the ships on display: Vice Admiral Sir William Hewett remarked that 'much of what you see is mere ullage'. Yet the vessels all represented significant combat value: broadside ironclads, centre-battery ships and turret ships, all had their advantages and disadvantages. The Channel Squadron covered the Atlantic and acted as a ready reserve. Thus it still needed long-range ships that previously had required sail and steam power, such as the pioneer turret ship *Monarch* and the larger broadside ironclads that were only now paying off into reserve as more modern vessels were acquiring the range to replace them. The earlier mastless turret ships were only really suitable for the Mediterranean but the advent of the triple-expansion engine was changing that. The Review and the contemporary pause in big-ship building marked a caesura in warship design. The fleet on display in 1887 was still ruling the waves, but such was the pace of naval development, it would very soon be totally obsolete. In the next ten years a totally new navy would be built.

In some ways the early years of the Salisbury Administration are more appropriately called the 'Dark Ages of the Victorian Navy' than the era of Gladstone and Disraeli. Its first year saw a reduction in the Estimates from 13.3 million in 1886–7 to 12.5 million for 1887–8, just over 14 per cent of a reduced total budget.[11] Key argued for a continuation of building on the scale of the Northbrook Programme, but expenditure on new construction fell from an annual average of £3.6 million in 1885–7 to £2.5 million in 1888–9.[12] Hamilton put the best face on it. In 1887 he claimed that because of 'exceptionally large' expenditure during the preceding years 'it would be possible for some years to come to associate a reduction of expenditure with an increase of naval efficiency and strength'.[13] Others might be more cynical. At the end of 1887 penny-pinching even included cutting the salaries of the officers in charge of the

NID. This stimulated Beresford to resign, to take up the Navy's cudgels in Parliament. The only bright spot was an increased number of seamen, boys and marines borne, reaching 62,600 by 1888.[14]

Early 1888 also saw a French war scare. From January, concern grew about preparations to mobilize the French fleet in the Mediterranean in increased strength. This reflected the recovery from the excesses of the Jeune Ecole, and the Admiralty reacted with wise caution, but public opinion was nervous, with a major public meeting in London in May passing resolutions for naval increases. By June the Queen was expressing her usual concern at the 'very unsatisfactory state' of the fleet. Thanks to Beresford a Select Committee of the House of Commons on the Naval Estimates was set up. Hamilton and the Naval Lords defended the current situation, claiming, rightly, that the fleet's strength was 'relatively greater as compared with the strength of the next naval power than it has been for many years past'. Hood explained that Victorian naval policy making involved receiving a sum of money from the Government and trying to obtain maximum value from it. He foresaw a limited programme of replacements into the next decade. Sir Anthony Hoskins, the Second Naval Lord, stated that he thought Britain should maintain a two-power standard over other naval powers, arguing such was already in place: in 1889 Britain possessed 22 first-class battleships, France 14 and Russia 7.[15]

The line presented by most Admiralty witnesses before the Select Committee was a reassuring one. The pressure was beginning to tell, however. The following month Hood and the other Naval Lords were asked to report on the fleet requirements in a war with France and Russia, to protect the British coast, Malta and Gibraltar from invasion or bombardment, to provide a reasonable level of protection for trade routes and coaling stations and to defend Constantinople. They recommended a five-year Special Programme of ten battleships, eight first-class and two second-class; eight first-class cruisers, 25 second-class and four third-class; and 18 torpedo gunboats. They also said steady new construction should continue after the conclusion of the Special Programme.[16]

Although Goschen, now Chancellor, publicly opposed Beresford on higher naval expenditure, his financial work made the new ambitions of the Admiralty practical. As Sumida points out, in 1888 he put through a conversion scheme that achieved a considerable decrease in the cost of servicing the National Debt. It became effective from April 1889. It had thus become possible to spend much more on the Navy without recourse, at this stage, to the politically dangerous alternatives of borrowing or greatly increasing taxation.[17]

Hamilton reacted to the Sea Lords' confidential report cautiously, although he did warn Parliament that he would lay before them in 1889 'a larger and more comprehensive programme than was provided by the current estimates'.[18] Then Parliament was presented with a report on the previous year's naval manoeuvres. It stated that the fleet was 'altogether inadequate to take the offensive in a war with only one Great Power... supposing a combination of two Powers be allied as her enemies, the balance of maritime strength would be against England [sic]'.[19] The authors called for a two-power standard to be clearly established. Navalist agitation thwarted attempts by Hamilton to downplay these warnings and the Naval Lords now had the situation they needed. Hamilton presented their proposed programme, which included five additional cruisers, to the Cabinet. The Naval Defence Bill was presented to Parliament in March. In introducing it, Hamilton declared to the House of Commons that Britain's battlefleet 'should be on such a scale that it should at least be equal to the naval strength of any two other countries'. These ships were to be of the newest type and 'most approved design', combining equivalent armour and armament to foreign vessels with more powerful engines for improved speed and endurance.[20]

The new five-year construction programme was costed at £11.5 million to be spent in the Royal Dockyards (plus £4.75 million to complete ships already building) and £10 million to be spent in private yards. Any annual underspend was to go into a special fund to be used later in the programme. The seven annual payments to the special fund for contract ships was about the same as the £1.4 million saved every year by Goschen's Debt Conversion Scheme. The average increase in the Estimates to cover shipbuilding was only £600,000 per annum. In all it was an elegant solution in line with Tory principles, involving no major tax increases or unwelcome borrowing.[21]

Hamilton hoped that the Naval Defence Act, which became law on 31 May 1889, would give Britain a permanent lead and might allow future economies. He announced a programme 'which I do not think all the Dockyards of Europe could complete in the time we propose; and if there are any nations abroad who do wish to compete with us in naval armaments, the mere enunciation of this scheme will show to them the utter futility of this desire'.[22]

The ships were an impressive bunch. To please the First Naval Lord, who retired in October 1889 and was replaced by Sir Richard Vesey Hamilton, one of the first-class battleships was an old-style low-freeboard turret ship, appropriately named HMS *Hood*. She was, in reality, the last and greatest (14,150-ton) coast-attack ironclad and, not surprisingly, proved unsuccessful as a seagoing battleship. In the others, White exploited the potential of new, lighter compound iron and steel armour which gave a high freeboard with armaments well clear of the water. With similar displacement to *Hood*, they fully lived up to their battleship designations and no less than seven were laid down subsequent to the Act. They were known as the Royal Sovereign class and had twin 13.5-inch breechloaders in open barbettes at bow and stern, with five 6-inch guns on each side.

The latter guns were of a new design, allowing much more rapid fire. These quick firers had been developed in the 1880s as light anti-torpedo guns, then in larger calibres. In 1887 a 4.7-inch quick firer (QF) proved able to fire ten rounds in almost 50 seconds, five times the rate of fire of the older 5-inch breechloader.[23] This promised devastating damage to the unprotected parts of enemy ships and an effective longer-range capability through sheer rapidity of firing. The new guns were therefore adopted before completion on the Trafalgars and a larger 6-inch version firing a shell of twice the weight chosen for the new ships. In many ways the 6-inch guns were the Royal Sovereigns' main armament. The two second-class battleships, for the China and Pacific Stations, were of 10,500 tons but faster and longer-ranged than their bigger cousins. *Centurion* and *Barfleur* carried twin 10-inch guns in covered barbettes. These new-style mountings would soon take over the term 'turret'. Their lighter QF armament was 4.7 inches in calibre. With the increased rate of fire of both sizes of weapon and the state of contemporary gunnery,

Centurion and *Barfleur* gave away little in real firepower to the first-class ships.

The lavish cruiser-building programme reflected the doubts over Britain's capacity to defend her trade. Nine were the Edgar class, smaller versions of the Blakes, a reduced machinery plant allowing a reduction of displacement at a cost of 2 knots in speed (20 knots on forced draught). Armament was the same, a 9.2-inch gun at each end and a powerful battery of five 6-inch QFs on each beam. No less than 30 second-class steel protected cruisers were ordered, the 3400 ton Apollo class. Armament was entirely QF – a 6-inch at each end and three 4.7-inch down each side. Four Pallas-class third-class cruisers, more powerful versions of the Pelorus design, were also laid down. The continued popularity of the torpedo gunboat as the preferred torpedo vessel was reflected in orders for 18 more. Not all were built, as thinking about larger torpedo craft for offensive and defensive use began to change.

Some problems were experienced in implementing the novel financing arrangements of the Naval Defence Act: the large orders, coinciding with increased demand for merchant ships, had an inflationary effect. Modifying the second-class battleships and enlarging the last eight second-class cruisers into the Astraea class and the torpedo gunboats into the Alarm and Halcyon classes also increased costs. In 1893 Earl Spencer, who had replaced Hamilton in 1892 after Gladstone's narrow election victory, had to ask for an extra £1.35 million as part of an extension of the programme and a revision of its accounting procedures. Nevertheless, as Sumida argues, the Act was:

a success from the standpoint of shipbuilding and finance. The continuous availability of funds, taken together with the administrative reforms and improvements in ordnance design of the late 1880s, resulted in the completion of most of the programme on schedule, which minimised excess spending... On average, expenditure above the original cost estimate for each warship ran to about 3%, which was a great improvement over the figures of 20 to 30% that had been the case between 1875 and 1885. The vessels provided under the Naval Defence Act nearly doubled the effective battleships and cruisers available to the Royal Navy.[24]

The torpedo gunboats were the least successful of the programme and were replaced by a new type of vessel while it was being implemented. The French had built torpedo boat stations along their coast from Dunkirk to Brittany and were constructing larger torpedo boat types to operate from them. This was a real challenge to British shipping in the Channel and countering it was the theme of the 1890 exercises. A flotilla of British torpedo boats, operating from Alderney and commanded by Commander J. Barry and Lieutenant Doveton Sturdee, mounted a surprise attack on Admiral Tryon's battlefleet in Plymouth Sound. The latter was forced to retire to the Scillies and the British torpedo boats were left free to roam the Channel attacking both merchantmen and Tryon's colliers. As Cowpe says: 'Clearly the French dispositions constituted a major threat to British naval supremacy in narrow waters; the question to be decided was the extent of the threat and how it could be countered.'[25]

In February 1891 Fisher, now both a Rear Admiral and Controller, wrote a memorandum stating that the only way the Channel could be defended, especially at night, was to destroy the torpedo boats' bases and or blockade them by 'vigorous offensive patrolling'. This required 'a cheap, tough vessel of light draught with just sufficient sea-keeping properties to maintain itself off the French coast and sufficient size to give an advantage of speed in rough weather over the torpedo boat'.[26] The torpedo gunboats proved disappointing in service, being too slow. Increasing their size, as done in the later classes to improve their speed and endurance, only made them better targets in night coastal engagements. William White admitted himself baffled; not so the torpedo-boat builders. Yarrow and Thornycroft both offered new designs: larger 26-knot vessels, built on torpedo-boat lines but with a heavy armament of a 12-pounder, quick firer and three 6-pounders, as well as three 18-inch torpedo tubes. A pair was ordered from both builders and the new 'torpedo boat destroyers' were laid down in July 1892. Yarrow's pair, *Havock* and *Hornet*, came into service in 1894.[27] Even before *Havock* was completed, two more 26-knotters had been ordered from Lairds in 1893, and the 1893–4 programme included 15 improved 27-knot boats from a number of builders.

The Estimates in the early 1890s averaged £14.2 million, the highest since the Russian War, between 16 and 17 per cent of the total budget.[28] This did not seem to be enough, however; by 1900 naval expenditure would double. The year 1893 saw this process begin with yet another full-scale naval panic. The Naval Defence Act had provoked, not demoralized, Britain's rivals. Between 1889 and 1893 France and Russia (formal allies from 1891) together laid down a dozen battleships. At the end of 1893, their amity was consummated by a much-publicized Russian visit to Toulon. France announced an intention to lay down five more battleships at the beginning of the next year. In the same period, Britain had built ten under the Naval Defence Act and the 1892–3 Estimates contained an eleventh, *Renown*, an improved second-class ship with 10-inch and 6-inch guns. Two more new and improved first-class battleships, *Majestic* and *Magnificent*, were planned for 1893–4, which left a shortfall in terms of the two-power standard. In July the Admiralty drew up a provisional programme of five more battleships but the Prime Minister, Gladstone, and Sir William Harcourt, the Chancellor, opposed it.

The Board of Admiralty that confronted these strong politicians was equally formidable. Sir Frederick Richards became First Naval Lord in 1893, replacing Sir Anthony Hoskins who had been in post since 1891. Marder speaks highly of Richards: 'a brilliant administrator whose contributions to the service have never received due recognition, from the beginning determined to quash any cheeseparing tendencies. His stern exterior, indomitable will, stolidity and disdain for verbiage made him a standing terror to the Chancellor of the Exchequer and those politicians who had too much regard for fiscal considerations'.[29]

Fisher testified to the First Naval Lord's 'stubborn will' and 'astounding disregard for all arguments'.[30] In August 1893, as Second Naval Lord, Richards had argued that France and Russia had to be regarded 'as one in the determination of the naval policy of England [sic]' and that Britain had to reply to their building.[31] In November, the new First Naval Lord met Fisher, Bridge and White to draw up two programmes, one a 'minimum', calling for seven new first-class battleships for bare two-power parity; the other the 'desirable', asking for ten to give a margin of superiority. As for cruisers, the 'minimum' total was set at 30 and the 'desirable' at 42, plus 82 destroyers (including the six already building) in both programmes. The following month the 'minimum' programme was adopted by Spencer, with an option on three more battleships if more were laid down abroad.

Despite enormous political pressure, Gladstone refused to budge as he saw the naval programme as both financially and politically destabilizing. The old man became isolated in his opposition and was forced to resign on 1 March, with a cover story of failing eyesight.[32] Lord Rosebery took over and the new Cabinet approved the £21 million five-year 'Spencer Programme' on 8 March. The Naval Estimates of 1894–5 were set at £17.64 million, a 20 per cent increase on the previous three years' annual figures. Harcourt was forced to increase the income from death duties, by introducing graduated rates. The programme promised still greater expenditure in the following year (the Estimates totalled £19.6 million). This was more than could be covered by the revised death duties. Spencer proposed a special naval works fund, to be financed by a system of borrowing called terminable annuities, to be repaid out of future Navy Estimates. A Naval Works Act with these provisions was passed in 1895.

The Spencer Programme rivalled the Naval Defence Act in its ambition. Seven more Majestics were added to the original two, making the battleship class the biggest ever. Nine-inch Harvey all-steel, face-hardened armour gave as much protection as twice the thickness of the composite armour in the Royal Sovereigns; 12-inch guns in covered barbette turrets were adopted as the best compromise of weight of shot and rapidity of fire (Fisher was an enthusiast for rapid-firing medium calibres and would have been happier with repeat Renowns). The last two units, *Caesar* and *Illustrious*, had improved circular barbettes that allowed loading at all angles instead of just fore and aft. A dozen 6-inch guns provided the effective main battery. These 14,900-ton vessels set the pattern for British battleships for a decade.

Even more impressive were the two huge 14,200-ton first-class protected cruisers, *Powerful* and *Terrible*. Over 100 feet longer than the Majestics, these two four-funnelled ships were direct answers to large Russian cruisers. They were designed for a speed of 22 knots and to steam 7000 miles at 14 knots. They were fitted with the new Belleville water tube boilers, which gave many problems despite their theoretical advantages. Armed with two 9.2-inch and twelve 6-inch guns they were powerful ships although their complements of 894, compared with a contemporary battleship's 672, made them expensive to operate. The coming of the armoured cruiser also made them rapidly obsolete. Their sheer bulk was, however, a sign that the large cruiser was beginning to rival the battleship as a capital (and expensive) asset. The original 30 cruisers of the December 'minimum' programme had included six reduced, 11,000-ton versions of *Powerful*, the Diadem class; twelve 5600-ton second-class Talbots; six third-class Pelorus class and six Arrogant class ram cruisers, for use with the fleet (an interesting vote of confidence in this old concept, perhaps confirmed by the sad accidental loss of HMS *Victoria* and Admiral Tryon to the ram bow of HMS *Camperdown* in the Mediterranean in 1893).[33] These programmes were trimmed with only nine Talbots being laid down. Work on the Arrogants and the Pelorus class was delayed until 1895 and the Diadems were held over indefinitely.

The mushroom growth of the destroyer flotilla was a final remarkable dimension of the Spencer Programme. As still more builders were involved, another twenty-one 27-knotters were laid down in 1894. Armament was standardized at one 12-pounder, five 6-pounders and two 18-inch torpedo tubes. That year, 30-knot designs were considered and in 1895 eight were laid down and more were planned to meet the Spencer Programme's ambitious total of 82. The destroyer was now the Royal Navy's standard torpedo craft, both offensive and defensive. Plans to build seven new torpedo gunboats were abandoned, as were the last two vessels of this type planned under the Naval Defence Act. Also abandoned were plans to build 30 small torpedo boats and another torpedo depot ship. Constabulary duties were not entirely forgotten: the Spencer Programme included two fully rigged Phoenix-class steel sloops.

While these ships were being built, Lord Salisbury came back to office after the victory of the Unionists (as the Tories now styled themselves) in the 1895 election. George Goschen returned as First

Lord. The new Government was more open to the requests of Richards and the Naval Lords, and navalist opinion was becoming more focused with the founding of the Navy League. The new Government expanded destroyer orders to a grand total of 89, either building or in service, by the end of 1886. The cruiser total was brought up to the 'desirable' programme of 1893 by beginning the Diadems, expanding their numbers to eight units at the expense of two rams and pressing ahead with the Pelorus class, to a total of 11 ships. Together with the eight cruisers building at the time the programme was drawn up, the 34 new cruisers amounted to 42.

The Naval Lords had presented the previous government with a recommendation for five more battleships. This was an extension even of the 'desirable' programme and, on assuming office, Goschen demanded reasons that would stand up in Parliament for the new ships. The Naval Lords based their argument on the fighting power of the latest second-class French and Russian battleships. These were surprisingly and disturbingly powerful and promised seriously to undermine the two-power standard. The rising power of the USA and Japan had also to be borne in mind. Goschen accepted the arguments and put five Canopus-class ships into the 1896–7 Estimates. These were innovative vessels with water tube boilers and the new Krupp armour, which had tougher backing than Harvey plates.[34] A 6-inch Krupp belt gave similar protection to the 8-inch Harvey belt of the Majestics and a greater proportion of the ship's sides could be armoured against lighter guns. The Canopus-class ships were slightly smaller than the Majestics but were faster (18 knots), drew about a foot less and carried the same armament. They could easily get through the Suez Canal (Majestics tended to ground) and were designed with the China Station in mind, where all but one eventually served. Four more were planned for 1897–8 but the increasing size of rival ships led to the desire for a bigger version. In the middle of 1897, the Board decided that three of the new battleships should be of Majestic size. These were laid down in 1898 as the Formidable class, enlarged versions of the Canopus with 9-inch Krupp armour belts.

The summer of 1897 saw the fleet paraded in the Diamond Jubilee Review: 164 vessels of all classes were on display, 30 miles of ships in five lines. The modern battleships and cruisers made a great impression on all who saw them.[35] The effect of the Review was to increase confidence in both the fleet and the Government's naval policy, which had taken over 20 per cent of the total national budget the previous financial year.[36]

The Review also helped stimulate yet more naval building by France and Russia – and Germany, which passed its first Navy Law in 1898, looking towards a fleet of 19 first-class battleships to coerce Britain into entente against her traditional rivals. These developments necessitated more British battleships. Three were included in the 1898–9 Estimates, even better-armoured developments of the Formidables, the London class. This was not deemed to be enough, given the Russian occupation of Port Arthur and their building of more battleships of apparently higher speed. A Supplementary Estimate was therefore presented to Parliament in July. This requested the construction of four improved smaller 19-knot Duncan battleships, designed to match the Russians in the Far East. Two more were included in the 1899–1900 Estimates and two more Londons in 1900–1. The improved design of these ships made them more expensive, about a million pounds each, instead of £800,000–900,000 for their predecessors.[37]

The coming of face-hardened armour allowed the first-class cruiser to rival the battleship as a capital asset. The French had begun building experimental armoured cruisers in the late 1880s but their 1896 programme included a much larger vessel, the 11,000-ton 23-knot *Jeanne D'Arc*, with a 6-inch Harvey belt, two 7-inch guns and 14 5.5-inch quick firers. More were planned. In May 1897 the Director of Naval Intelligence prepared a memorandum that exposed the threat to British trade – these new ships could outclass all existing British cruisers. A Supplementary Estimate was therefore introduced in July to cover the construction of armoured cruisers. Based on the Diadem design, but with 6 inches of Krupp armour (the same as a Canopus), these 12,000-ton ships were armed with two 9.2-inch and twelve 6-inch guns, giving them the effective firepower of a battleship. *Cressy, Hogue, Aboukir* and *Sutlej* were laid down in 1898 and two more the following year. White clearly saw them as part of the battlefleet as well as trade defence vessels.[38] These were followed in the 1898 programme by the 'gigantic' 500-ft., 14,150-ton Drake class with a 6-inch battery increased to eight each side. Four were laid down in 1899. These truly magnificent vessels were some of the greatest warships of their day. They were, however, too expensive and the 1898 Supplementary Estimates included four new Monmouth-class vessels of reduced size (9800 tons) but with the same speed as the Drakes. With their fourteen 6-inch guns, they were specifically designed as trade defence vessels rather than as capital ships, and six more were laid down in 1900–1.

The armoured cruiser had serious implications for the Naval Estimates. Spending on first-class cruisers tripled between 1895–6 and 1899–1900, from £828,000 in 1895–6 to £2.5 million in 1899–1900. Naval expenditure totalled £23.8 million in 1896–7, went down to £22.5 million in 1897–8 but increased to £26 million in 1898–9 and £29.4 million in 1899–1900, almost double the figure of the first year of the Naval Defence Act.[39] The Government was lucky that the buoyant state of the economy allowed a good return from the various forms of taxation; death duties were also more productive than expected. A second Naval Works Act in 1896 was therefore funded without borrowing. Delays in warship construction caused by excess demand and labour disputes (especially the engineering strike of 1897) also meant underspending of the shipbuilding parts of the annual budgets.

Numbers of personnel also increased. The number of seamen, boys and Royal Marines topped the 70,000 mark in 1892, reached almost 80,000 in 1894 and 100,000 in 1899 (104,239). Figures actually borne were less than those voted (100,050 men had been voted in 1897) so there was some truth in navalist complaints about under-manning.[40]

These global policemen had to be prepared for service afloat and ashore. Ships on overseas stations increased to 105 in 1895 from 91 in 1890 and remained at around that figure for the rest of the century.[41] In 1896 British-dominated Zanzibar suffered an anti-British coup. The third-class cruiser, *Philomel*, and the gunboat, *Thrush*, were at the island and the sloop *Sparrow* soon reinforced them. The ships landed men to guard British interests and more reinforcements arrived: the torpedo cruiser *Racoon* and the Cape Station flagship, the new protected cruiser *St George*. Rear Admiral Harry Rawson gave the rebel prince an ultimatum to haul down his flag by 0900 on 27 August. The ships opened fire, also engaging the Zanzibar gunboat *Glasgow*. The latter was put out of action and considerable damage ashore caused before the rebels complied at 0937. The British-backed Sultan was reinstated and duly saluted. Five hundred Zanzibaris were casualties, one British seaman wounded.[42] Thus ended what some have called the shortest war in British naval history.

In 1899 the Transvaal and Orange Free State invaded the British territories in South Africa. The British were short of artillery. Captain Percy Scott of the cruiser *Terrible* was at the Cape on the way to China and dismounted his guns, designing mountings for them to be used ashore. Naval Brigades played a significant role in the fighting ashore until they were withdrawn in 1900.

That year also saw the Boxer Rebellion in China. Royal Marines helped defend the Legations at Peking and a Naval Brigade landed from the ships of the China Station to operate as part of the international force ashore. A maritime attack was carried out on the Peiho Forts. The new sloop *Algerine* took part in the bombardment and Commander Craddock, of the despatch vessel *Alacrity*, led an international assault party that captured the forts. The destroyers *Fame* and *Whiting* captured the four Hai Hola-class Chinese destroyers at the Taku dockyard. The boats were divided between the British, French, Germans and Russians.

October 1900 saw a General Election in Britain. Capitalizing on the apparent Boer defeat, Salisbury and the Unionists were returned to power. The Cabinet was reconstructed and Lord Selborne became First Lord. He 'was a man with no previous interest or experience in Naval affairs' and the Prime Minister insisted that he take Hugh Arnold-Forster as his Parliamentary Secretary to lead for the Admiralty in the House of Commons. As Nicholas Lambert says, 'Arnold Forster's peers regarded him as something of an expert on defence matters. As a journalist and as a Member of Parliament he had made his reputation amplifying complaints about the inadequate strength of the armed forces made by various interest groups. His selection promised the jingoes in the party a voice in naval policy making.'[43]

The new team would need all the junior minister's enthusiasm and powers of advocacy as it was facing an imminent crisis over naval expenditure. The South African War had caused such an increase in defence expenditure that taxes had been raised and borrowing increased, so the National Debt ballooned by 25 per cent. In 1901 Michael Hicks Beach, the Chancellor, warned the Admiralty that the apparently unstoppable growth in naval expenditure would lead 'straight to financial ruin'.[44] The previous year had seen naval expenditure of over £33.2 million, over £3 million more than the Estimates themselves, thanks to Naval Works loans. Unfortunately, however, the repayments on the first Act were due in 1901–2.[45]

Selborne argued that Britain's credit depended on her fleet and that he could encompass no hopes of 'such a slackening of our efforts. To do so would surely entail our falling into an inferiority of strength in respect to France and Russia, and would leave our mercantile marine inadequately defended – a responsibility which I take it, no one would readily accept'. He argued for superiority in strength over the French and Russian battlefleets and more armoured cruisers to match the French programmes.[46]

The 1901–2 Programme had included three new, larger (and 20 per cent more expensive) King Edward VII-class battleships armed with four 9.2-inch guns, in addition to 12-inch and 6-inch, to help penetrate the increasingly formidable armour of potential enemy vessels. Six more trade-defence armoured cruisers were also included, of a somewhat enlarged and more heavily armed 10,850-ton Devonshire type. These carried four 7.5-inch guns in addition to six 6-inch, but were considered under-armed and, in the following year, the Admiralty reverted to capital ship armoured cruisers in the two Duke of Edinburgh class, armed with six 9.2-inch and ten 6-inch on a displacement of 13,350 tons. These ships could make 23 knots compared to the contemporary battleship's 18.5. They cost over a third as much as the Devonshires.[47] Two more King Edward VII-class battleships were also ordered.

In October 1902 Selborne presented his programme designed to obtain 'equality plus a margin' to the Cabinet. In the light of Germany's naval ambitions (made even more clear by the 1900 Navy Law), he was asking for, in effect, a three-power standard – of six battleships and no less than 14 armoured cruisers over the Franco-Russian total by December 1907. This would require three battleships and four armoured cruisers per year in the four financial years 1903–4 to 1906–7. The Cabinet, now led by Arthur Balfour following Salisbury's resignation that summer, approved, but Ritchie, the Chancellor, facing a gloomy economic outlook, expressed 'considerable concern'. He feared a 'violent reaction' to inflated taxation, which might mean lower Estimates in future, but felt compelled to go along with Selborne because of the new triple threat.[48] The 1903–4 Programme contained four more heavily armed (six 9.2-inch and four 7.5-inch) versions of the Duke of Edinburghs, the Warriors. Three more King Edward VIIs were also programmed.

Between 1902–3 and 1903–4 naval expenditure increased from £35 million to £40 million, over £4 million above the Estimates and almost 23 per cent of the total budget.[49] Selborne had warned the Admiralty that the Estimates were 'very near their possible maximum' and that economies would be required. One reason for the inflation in 1903–4 was the purchase of two ships under construction for Chile, to stop them being purchased by Russia – in confrontation with Japan with whom Britain had signed an alliance in 1902. They became *Swiftsure* and *Triumph*. This eliminated a battleship and an armoured cruiser from the 1904–5 Programme. Nevertheless the latter still included the still more powerful battleships *Lord Nelson* and *Agamemnon* to be armed with powerful armaments of four 12-inch and ten 9.2-inch guns. The three armoured cruisers were of an enlarged Minotaur class with four 9.2s and ten 7.5s. All these ships cost £1.4–1.5 million each.

British naval policy was approaching a major crisis. In October 1903 Selborne expressed his despair to Balfour about the financial outlook. In January he reduced the building programme slightly but this was not enough for the formidable new Chancellor, Austen Chamberlain. In April 1904 the latter stated plainly that 'the time has come when we must frankly admit that the financial resources of the United Kingdom are inadequate to do all that we should desire in the matter of Imperial Defence'. Selborne was allowed a last slight increase of Estimates to £37 million (total expenditure was £41 million, almost a quarter of the total national budget), but he had to agree that the Estimates would be much decreased in 1905–6, at a time when Naval Works Act loan repayments would be taking the equivalent of the 1904–5 increase.[50] Someone had a solution: his name was John Arbuthnot Fisher.

A man of considerable, if erratic, genius, Fisher had demonstrated his reforming zeal and energy as Second Sea Lord in 1902–3.[51] A major training reform was carried out, with a common entry for seaman and engineering officers. This was done more to make the engineering officers like seamen than vice versa and the effect was to make the Naval Officer Corps more rather than less socially exclusive, as the course length was doubled and fees were still charged.[52] Entry age was reduced to 12½ (then raised to 13). A Royal Naval College was opened at Osborne in 1903 to take the Selborne Scheme entries. A college at Dartmouth was being built, under Naval Works Act funding, to replace the *Britannia* and *Hindostan* hulks moored there. It opened for the second half of the new course in 1905. The syllabus taught at the Colleges was a progressive one by the standards of the day, being technologically and scientifically orientated. Fisher also improved the training and prospects of the lower deck. Commissioning was opened to warrant officers, stokers were given a warrant mechanician rank and a boy artificer's training establishment set up.

In 1903 Fisher was already convinced he could reduce naval expenditure by radical reforms involving increased efficiency. This fitted Selborne's agenda perfectly. When Fisher was appointed, in October 1904, the Naval Lords became officially First, Second, Third and Fourth Sea Lords. The last three were in charge of personnel, material and logistics; the First Sea Lord was in charge of major questions of naval policy and the organization, efficiency, mobilization and movements of the fleet.

Selborne presented Fisher's proposals, somewhat modified by his Board colleagues, to the Cabinet on 6 December 1904. Much emphasis was placed on the role of the armoured cruiser in providing a fast and mobile reserve capable of replacing deployed squadrons of weaker ships. The Navy would henceforth comprise three main commands in European waters. The eight battleships of the Channel Squadron would become the Atlantic Fleet, based at Gibraltar. The

Home Fleet would become the Channel Fleet, reinforced by four battleships from the Mediterranean to 12 units. The Mediterranean Fleet would have eight units; the China Fleet would retain five battleships until the outcome of the Russo-Japanese War became clearer (Fisher wanted to bring them home). Each European-based fleet would have attached flying squadrons of armoured cruisers 'ready to go anywhere' as required.[53]

The system of manning ships was to be drastically reformed, with shorter commissions and a reduced reserve based on a system of nucleus crews who could maintain vessels at adequate levels of fighting efficiency, something the previous system had notably failed to do. The fleet was to be drastically reduced by scrapping older and less capable vessels. So drastic was the proposed pruning that the Admiralty was reluctant to produce figures.[54] In order to man the vital armoured cruisers, about 60 older cruisers were scrapped – including the Naval Defence Act armoured cruisers left behind by recent developments – as well as a similar number of smaller sloops, gunboats and torpedo gunboats, some to scrap, some to reserve. By 1914 'there were scarcely a dozen seagoing sloops and gunboats left in service'.[55]

Also for disposal or hulking were old ironclads, despite the considerable sums spent on their modernization for coast defence duties in the 1890s. Fisher had a cheaper alternative for coast defence duties: 'flotilla defence', using torpedo armed destroyers and submarines. The torpedo had come of age through the addition of a gyroscope to ensure straight running. This made it a much more serious threat at ranges of 2000–3000 yards. Such weapons transformed the capabilities of surface torpedo craft and, together with improvements in internal combustion engines, made submarines useful weapons platforms. Despite doubts among the Naval Lords (that have been consistently overrated by most historians), the Admiralty, prodded by Arnold Forster, decided in 1900 to build five submarines, of the American Holland type, at Vickers. These were intended for experiments and to act as targets for anti-submarine exercises. All were in service by 1903, by which time 13 modified boats were on the way. Foster had convinced Selborne that the submarine was the answer to the invasion threat.[56]

Fisher was a great enthusiast for the new vessels and saw them, together with destroyers, as vital components of his concept of flotilla defence, based on groups of destroyers and submarines that would cheaply, economically and effectively deny the narrow seas to any opponent. Fisher persuaded the Earl of Cawdor, Selborne's successor, of the concept and it was secretly adopted the month Cawdor took office, March 1905.[57] A class of larger, more seaworthy, destroyers, the River class, came into service at this time. Fisher cancelled orders for more of these and instead ordered numerous Cricket-class coastal destroyers, half the size, for his flotillas. A long production run of C-class submarines was also put in train, 38 eventually being built.

Fisher did not like battleships, as he made clear in his writings.[58] He conceded that, for the time being, construction of them would have to continue but he planned to build vessels of radical, new, all-big-gun design. At the end of the previous century Captain Percy Scott had introduced a new method of employing quick-firing guns by keeping them continuously aimed on the target. This further enhanced their potential as long-range weapons but techniques were soon being evolved to increase the effectiveness of slower-firing big guns at the still longer ranges required to avoid the new torpedoes. In 1898–1900 the Mediterranean Fleet had pioneered experiments with controlled salvos at ranges of around 5000–6000 yards, and Captain Edward Harding, Royal Marines, published a paper on the technique in 1903. Scott, by now commanding *Excellent*, supported the idea of fire control. Harding, working for the Ordnance Department, carried out experiments in the battleships *Venerable* and *Victorious* and prepared a secret report. These newer battleships, with guns that could be loaded at any angle, could fire their 12-inch guns almost once a minute. Harding argued that fire control had turned naval gunnery on its head: no longer were medium guns the optimal long-range weapons. Twelve-inch weapons, with their flatter trajectories, could now be brought on to the target more easily at ranges of three miles or more and the effect of a 12-inch projectile was 4–5 times that of a 6-inch, more than making up for the larger gun's slower rate of fire.

By 1904 Fisher was calling for large armoured ships with a uniform armament of big guns capable of dealing catastrophic blows at ranges of six miles. These ships would be faster than previous vessels, as Fisher saw speed as the ultimate qualitative superiority in operational terms; no practical amount of armour could provide protection for 12-inch shells at ranges up to about 9000 yards. Therefore, he saw the all-big-gun armoured cruiser as his ultimate capital ship.

The arguments were thrashed out in a Committee on Designs for the 1905–6 Programme that met in January and February 1905. Four ships were to be built instead of seven, a catastrophic revenue crisis in late 1904 causing a reduction in the Programme. Fisher argued strongly for concentrating on the 12-inch gun-armed armoured cruiser but it was decided instead to build an all-big-gun battleship first. To Fisher's delight, however, the other three would be the new cruisers.

Although the all-big-gun ships were individually more expensive than their predecessors, their superior fighting power was the key to cost-effectiveness. The Committee on Designs pointed out that the proposed ships could take on superior numbers of more conventional vessels, so that fewer ships would have to be built, at least in the short term. It even said that the financial advantages were the most important aspect of the all-big-gun ships. It was crucial, however, both to build up a lead in them as quickly as possible and to gain experience with their armament and turbine power plants. This encouraged Fisher's showmanship. The new battleship, HMS *Dreadnought*, was laid down at Portsmouth on 21 October 1905 and was officially commissioned for trials with a nucleus crew on 1 September 1906. She carried out those trials in October and a battle practice in December. This was the new long-range (5000–7000 yard) gunnery test adopted earlier that year. Guns and mountings were obtained from the previous year's battleships and another set made, to give her the unprecedented armament of ten 12-inch guns. Her four shaft-geared turbines gave her a speed of 21 knots. Maximum armour thickness was 11 inches.

Dreadnought threw foreign building programmes into confusion. The Germans, with their finely tuned Naval Laws, were especially badly affected. Not until 1907 were all-big-gun ships laid down, and limited German industrial facilities meant they did not have turbine engines. This made them slow, less than 20 knots, and they were not completed until 1910, by which time Britain had seven Dreadnoughts and three Invincibles. The USA had already designed a pair of all-big-gun ships but these used reciprocating engines and were not completed until 1910, the year the first US Dreadnoughts proper appeared. Russia, Japan and Italy only began their first Dreadnoughts in 1909 and France and Austria in 1910.

Although Dreadnought would forever be associated with Fisher's name, the radical First Sea Lord saw her as an 'Old Testament' ship. His 'New Testament' 25-knot 12-inch gun armoured cruisers were designed – in some secrecy, as Fisher did not want their radical characteristics to be known – by mid-1905. The financial climate, however, did not allow their laying down until early the following year. By this time Fisher was contemplating a fusion design of ship 'combining the speed of the armoured cruiser with the offensive and defensive strength of the battleship'.[59] The 'Cawdor Memorandum' on Admiralty Policy, published in December 1905, left their characteristics open in its call for four large armoured ships annually.

Almost simultaneously Fisher called together an Admiralty committee to examine these characteristics. This 'Fusion Design' committee recognized the huge strategic changes that had taken place in the previous two years. Britain had effectively changed the whole strategic calculus of defence policy by her Entente with France in 1904 and backing Japan to smash Russia's power in the Far East. With little threat in the latter theatre, the China battle-ships had just been recalled home, boosting the Channel Fleet to 16 battleships by 1906. Germany was now the main – but not the only – threat and the Committee worried that going to the 'fusion' type would mean ships of such size and expense that by 1909 the British would have only have 'a bare numerical superiority over Germany in new armoured vessels'.[60] The Germans, with their more limited horizons, might also produce vessels of greater fighting power. In any case, the Germans were concentrating on battleships and their armoured cruiser force was weak. The committee therefore recommended that the next four armoured ships should be mainly battleships.

The terminally split Balfour Government finally fell at the end of 1905. Sir Henry Campbell-Bannerman became Prime Minister, with Lord Tweedmouth as his First Lord. The new government of Liberals and allies won a landslide victory in the January 1906 election, with a commitment to social reform. This meant limiting the defence estimates. In fact, Fisher's reforms had already allowed significant cuts in the Estimates, which fell from £37 million in 1904–5 to £33.15 million in 1905–6 and £31.5 million in 1906–7.[61] Naval expenditure was reduced to less than 22 per cent of the total budget.[62] Asquith, however, the Chancellor of the Exchequer, looked for further cuts in a review begun in May 1906.

Asquith considered that new construction was unnecessary as the strength of the fleet was far above the two-power standard. Tweedmouth replied that the need to build modern ships required limiting any cuts. Indeed, the moving of works expenditure would require an increase of the estimates of £750,000. The Chancellor opposed this strongly. He questioned the relevance of the two-power standard in contemporary strategic circumstances, as Germany (second of the two-power navies since May 1905) was unlikely to be on the same side as France in any war. In any case, Britain had 49 modern battleships, compared to France and Germany's combined total of 29.[63] A compromise was reached. The Admiralty dropped the armoured cruiser from its 1906–7 Programme and just ordered three Dreadnoughts of the Bellerophon class to complete a squadron of four. The 1907–8 Estimates were kept down to £31.25 million.

In order to achieve this figure, while still keeping the three new Dreadnoughts, the Admiralty reduced the number of large warships in commission by seven battleships (later reduced to six) and four armoured cruisers. These were to be placed in nucleus crew reserve. The news was leaked and led to an outcry. Fisher responded by announcing that they would be formed into a 'Home Fleet' with 60 per cent of war complement and capable of rapid mobilization. The most ready reserve ships at the home ports were also added to the new force. Although battleships were the subject of discussion, the Home Fleet had its main strength elsewhere. Over a hundred flotilla craft, crewed to 80 per cent, were allocated, and the new force was more a flotilla defence organization than a battlefleet. According to

Nicholas Lambert, it was intended to be the basis of the naval capability in home waters, leaving the Channel and Atlantic fleets for more distant deployment if necessary.[64]

The new fleet, however, was highly controversial, especially when, in a misconceived publicity move, Fisher decided to allocate the new all-big-gun ships to its Nore Division, fully manned. This only confused the Home Fleet's function, 'neither a reserve nor a striking force', but Fisher may have had other motives. He did not want his beloved new all-big-gun armoured cruisers going to Lord Charles Beresford's Channel Fleet, as originally intended.[65] Beresford and Fisher were by this time at daggers drawn for personal and political reasons, a dispute that increasingly split the service.[66]

Fisher did not fully explain the reasoning behind his policies. In 1907 he came under increasing pressure from two sides – from the cost-cutting Government and from his conservative opponents, Beresford's 'Syndicate of Discontent' within and without the service. He was unable to continue his passion for large armoured cruisers and an improved Invincible, planned for 1907–8, was dropped. He and Tweedmouth were, however, able to obtain another three Dreadnoughts, the St Vincent class, in 1907–8.

At the end of 1907 there was a back-bench revolt against defence spending. Asquith had to find space in his budget for old age pensions and in November 1907 the Admiralty was informed it could expect no increase in expenditure in 1908–9. In retaliation, the Board threatened resignation. Campbell-Bannerman accepted the Admiralty's position, an increase of £1.4 million over the previous year that would allow the building of only one battleship, HMS *Neptune*, built to maintain demand for armour plate and heavy gun mountings, plus two cheaper armoured cruisers armed with 9.2-inch guns to match the German 8.2-in gun Blucher of their 1906–7 programme. Then the Prime Minister suffered a heart attack. Asquith, as the heir apparent, was once more in the ascendant and Fisher was summoned before the Cabinet to be told that the 1908–9 Estimates would be reduced.[67]

Fisher used his press connections to publicize his struggle and the Cabinet restored most of their cut, although the armoured cruiser programme was reduced to a single ship. Asquith duly became

Prime Minister in April 1908 and replaced Tweedmouth with Reginald McKenna. Much to Fisher's disgust, Winston Churchill turned the post down. McKenna was Asquith's former assistant at the Treasury and therefore safe, or so Asquith hoped. McKenna had, however, not helped his cause when, in March, he referred to the new armoured cruiser as a 'battlecruiser', the name beginning to be used for the new all-big-gun armoured cruisers, *Indomitable, Inflexible* and *Invincible*, approaching completion. Fisher arranged for a 12-inch 'Sans Pareil', later officially named *Indefatigable*, to be substituted for the 9.2-inch ship. This coincided with the German announcement that they intended to build 11-in gun battlecruisers, after their false start with *Blucher*.

The 1908–9 British Programme also included a new class of unarmoured cruiser. According to John Jellicoe, the Director of Naval Ordnance, these ships were required to support an inshore watching squadron of destroyers off an enemy coast.[68] Following the failure of HMS *Swift*, a larger destroyer-type ship, the previous year's programme had included the first of six 3300-ton 'scouts' to lead the flotillas. The new, larger 5000-ton ships were modern turbine-powered variants on the protected cruiser theme, capable of 25 knots and named after cities. Five were built in 1908–9, four the following year, the latter with an armament of 6-inch guns rather than a mixed armament of 4-inch and 6-inch. As well as his Crickets – re-rated torpedo boats – Fisher had built 1000-ton Tribal-class oil-burning destroyers capable of ultra high speed; 33 knots for eight hours. The result was both expensive and unsatisfactory. A new class of 16 slightly smaller, coal-burning destroyers, the Beagle class, was therefore designed for the 1908–9 Programme, to replace the worn-out first-generation destroyers. These were seaworthy and successful vessels. The first of a new class of larger long-range D-class diesel submarines was also delivered.

These new torpedo craft were equipped with new heater torpedoes. By heating the air of the torpedo engine, greater range was possible. The Mk. VII 18-inch could travel 6000–7000 yards at 31 knots; the Mk. VII 21-inch, fitted to the Beagles, 12,000 yards at 30 knots. By 1908 these weapons were making the case for still longer-range shooting. Since 1905 the Admiralty had been experimenting with advanced systems to make its long-range fire more certain. Arthur Hungerford Pollen, a civilian inventor, had offered a system that used a mechanical analogue computer to work out the area in which an enemy ship would be when the shells arrived. Pollen, aware of the revolutionary nature of his equipment, was unwilling to work by normal Admiralty contract methods and asked for large fees. The Royal Navy's leading gunnery officer, Frederic Dreyer, together with Admiral Sir Arthur Wilson, worked out a simpler, if more labour-intensive manual system. In 1908 both systems were tested in trials commanded by Wilson, involving the cruiser *Ariadne* and battleship *Vengeance*. In highly controversial circumstances, the Wilson–Dreyer system was adopted, although it did not prove successful and many gunnery officers bought simple manual versions of Pollen's equipment to improve their performance in battle practice.[69]

Perhaps partly because of Pollen's equipment, battle practice results were very good and Fisher was reassured of the practicability of long-range action where speed would be used to control the range. This strengthened the argument for battlecruisers and in 1908 Fisher was able to get a splendid example into the 1909–10 Programme. Over 26,000 tons in displacement and over 100 feet longer than *Indefatigable*, HMS *Lion* had 42 boilers that drove her at 27 knots. She was armed with the new 13.5-inch gun in four twin mountings and was intended to overmatch the new German battlecruisers.

Before she was laid down, naval policy suffered a fully fledged naval scare. The Admiralty's total Programme for 1909–10 called for six large armoured ships, two 12-inch Dreadnoughts of the Colossus class, three 13.5-inch Super Dreadnought battleships and the new battlecruiser. Fisher wanted an extra 13.5-inch battleship and battlecruiser. Radical members of the Government, led by social reformers Churchill and Lloyd George (in unholy alliance with the Syndicate of Discontent) tried to bring the total number down to four, but public concern at German building forbade it. Fisher connived at this concern, not because he needed the new ships against the Germans, but in order to safeguard British naval facilities.[70] Paranoia about Germany rose to unreasonable heights, and Fisher shamelessly exploited it. Unrealistic projections of German building were produced and public opinion mobilized by the slogan 'We want eight and we won't wait!' McKenna, under attack also in part because of his opposition to the new land taxes supported by Chancellor Lloyd George, threatened resignation. The emollient Asquith produced a most attractive compromise: four ships in the short term plus four more, if required. As Churchill said: 'the Admiralty had demanded six ships; the economists offered four; and we finally compromised on eight'.[71] The full eight-ship Programme was eventually put into effect; *Colossus* and *Hercules* were laid down in July 1909, *Lion*, in September, the Super Dreadnought, *Orion*, in November, her sisters *Monarch, Conqueror* and *Thunderer* in April 1910 and a second 'Lion', *Princess Royal*, in May. In addition to the larger ships, 20 800-ton Acorn-class oil-burning destroyers and another four Town-class cruisers were included in the 1909–10 Programme.

This orgy of ship building cost money. Expenditure for 1909–10 was up £2.5 million to £36 million. The trajectory was upward once more, but the Chancellor had a mechanism to cope. His 'People's Budget', disguised by its commitment to social reform, was, in fact, a mechanism to deal with the growing naval concern with Germany. It involved substantial increases in both direct and indirect taxes (including the introduction of car tax), increased death duties and a new duty on the increased value of land. This led to a constitutional crisis when the House of Lords threw the budget out in November. Not until the passage of the Parliament Act in August 1911 did the situation settle down, although after the victory of the Liberals and their allies in the election held in early 1910, the Lords belatedly passed the budget in April. There was a substantial shortfall in taxation in 1909–10 but this was compensated the following year. This, and a booming economy, allowed naval expenditure to rise still further, to £42.6 million in 1910–11. As Sumida has pointed out, increases in social welfare spending up to 1913–14 were matched by increases in naval expenditure.[72] Its proportion of the total budget rose to over 24 per cent.[73]

Assistance was also obtained from the Dominions. With the 'We want eight' crisis, New Zealand offered to fund up to two battleships. Canada also offered assistance, as did Australia. Simultaneously, but unconnected, the C.-in-C. China Station expressed serious concern that his remaining weak forces 'had lost command of the sea in Eastern waters'.[74] The Admiralty stressed that the Mediterranean Fleet was available to reinforce the Far East in just over three weeks and more units, up to 20 battleships plus armoured cruisers, could be sent, even if at war with Germany. The Committee of Imperial Defence strengthened the China Squadron and considered the Dominion offers to strengthen the imperial Pacific presence, to increase Dominion confidence against Japan, which, despite the alliance, was seen as a potential threat.

Unsurprisingly, Fisher saw the battlecruiser as the answer to the Dominion worries, with each the core of a powerful Fleet Unit, a number of which would give the Empire command of the Pacific. The mind of the 'Fishpond', as the First Sea Lord's party was known, was clearly moving towards the abandonment of the traditional battlefleet. This was the result of the joint threat of heater 21-inch torpedoes and the latest guns and projectiles at expected combat ranges. In a paper given to the Institute of Naval Architects in March 1910, Rear Admiral Reginald Bacon called for the end of massed battlefleets and their replacement by units of battlecruisers with accompanying seagoing flotilla craft.[75]

The Admiralty proposed four units in the first instance: an Australian one at Sydney, a Canadian one at Vancouver and two British ones (partially subsidized by New Zealand) at Hong Kong. As a first step, two sisters of *Indefatigable* – a design considered adequate for Pacific service – were ordered with Dominion funds. These, *Australia* and *New Zealand*, were laid down in mid-1910. In typical style, Fisher made clear his intentions in correspondence with Lord Esher: 'It means *eventually* Canada, Australia, New Zealand, the Cape (that is South Africa) *running a complete Navy*! We manage the job in Europe. They'll manage it against the Yankees, Japs and Chinese, as occasion requires.'[76]

By that time Fisher was out of office. The Fisher–Beresford feud had continued, with personal factors combined with strategic. Beresford considered a close blockade of Germany possible and lamented the Channel Fleet's shortage of cruisers and destroyers for such work. Fisher and his supporters wanted to leave the North Sea to the flotillas of the Home Fleet, with the Channel Fleet as a reserve.[77] In 1908 orders were issued to Beresford that were more in accordance with his views but there is strong evidence that these were only intended to keep him quiet.[78] In order to silence him more permanently it was decided to abolish his command. Admiralty plans to combine the Channel Fleet with the Home Fleet were put to the cabinet late in 1908 and in March 1909 Beresford hauled down his flag.

The following month he wrote a powerful letter to Asquith, asserting that the Navy was not properly organized for war. The Prime Minister called a subcommittee of the Committee of Imperial Defence to enquire into the situation. It met between April and July 1909 and refused to take sides in the quarrel. It did, however, come out in favour of 'the further development of a Naval War staff, from which the naval members of the Board and Flag Officers and their staffs at sea may be expected to derive common benefit'.[79] Fisher strongly opposed such a body, as a bureaucratic brake on his authority. Fisher felt he had been fundamentally undermined and, in October 1909, agreed to step down. He duly retired on 25 January 1910, being replaced by Sir Arthur Wilson.

Wilson was authoritarian and obstinate, and was chosen by McKenna as a 'stone wall' to protect Fisher's reforms.[80] But Wilson had ideas of his own, beginning notably with a move towards a concept of 'The Grand Fleet of Battle' that would group all Britain's major units in a single force with battleships and a fast squadron of battlecruisers screened from torpedo attack by cruisers and destroyers. This caused considerable controversy, as the problems of commanding such an unwieldy formation were recognized, but exercises demonstrated the dangers of trying to operate fleets in more autonomous divisions. The Germans clearly intended to use their larger torpedo boats with the fleet and this threat, it was argued, was best met in kind.

The 1910 Programme included four more Super Dreadnoughts of an improved King George V class and an improved Lion, HMS *Queen Mary*, all laid down in early 1911. There were two Active-class scouts and three larger Chatham-class cruisers with side armour to enhance their protection. Another 20 778-ton destroyers, the Acheron class, were also ordered. The rest of the Australian fleet unit was also ordered: two of the new light cruisers and six Acherons. This procurement pattern fitted the new Grand Fleet ideas well and was repeated the following year. A departure was the restoration of full 6-inch secondary armament on the capital ships, the Iron Duke-class battleships and the battlecruiser *Tiger*. This move reflected the enhanced flotilla threat but with a more important motive. Battle ranges in the North Sea would be unlikely to exceed 6000 yards, given both the weather and the perceived intentions of the Germans, and 6-inch guns would prove useful in damaging the less well-protected parts of enemy major units. There were four slightly more heavily armed light cruisers and 20 more destroyers of a 1072-ton Acasta design.

Late 1911 saw a sudden transformation at the Admiralty, caused by the Agadir crisis with Germany. The German attempt – symbolized by the despatch of the gunboat *Panther* to Agadir – to gain a presence in Morocco, or at least be compensated for a French take-over, led to Britain making clear its strong support for France. Tension was high although the Admiralty did not take it very seriously. The Atlantic Fleet was at Cromarty and the Home Fleet divided between Berehaven and Portland, with its older ships reducing to nucleus crews at Devonport, Portsmouth and the Nore.[81] The Government was unimpressed by Wilson's performance at a key meeting of the Committee of Imperial Defence on 23 August. The Army skilfully explained their plans to move to the left flank of the French Army. Wilson revealed a plan he had not even discussed with his subordinates, which called for the capture of Heligoland and a close blockade of Germany, while maintaining the Army as a mobile reserve for possible deployment in the Baltic.[82]

Under pressure from Haldane, the Minister of War, Lloyd George and Churchill, Asquith decided to appoint his most energetic minister, Winston Churchill, as First Lord in exchange for McKenna. Churchill wanted Prince Louis of Battenberg to replace Wilson, but the Prince's German birth stood against him and Churchill was forced to take Sir Francis Bridgeman, who took up office in December, with Battenberg as Second Sea Lord. A Naval War Staff came into being at the beginning of 1912 with three divisions – Operations, Mobilization and Intelligence – and a Chief of the War Staff, a Rear Admiral (not a member of the Board of Admiralty) at its head.

First Churchill tried to cut the Estimates. He was influenced by Fisher into adopting a policy of concentration on battlecruisers and flotilla craft. Churchill's colleagues, however, disagreed and he was forced back to planning substantial reductions to the number of ships in commission, in the process decommissioning the Mediterranean Fleet battleships and abandoning plans to send British battlecruisers to the Pacific. This was overtaken in early 1912 by the new German Navy Law, the Novelle, that promised over two dozen German capital ships in commission. There was no way the British could make reductions or indeed rely on flotilla defence. Numbers of capital ships (as battleships and battlecruisers were now collectively known) had a political salience that could not be ignored. The Home Fleet had to be built up to no less than 33 ships, plus eight with nucleus crews. Because of scarcity of personnel, increasing the planned number of big ships meant taking crews from flotilla vessels, a major reversion of Fisherite values.[83]

Churchill announced the new policies in Parliament on 18 March 1912. This important speech officially announced the adoption of a new naval standard of 60 per cent superiority over the German Fleet in capital ships. This is often seen as a concession of weakness but, given the size of other fleets, it was in effect still a two-power standard. On 1 May a new Home Fleets Command was set up, composed of a First, Second and Third Fleet. The First Fleet was composed of Four Squadrons: two being the previous two Divisions of the Home Fleet, the third the former Atlantic Fleet based at Portland and the fourth the former Malta-based battleships moved to Gibraltar. The Second Fleet comprised the two battle squadrons with 50 per cent nucleus crews and the Third Fleet two reserve squadrons on a care-and-maintenance basis only. Only an armoured cruiser squadron was to remain at Malta. This sparked a controversy over Britain's position in the Mediterranean and later in the year four battlecruisers reinforced the four armoured cruisers, thus maintaining a fleet equal to the next strongest power in the region after France, which by agreement was to concentrate its fleet in this region.

Fisher was unsuccessful in pressing Churchill to make the 1912 Programme capital ships battlecruisers. Instead they were fast battleships of 27,500 tons with 13-inch belts and capable of 23 knots. Their main new feature was the 15-inch gun carried in four twin turrets. These were exceptionally powerful ships. Two, *Queen Elizabeth* and *Warspite*, were laid down in October 1912 and two, *Valiant* and *Barham*, at the beginning of 1913. Malaya funded a fifth, laid down in October 1913. They were destined for long and distinguished service lives. Importantly, they were oil-burning. Churchill, influenced by Fisher, was a strong advocate of oil. The First Lord appointed Fisher Chairman of a Royal Commission on Fuel Oil to examine the implications of its general adoption, and this led directly to Britain's purchasing a controlling share in the Anglo Persian Oil Company.

Churchill was also an enthusiastic convert to the Grand Fleet of Battle idea. It appealed to his romantic and political instincts. He set up a committee to develop the optimal fleet light cruiser: the result was the Arethusa class of eight 3750-ton 'light armoured cruisers' with a 3-inch belt and mixed armament of 4-inch and 6-inch guns. These were specialist North Sea vessels. The 1912 Programme also included 22 1000-ton destroyers. Together these ships would provide the screen for the capital ships.

Without Fisher, submarine policy was in a state of flux. A new type of improved seagoing submarine, the 'E' class, had been ordered for 1910–11, and this successful design was continued. Numbers remained limited, however, as attempts were made to diversify construction, which led to the procurement of boats of various, mostly unsuccessful, designs. The search also began for a fast submarine to operate with the fleet – the final addition to the Grand Fleet of Battle.

A significant new technology in the Royal Navy was the aeroplane. Churchill found the Navy experimenting with aeroplanes, after the abject failure of the Admiralty's first attempt to build a rigid airship. The aptly named *Mayfly* never did, and was wrecked in September 1911. By this time, however, naval officers were being trained to fly aeroplanes on the initiative of Francis McClean of the Royal Aero Club, who placed his Eastchurch airfield at the Admiralty's disposal. This was taken over by the Admiralty as the Naval Flying School at the end of 1911 and on 10 January 1912 one of the first four naval pilots took off in a Short biplane from a platform built over the forecastle of the battleship *Africa* at Sheerness. The First Lord was greatly attracted to the new machines, and, under his protection, the naval wing of the Royal Flying Corps (RFC), formed in 1912, developed as the autonomous Royal Naval Air Service (RNAS). Experiments were made in flying from battleships underway and the cruiser HMS *Hermes* was fitted to operate seaplanes at sea for the 1913 exercises. Following this innovation a new mercantile keel and frames formed the basis of a purpose-built aircraft-carrying ship, HMS *Ark Royal*.[84] Three non-rigid airships were also acquired and a new rigid airship ordered. In the summer of 1914 no navy in the world had a larger air component than the RNAS's 91 aeroplanes and seaplanes and 7 non-rigid airships. Six seaplane stations provided reconnaissance for flotilla defence, although providing air support for the Grand Fleet of Battle remained highly problematic without rigid airships. On 1 July an Admiralty circular letter, issued on the organization of the RNAS, established a dual rank structure, from Flight Lieutenant to Wing Captain, which would be parallel to but separate from the rest of the naval service. This is often seen as the birth of an RNAS as part of the Navy independent from the RFC but, as Roskill pointed out, this is not the case.[85] The letter is better seen as an exploitation of the RNAS's situation as a branch of the Royal Flying Corps, to confirm it as an autonomous fiefdom of the First Lord.

The year 1912 also saw important gunnery developments. Pollen's relations with the Admiralty had remained difficult. His association with Beresford hardly helped his relationship with Fisher and Wilson was an old enemy. Trials of his Argo system did, however, take place in HMS *Natal* in 1909 and 1910. These were quite successful but Admiralty orders were limited to gyroscopically stabilized range-finder mountings. Tests of the full Argo system were carried out in HMS *Orion* in 1912 and five Argo clocks ordered for the 1910 capital ships, in which they were combined with a Dreyer rate plotter in the Dreyer Table Mark II. Dreyer himself developed a cheaper mechanical fire control clock that was also tested and adopted for future construction. Controversy persists about this decision. Percy Scott's system of centralized director firing was also proved after trials in HMS *Thunderer*.[86] During these trials and connected exercises, a new doctrine was developed which emphasized rapid, accurate fire over medium ranges, followed by a turn away to avoid long-range torpedoes. Great emphasis was placed on the ability of individual gun layers to engage in rapid independent fire using continuous-aim techniques made possible by the latest mountings.[87]

In 1911–12 in the atmosphere of social reform, dissatisfaction on the lower deck became an issue. Churchill, still the social reformer, increased pay, abolished certain punishments, limited the power of the ships' police, gave better leave, the right to trial by court martial to petty officers and introduced a system to give the best warrant and petty officers commissioned rank. Churchill, however, took his attitude to juniors to extremes. His habit of touring the fleet and inviting juniors to comment unfavourably on their superiors understandably caused much offence. This culminated in a major row in late 1913 when Churchill backed a junior RNAS officer against the captain of *Hermes* and the C.-in-C. Nore, Admiral Sir Richard Poore. The Sea Lords threatened resignation and the affair faded away when the principals were persuaded to apologize.[88] Churchill was lucky to avoid a major crisis. Marder sums up well the contemporary view of the First Lord: 'He was regarded as a blusterer, an opportunist, and a showman, totally devoid of integrity.'[89]

Churchill soon tired of Bridgeman, who resented the First Lord's constant interference, which had bad effects on the First Sea Lord's health. Thus in November 1912 Churchill suggested retirement but the First Sea Lord was feeling better and wanted to stay on. Churchill, however, insisted he go and the affair became a matter of political controversy. Churchill lost face by publicly reading private correspondence between Bridgeman and other officers in which the former complained of ill health and a desire to resign. As Marder says, 'the whole politico-naval storm did the Navy no good'.[90] Battenberg, rather more amenable to the First Lord's whims, succeeded Bridgeman.

In the autumn of 1912 Churchill made a volte face on the question of the substitution of flotilla vessels for capital ships. There was a growing crisis in naval funding. The abandonment of Fisherite policy inevitably meant greater expenditure. The 1912–13 Estimates had reached £45 million and total expenditure £47.4 million; 1913–14 looked more like £50 million. And 1914–15 might total £53 million.[91] Churchill hoped he could solve this problem by a new concentration on submarines, given the success of the latest boats, but in the event it was not necessary. Higher than expected taxation yield and Churchill's political support for Lloyd George's land-tax policies, plus the subventions of both Malaya and New Zealand to the capital-ship building programme, staved off the immediate crisis and allowed the maintenance of the 60 per cent battleship standard for another year.[92]

The 1913 Programme finally looked conventional, even reactionary. Five new 15-inch-gun battleships of the Revenge class reflected the new short-range tactical doctrine, with improved vertical protection and steadier motion that suited rapid independent fire. Speed was not seen to be an advantage and they reverted to coal burning with a speed of only 21.5 knots. Another eight light-armoured cruisers were ordered, six Carolines and two two-funnel Calliopes with geared turbines that proved successful and set the design for succeeding classes. Sixteen faster M-class destroyers comprised the year's surface flotilla.

The funding crisis had only been postponed. When, at the end of 1913, Churchill did ask for over £50 million for 1914–15 he suffered a storm of opposition from the Cabinet, the Government back benches and the Liberal press. The Cabinet argued that the plans for four capital ships, three more Revenges and a battlecruiser version of the Queen Elizabeth, *Agincourt*, should be reduced to two. Much of the Cabinet was convinced that Churchill thrived on high estimates and Lloyd George joined the opposition. In the end, Lloyd George accepted £53 million for 1914–15, on condition that there was a reduction to under £50 million in 1915–16. Churchill's solution to the problem was to revert to submarine substitution. Fourteen E-class submarines were to be built instead of the projected Revenge-class *Resistance* and six armoured semi-submersible torpedo craft of a new Polyphemus class in place of *Agincourt*. The destroyers were also to be replaced by submarines, except for four new destroyer leaders of the newly developed Lightfoot design.[93] Nicholas Lambert argues that these radical plans presaged the abandonment of a capital ship standard of naval power. There also seen to have been plans to use the battle cruisers in smaller, more dispersed squadrons, somewhat along the lines of the earlier fleet units.[94]

Yet there was not time for this 'strategic revolution' to bear fruit.[95] The crisis of July 1914 intervened. It found the Royal Navy fortuitously well prepared. A test mobilization of the Home Fleets had been announced in Parliament in March and, with the war clouds gathering over Europe, it duly began on 15 July. A review was held at Spithead and then the fleet sailed for exercises in the Channel. Demobilization and dispersal was beginning but was quickly stopped by Battenberg on 26 July, when news of the Austrian rejection of the Serbian reply to their ultimatum was received. On 29 July the First Fleet left Portland for its planned wartime North Sea anchorage at Scapa Flow. On 4 August Admiral Jellicoe was appointed its Commander in Chief and soon the name Grand Fleet was officially adopted for its impressive mass of 20 Dreadnoughts and Super Dreadnoughts, four battlecruisers, eight armoured cruisers, 13 pre-Dreadnought battleships, six light cruisers and 41 destroyers.[95] The Navy was ordered to commence hostilities against Germany at 23:00 that evening. Despite the radicalism of the Fisher era, the Royal Navy was to fight Germany with a traditional battlefleet, the most impressive 'Grand Fleet' ever deployed.

5 The First World War

The Grand Fleet at Scapa Flow under Admiral Sir John Jellicoe was the foundation of a strategy of distant blockade. This had been adopted in 1913 and was maintained in war despite its leaving open the North Sea coast to enemy attack, a vulnerability that had been demonstrated in the last major prewar fleet exercise. To help solve this problem, Vice Admiral David Beatty was forward-deployed at Cromarty in command of Cruiser Force 'A', which comprised the Grand Fleet's battle-, armoured and light cruiser component. In mid-August Cruiser Force 'K' was formed, in the Humber, with the battlecruisers HMS *New Zealand* and *Invincible*. The southern North Sea was protected by the Harwich Force of 35 destroyers and two light cruisers under Commodore Reginald Tyrwhitt. Also at Harwich was Commodore Roger Keyes's flotilla of longer-range submarines. The Admiral of Patrols, Commodore George Ballard, provided co-ordinated coast defence and commanded a force of light cruisers, old destroyers and small submarines at Dover. A pre-Dreadnought Channel Fleet was established and more cruiser patrols were set up using reserve units as they were mobilized. Ten older cruisers enforced the blockade in the north.[1]

The Harwich Force was first in action on 5 August when the scout cruiser *Amphion* and destroyers *Lance* and *Landrail* sank the converted ferry minelayer *Konigin Luise*. Early the following day *Amphion* hit a German mine and sank.[2] The Germans sent out their First U-boat flotilla to investigate British dispositions. One submarine attacked the battleship *Monarch* while detached for gunnery practice; another was lost to a cruiser operating ahead of the Grand Fleet. This increased Jellicoe's concern and, rightly anxious about the security of Scapa, he withdrew the Fleet first to the Western Isles and then to

Lough Swilly in Northern Ireland. The move was not totally successful. The converted German liner *Berlin* laid mines to the northwest of Lough Swilly and on 27 October one of the Grand Fleet's most powerful battleships, HMS *Audacious*, hit one and sank.

Keyes had used his RN submarines to reconnoitre the Heligoland Bight and, supported by Tyrwhitt, he called for a major operation to deal with the German patrols. Churchill supported the idea but the Staff was unenthusiastic. Its chief, Vice Admiral Doveton Sturdee, told Jellicoe the support of his full fleet was unnecessary but that he might send down the battlecruisers of Cruiser Force 'A' to join with the Humber battlecruisers to give extra cover. Keyes and Tyrwhitt were unaware of Beatty's possible presence, being out of wireless range when his deployment was decided upon.

The weather was foggy and action confused. The Germans sent out cruisers that outgunned the British destroyers and Beatty decided to storm in. Three German light cruisers and a destroyer were sunk for no British losses, although some damaged British ships had to be towed home. This Battle of the Heligoland Bight was lauded as a great victory, not least by Churchill, but Keyes considered it an 'absurd affair' and a missed opportunity to inflict twice as much damage.[3]

The Germans continued their naval offensive. U21 sank the scout cruiser *Pathfinder* off St Abbs Head on 5 September and U9 scored a signal success on 22 September by sinking most of Cruiser Force 'C', *Aboukir, Hogue* and *Cressy* off the Dutch coast; 1459 men and boys were lost. U9 had another success on 15 October, sinking the cruiser *Hawke* off the Scottish coast. British submarines retaliated. Lt. Cdr. Max Horton of E9 sank the cruiser *Hela* off Heligoland and a German destroyer off the Ems.[4]

Horton was sent to the Baltic in October, together with Lt. Cdr. Noel Laurence in E1. Laurence broke an agreement not to engage the enemy until all three intended deployments were complete and his abortive attack on the training cruiser *Viktoria Luise* gave early warning to the Germans. Horton had problems passing through the straits and Martin Nasmith in E11 was forced to turn back. Also the Germans withdrew their ships from the training areas, thus depriving the British boats of targets.[5] British submarines thus initially were unsuccessful and the incident led to a lasting feud within the submarine service.[6]

The Mediterranean Squadron at the outbreak of war was under the command of Admiral Sir Archibald Berkeley Milne. It was composed of the Second Battle Cruiser Squadron *Inflexible, Indomitable* and *Indefatigable*, the armoured cruisers *Defence, Warrior, Black Prince* and *Duke of Edinburgh* (of Rear Admiral Troubridge's First Cruiser Squadron), four Town-class light cruisers and 16 destroyers. The Germans had the battlecruiser *Goeben* accompanied by the light cruiser *Breslau*. On 30 July Churchill sent Milne a very confusing signal telling him to concentrate on the defence of the French troop transports in the Western Mediterranean and forbidding him to engage a 'superior force' except in combination with the French 'as part of a general battle'. By superior force, Churchill meant the whole Austrian Fleet but the signal implied that any such force must not be engaged and Troubridge considered that his whole squadron was inferior to *Goeben*. The stage was set for a significant débâcle.[7]

The German Mediterranean Division were found and shadowed by *Indomitable* and *Indefatigable* on 4 August, but war had not been declared, so fire could not be opened. The German ships drew away and contact was lost. That day the Division was ordered to proceed to Constantinople. Milne, concentrating on his primary directive, was unaware of German intentions and put his capital ships between the French troopships and *Goeben*. Troubridge was at the entrance of the Adriatic when the German ships were again spotted and he realized that by the time he engaged *Goeben* it would be daylight. This made the German battlecruiser a 'superior force'. The traditions of the service dictated attacking but his flag captain, Fawcet Wray, talked the admiral out of it. The *matériel* advantage of the Germans seemed too great.[8] The shadowing cruiser *Gloucester* ran out of coal and had to give up the chase while Milne was drawn away by a premature signal to commence hostilities with Austria. The German Admiral Souchon thus brought his two ships safely to the Turks, into whose fleet they were officially absorbed, complete with German crews.

The arrival of the *Goeben* swung Turkey's entry into the war on Germany's side and partially made up for the loss of its two battleships completing in Britain (they were seized and absorbed into the British fleet as HMS *Agincourt* and HMS *Erin*). Troubridge was recalled and a court of enquiry held which found his actions 'deplorable and contrary to the tradition of the British Navy'. He was court-martialled but acquitted.[9]

British naval reverses and the lack of the anticipated great victory over the German High Sea Fleet led to criticism of the Admiralty. Much of it was directed at Churchill whose amateur interference had been responsible for many of the problems. His reputation was not helped by the débâcle at Antwerp, stemming from his ill-considered attempt to reinforce the Belgians, which saw the loss of much of the first Royal Naval Division, a scratch force formed of a brigade of Royal Marines and two of naval reservists. Despite amusement at his request to take personal command at Antwerp, Churchill's position in the Cabinet was still strong and the campaign was diverted onto Battenberg, the First Sea Lord, whom it was thought was too much under Churchill's spell. Battenberg was also in poor health and his German name rankled in the prevailing xenophobia. In late October he was asked by the Cabinet to resign and was replaced, at Churchill's insistence, by Lord Fisher.[10]

The new First Sea Lord was immediately faced by a serious crisis in South American waters. The German East Asiatic Squadron, based at Tsingtau, Germany's equivalent of Hong Kong, was commanded by Vice Admiral M. Graf Von Spee and composed of two powerful final-generation armoured cruisers, *Scharnhorst* and *Gneisenau*, and three light cruisers. Given the weaknesses of the Royal Navy's China Station, it was fortunate that Spee was in mid-Pacific at the outbreak of war. He detached his light cruiser *Emden* to raid (very successfully) into the Indian Ocean and concentrated his forces off Easter Island where he was joined by *Dresden*, which had been operating off the east coast of the Americas.

The British forces in the area were weak. Rear Admiral Christopher Craddock, an officer of great gallantry, only had a small cruiser squadron to protect trade in South American waters. He flew his flag in the armoured cruiser *Good Hope*, a fine but outdated ship with armament of 6-inch weapons supplemented by two 9.2-inch guns. The other armoured cruiser, *Monmouth*, had been built smaller for economy and was only armed with 6-inch guns. These armaments would have been fine in the early years of the century but now the British ships were decisively outclassed by the German cruisers' heavier and uniform armament. Also, the German squadron's gunnery was particularly good whereas the British ships were manned by mobilized reservists. Craddock also had the modern light cruiser *Glasgow* and the armed merchant cruiser *Otranto*, but the German light cruisers outnumbered these.

Nothing illustrates the problems of the Churchill–Battenberg Admiralty better than the errors made in meeting Spee. The only reinforcement sent early was the pre-Dreadnought *Canopus*, with an effective speed of only 12 knots, half that of the armoured cruisers. The First Lord's idea of using the battleship as a 'citadel' around which cruisers might find absolute security was amateurish, even by Churchill's standards.[11] *Canopus* was a terrible tactical handicap and Craddock used it to escort his colliers when he sailed into the Pacific. He hoped the modern armoured cruiser *Defence* would join him from the Mediterranean, but *Defence* (a match for the German vessels) was held back in the Atlantic where another cruiser squadron was being built up, under Rear Admiral Stoddart, in case the German ships avoided Craddock.

Admiralty orders implied that Craddock's constituted a sufficient force to deal with *Scharnhorst* and *Gneisenau*. He did not want to emulate Troubridge and any action he instigated might inflict damage on a German squadron far from home and repair facilities.[12] Too late did the Admiralty seek to restrain him. The four armoured cruisers met in the late afternoon of 1 November. The heavy seas diminished the fighting power of the British still further as they prevented use of the lower 6-inch batteries. The British ships, silhouetted against the setting sun, provided excellent targets at a range of 5500 yards. *Good Hope* blew up after taking 30–40 hits. *Monmouth* was reduced to a listing wreck and was finished off by the light cruiser *Nurnberg*. *Glasgow* and *Otranto* had no alternative but to flee. Poor Craddock and about 1600 men were lost: it was the worst British defeat on the high seas for over a century.[13]

German claims of victory arrived in London on 4 November. Fisher at once persuaded Churchill to detach the battlecruisers *Invincible* and *Inflexible* to reinforce Stoddart, and *Princess Royal* to reinforce the West Indies Squadron. *Invincible* and *Inflexible* were hustled through Devonport and sailed on 11 November. They were commanded by former Chief of the War Staff, Doveton Sturdee, whom Fisher blamed personally for the débácle. As C.-in-C. South Atlantic and South Pacific, Sturdee was ordered to meet Stoddart and then base himself in the Falklands to find and destroy Spee. He arrived at the Falklands on 7 December with his two battlecruisers, four armoured and two light cruisers and an armed merchant cruiser.

Spee, deciding to attack the Falklands on his return to Germany, sailed into the jaws of a trap. At 07.50 on 8 December *Gneisenau* and *Nurnberg* were spotted reconnoitring the island. Sturdee's squadron was coaling but 12-inch shells from *Canopus* caused the Germans to sheer off, giving the British time to leave harbour. Sturdee hoisted 'general chase'. It was classic battlecruiser battle, the British ships using their superior range and speed to dictate the action. The vibration of high-speed movement interfered with the British fire control instruments, but *Scharnhorst* was sunk with all hands at 16.17. *Gneisenau* was scuttled in the process of being pounded to a wreck. *Leipzig* was sunk by *Glasgow, Nurnberg* by *Cornwall* and *Kent. Dresden* escaped but was run down by *Glasgow* the following March.[14]

This was exactly the role for which battlecruisers had been designed and Fisher exploited this success. On 26 August 1914 orders for the last three Revenge-class battleships had been suspended in anticipation of a short war. Fisher now wanted two of these ships reordered as larger, 30-knot 'light battle cruisers' armed with six 15-inch guns.[15] Shallow draught kept the displacement of these very lightly protected (6-inch belt) ships down to 27,650 tons. Churchill opposed starting new capital ships but Cabinet sanction was obtained and *Renown* and *Repulse* were laid down in January 1915. Fisher now planned three 19,000 ton 32-knot ships that, as 'large light cruisers', could be built without Cabinet approval. The first two, *Courageous* and *Glorious*, were to be armed with four 15-inch guns and the third, *Furious*, with two 18-inch guns; they were laid down between March and June 1915.[16] Fisher also added two more conventional 'C' class light cruisers to the four already building under the 1914 programme. The shallow draught of many of the new ships was part of Fisher's ambition to make an offensive move into the Baltic. His building plans included 24 mass-produced Flower-class sloops for minesweeping, 250 powered lighters for landing troops and a mixed bunch of shallow-draught monitors for coastal bombardment.

In January 1915 a rather different offensive operation was planned – against Turkey. Churchill backed a purely naval operation to force the Dardanelles. Fisher, albeit dubiously, initially went along with this and the idea was accepted by the War Council on 13 January, to be executed the following month.

Meanwhile there occurred another major clash in the North Sea. In November Rear Admiral Hipper's First Scouting Group of battlecruisers raided Yarmouth. Another raid was planned on Scarborough and Hartlepool in December and the whole German High Sea Fleet sailed to support. Although the code-breakers in the Admiralty (Room 40) gave warning of the German sortie, the Admiralty was ignorant of the move by the High Sea Fleet and played into German hands by sending a single battle squadron to support Beatty. Its light forces were spotted by the High Sea Fleet, but Ingenohl, the German fleet commander, thinking he was facing Jellicoe, turned away. The German battlecruisers did bombard Scarborough, Hartlepool and Whitby but the British were well positioned to intercept and annihilate them. The cruiser screens of the two forces came into contact, but Commodore Goodenough of the First Light Cruiser Squadron broke off contact 'by the authority of a signal that had been made without citical information' and Hipper got away.[17]

To counter more raids, Beatty and Goodenough were moved south to Rosyth on 21 December. In January the First Scouting Group made another sortie, with four battlecruisers, four light cruisers and 18 destroyers. The intention was to reconnoitre the Dogger Bank and engage any British forces found there. Again Room 40 gave warning and Beatty, Goodenough and Tyrwhitt were sent to intercept. The British had a superior force of three 13.5-inch armed battlecruisers and two 12-inch armed ships.

The battlecruisers came into contact on the morning of 24 January. *Lion* bore the brunt of enemy fire and, hit by three shells, dropped back. The rearmost German ship, *Blucher*, was also heavily damaged and, due to signalling confusion, the remaining battlecruisers concentrated on it rather than chasing the fleeing German force. *Blucher* sank, giving a good propaganda picture, but Beatty fumed at the 'terrible failure ... we were going to get four, the lot, and four we ought to have got'.[18] It was small comfort that his command grew to three squadrons and was redesignated 'Battle Cruiser Fleet' in February.

The focus of the naval war became the eastern Mediterranean as the assault on the Dardanelles defences began on 19 February. Vice Admiral Carden commanded only two modern capital ships, the new 15-inch gun *Queen Elizabeth* and his flagship, *Inflexible*. He also had 12 British and four French pre-Dreadnoughts. The latter, with their medium-calibre flat-trajectory guns, were not good for the engagement of land targets.

Nevertheless the outer forts were silenced by 2 March and the fleet was able to penetrate the straits for seven miles up to the main Turkish minefield. Going then became difficult. Some 21 minesweeping trawlers were allocated to the operation but they were vulnerable to mobile Turkish light artillery fire that proved to be a major problem. Churchill ordered Carden to move for an early confrontation, accepting losses if necessary. The strain was too much for the British commander and his health gave out. Thus it was that Rear Admiral John De Robeck, a more impressive figure than his chief, commanded the big push up the straits on 18 March.

Faced by 16 major Allied units, fire from the shore slackened. But then disaster struck from a previously unknown minefield. The French battleship *Bouvet* was hit and sank quickly. Then *Inflexible*, already damaged by gunfire, hit a mine and was forced to retire. *Irresistible* was a third mine victim. Abandoned, she was finished off by the enemy forts. While coming to her aid, HMS *Ocean* met a similar fate. The gunfire from the shore remained all too effective, preventing any minesweeping

Neither Churchill nor De Robeck were put off by the events of 18 March, but now, opinion was beginning to favour a land operation to take the Gallipoli peninsula. De Robeck came round to this view at a crucial meeting aboard *Queen Elizabeth* on the 22nd. On 25 April the landings took place, covered by the guns of a reinforced fleet. Aircraft from the Eastchurch Wing, operating out of Tenedos, provided air support.

On the night of 12–13 May a German-commanded Turkish destroyer sank HMS *Goliath*. U-boats were also on the way and Fisher, never happy about the campaign, became increasingly worried.

He threatened resignation to Asquith and on 13 May Churchill agreed to replace the valuable *Queen Elizabeth* by the pre-Dreadnoughts *Exmouth* and *Venerable* and two monitors. Fisher thought he and Churchill agreed on the reinforcements, but when he returned the following morning, he found that the First Lord had added vessels to the list. This caused a breakdown in the erratic old man, who sent letters of resignation to Churchill and Asquith and quit the Admiralty. Ignoring orders to return, he denounced Churchill to Bonar Law, the Leader of the Opposition, as 'a real danger' who had to 'go at all costs'.[19]

Fisher's resignation escalated the political crisis for the Asquith Government, following a huge scandal over inadequate artillery supplies for the Western Front army. A coalition government was formed and, in the ensuing Cabinet reconstruction, Churchill was replaced as First Lord by the former Prime Minister, Arthur Balfour, and Fisher by Sir Henry Jackson.

Fisher left behind a massive programme of flotilla vessels. While he was First Sea Lord the Admiralty ordered some 65 submarines. Five more destroyer flotilla leaders were ordered, bringing this type's total to 17 (four being taken over from a Chilean order). Some 50 more 'M' class destroyers were being built to add to the 20 ordered in September 1914. Eight destroyers were taken over from Turkish and Greek orders as well as two 5.5-inch gun Greek light cruisers that were commissioned as *Birkenhead* and *Chester*.

Other Fisher legacies were 24 600-ton patrol (P) boats, built to look like submarines. They were intended to replace destroyers in anti-submarine operations. Fifteen smaller whaler-type patrol craft were also built for similar work. The need for such vessels was urgent. On 4 February 1915 the Germans declared the waters round the British Isles a war zone, in which merchant ships would be destroyed, if necessary from underwater, and without consideration for crew or passenger safety. Neutral ships were also at risk unless their neutrality was obvious.[20]

German surface raiders had been successfully overcome and at first it seemed U-boats would be no more threatening. In the first six weeks of the campaign, fewer ships were sunk by U-boats than by the most successful surface raiders, *Karlsruhe* and *Emden*.[21] Although the sinking of the *Lusitania* in May was a dramatic, if politically embarrassing,

German success, Churchill left the Admiralty confident that the U-boat offensive had been unsuccessful.

Remarkably little progress had been made with anti-submarine measures before the war. The first anti-submarine patrols at Portland in 1914 saw picket boats carrying hammers and canvas bags to blind periscopes and thus force U-boats to the surface, to be engaged by gunfire.[22] A more successful system utilized an indicator net, towed by drifter, that, if snagged, revealed a submarine's presence by a flare buoy. Contact mines were also added to the nets. A drifter patrol was established in the Dover Straits, which, in April 1915, caused the Germans to abandon this route to the Western Approaches for High Sea Fleet U-boats. Production also began of the Sea (or Submarine) Scout SS non-rigid airship used for patrols in the Channel and Irish narrows.[23]

The RNAS as a whole had prospered under Churchill. It rapidly doubled in size and became an autonomous and innovative force. On the war's outbreak the Eastchurch Wing had been sent to Ostend to support forces at Antwerp. A forward base was established at Antwerp itself and raids were mounted on Zeppelin facilities in Germany. On 8 October an RNAS Sopwith Tabloid destroyed Zeppelin ZIX in its shed at Dusseldorf. Improvised RNAS armoured cars were also used both to rescue pilots and substitute for air reconnaissance.

The wing subsequently retreated to Dunkirk to assert aerial control over an area within a hundred miles of the port. This provided a context for more armoured-car operations and in October Churchill decided to form a Royal Naval Armoured Car Division as a branch of the RNAS. The RNACD gave the Admiralty an important role in the Landships Committee that would eventually lead to the tank. The Admiralty's superior understanding of and sympathy for technology was a vital factor in this application to land warfare. Without it, the project might have been stillborn.

The anti-Zeppelin air offensive continued. In November five RNAS Avro 504s were sent to Belfort in France to attack the main airship base at Cuxhaven. This raid, a 250-mile round trip by four of the aircraft, was an extraordinary feat for its day. Eleven bombs were dropped, a Zeppelin was damaged and the gas plant destroyed. The Dunkirk force kept up the pressure into 1915 when in March a new

No. 1 Squadron took over. Bombing attacks were carried out on submarine targets and Zeppelin sheds as well as spotting for shore bombardment by warships. On 7 June the squadron bombed a Zeppelin on the ground and another in the air, causing the German Army to withdraw its airships from Belgium.

Three converted cross-Channel steamers, *Empress, Engadine* and *Riviera*, were allocated to the Harwich Force as the world's first carrier striking fleet, with Zeppelin sheds as the main target (a large fast seaplane carrier, the converted Cunarder, *Campania*, was not commissioned for the Grand Fleet until April 1915). Tyrwhitt's initial carrier foray against the naval Nordholz Zeppelin base south of Cuxhaven was, however, a failure because of adverse weather.

In late November 1914 the attempt was repeated on a wider canvas that included the enticement of the High Sea Fleet into an action with the Grand Fleet. Again, the aerial portion of the operation miscarried, this time because of fears about the vulnerability of the carriers, which had to stop to operate aircraft; but the enterprise was pursued (unsuccessfully) by surface forces, the cruiser *Liverpool* being subjected to the first air attack in the Royal Navy's history.

In December there was a third try, with Keyes's submarines offering both protection to the carriers and rescue facilities for the aircrew. The forces sailed on Christmas Eve. Nine seaplanes were hoisted out. Two could not take off and the others were not able to attack their primary target because of fog. The Germans retaliated with Zeppelins, seaplanes and U-boats. Four British seaplanes and one German were lost and one German and two British battleships were damaged in collision. This brought British fleet strength down to the lowest level of numerical superiority of the entire war: 19 Dreadnoughts and Super Dreadnoughts to 17 German Dreadnoughts and five British battlecruisers to four German. The first ever carrier air strike was more a harbinger of the future than an operational or strategic success.[24]

Balfour and Jackson were, perhaps, the brightest combination in intellectual ability ever to be in charge of the service. Balfour's 'patience, cheerfulness and imperturbable charm had won him the reputation of being an easy man to work with'.[25] His weaknesses were a reflection of his strengths – a tendency for calm reflection that could infuriate the shallower and the more dynamic. Jackson was a reserved scientist, a pioneer of wireless and Fellow of the Royal Society, rather than a dynamic leader, and in less than perfect health. The Admiralty had 'jumped from one extreme to the other. In place of two men of driving power, initiative and resource, but occasionally lacking in judgement, there were now in charge two men of philosophic temperament and first-rate judgement, but less dynamic than their predecessors'.[26]

The new Board inherited both the U-boat threat and the Dardanelles campaign. Increased numbers of U-boats meant higher shipping losses: between June and September, submarines sank 365 merchant ships of 532,116 tons.[27] British countermeasures remained ineffective. The British submarine E16 struck lucky and caught and sank U6 while the destroyers *Maori* and *Gurkha* used the newly developed explosive sweep to sink U8. Decoy measures were the most successful. Small British submarines towed by trawlers scored two successes in June and July and armed trawlers sank two U-boats with gunfire. Q ships, merchant ships fitted with hidden armament, had their first successes, one per month, in July, August and September.

In September, a U-boat sank the liner *Arabic* and the USA exerted sufficient pressure for the Germans to call off the campaign. The U-boats had not been defeated as British anti-submarine patrols were inherently ineffective. Even the Dover barrage ceased to provide protection as smaller Flanders-based boats began to penetrate it from June 1915. More vessels were built to counter this enemy. Forty-nine new 'R' class destroyers, plus four more leaders, were ordered between July 1915 and March 1916 – plus 36 more sloops ordered in July 1915. Six sloops were ordered at the beginning of 1916 for use as Q ships. Unless they could be operated more effectively, however, this reinforcement was of little avail.

In July the Western Approaches command was enlarged; the efficient, hard-working and irascible Vice Admiral Sir Lewis Bayly was appointed as Admiral Commanding (C.-in-C. from May 1916). He had some 450 vessels of various shapes and sizes, including many trawlers and drifters of the Auxiliary Patrol Service which, by the end of the year, had grown to 2236 vessels deployed around British coastal waters and in the Mediterranean.[28]

The Germans sent U-boats to the Dardanelles in May and scored rapid successes, sinking the pre-Dreadnoughts *Triumph* and *Majestic* before the end of the month. Patrolling the restricted waters of the straits with small craft made more sense than in the wider waters of the western approaches and the U-boats were unable to interfere much with continued operations, especially when shallow-draught monitors replaced the more vulnerable pre-Dreadnoughts. British submarines had rather more success interfering with Turkish communications in the Sea of Marmora, both afloat and ashore.[29] E14 (Lt. Cdr. E. C. Boyle) and E11 (Lt. Cdr. M. E. Nasmith) particularly distinguished themselves. Pioneering torpedo seaplane attacks on Turkish shipping were also made from the seaplane carrier *Ben My Chree*, which replaced *Ark Royal* in June 1915.

The Allied front was broadened in August with fresh landings at Suvla but the operations ashore again fared badly. After a visit by Kitchener himself, in November 1915, it was decided to leave. A huge fleet covered the withdrawal, carried out in two stages in December 1915 and January 1916.[30] Ironically, it was by far the most successful part of the whole, sad campaign.

One reason for withdrawal was the growth of other Mediterranean commitments. Italy entered the war against her former allies in May and, to reinforce her fleet against that of the Austrians, four RN pre-Dreadnoughts and four light cruisers were sent to the Adriatic. In September an anti-submarine blockade was mounted at the Straits of Otranto, using British net drifters. These proved much less successful than they had been in the narrower, shallower English Channel with its more predictable currents.

The RN submarines in the Baltic were reinforced in the summer of 1915. E13 failed to pass through the straits and was interned but E8, E18 and E19 succeeded and joined the other boats in a campaign against merchant shipping that caused considerable dislocation.

In early 1916 the Grand Fleet again took centre stage in the naval war. In February a new commander took over the German High Sea Fleet, Vice Admiral Reinhard Scheer. An aggressive and able officer, Scheer had the authorization of the Kaiser to take risks. His options were, however, limited to raids on the British coast and other offensive moves designed to precipitate a battle at full German strength with a detached portion of the British fleet. The aim was to inflict disproportionate attrition, so that British strength might be worn down to that of the High Sea Fleet, thus making a full-scale fleet action practical. Room 40's work, however, made surprise unlikely. Often its intelligence was less than clear and the War Staff did not always use the Room's insights properly; but Scheer was at a major disadvantage.[31]

The British also had plans to lure the Germans to destruction. In March the Harwich Force, with its seaplane carrier *Vindex* (commissioned the previous November), carried out an anti-Zeppelin raid. The Germans were lured out but bad weather vitiated the enterprise. In April Scheer took the initiative with a raid on Lowestoft. Tipped off, all three British forces, Jellicoe's, Beatty's and Tyrwhitt's, put to sea. Tyrwhitt found the German Scouting Groups, which had already been weakened when the battlecruiser *Seydlitz* hit a mine. He tried to deflect the four remaining German battlecruisers but they pressed on and bombarded Lowestoft and Yarmouth. Tyrwhitt re-engaged and was in some danger of being destroyed. But Rear Admiral Bodicker, substituting for a sick Hipper, turned back to support Scheer's main fleet. Scheer, fearing an engagement with the enemy main fleet, turned for home. The Admiralty subsequently decided to take more measures to protect the southern East Coast, moving to the Nore the Third Battle Squadron of seven King Edward VII-class pre-Dreadnoughts, led by HMS *Dreadnought*.

In May *Vindex* offered another seaplane carrier bait in a raid also using *Engadine* (now the Battle Cruiser Fleet's carrier) escorted by the BCF's First Light Cruiser Squadron and First Destroyer Flotilla. Poor weather meant only three of the Sopwith Baby seaplane fighter-bombers got off the waves and the only aircraft to find the Tondern Zeppelin base missed. The two fleets also avoided contact but a Zeppelin that sortied to clarify the situation was shot down by the gunfire of the raiding force.

It was now Scheer's turn. In analysing the events of April, he decided he had chosen the wrong coastal targets. Sunderland, 200 miles to the north, would offer better rewards. Beatty could be engaged before Jellicoe would have time to come out in support. Scheer also integrated U-boats into his plans. An attempted, less restricted, submarine campaign against merchant shipping at the end of February had involved the sinking of a ferry, *Sussex*, and a real threat of war with the USA. On 24 April the U-boats were forced back to prize regulations. Scheer, therefore, thought the U-boats were best employed in his North Sea attritional plans, both as reconnaissance assets to be added to the Zeppelins and as a means of attrition in themselves. U-boats were sent out to lay ambushes for both Jellicoe and Beatty and to lay mines, but the raid had to be delayed from its originally planned date of 17 May because of delays in repairing *Seydlitz*. Then on the 29th, the next planned date, it was too windy to launch the Zeppelins.

Scheer's U-boats were at the end of their endurance and would have to start for home on 1 June. Without Zeppelins he could not prudently close the Durham coast. A last-minute compromise was decided upon. The two Scouting Groups, under a now recovered Hipper, would sortie into the Skagerrak with the main fleet 60 miles astern. This would draw Beatty and Jellicoe over the U-boats. Perhaps Beatty might also be enticed onto the guns of the combined German squadrons, but the latter would be close enough to home to be able to hasten out of danger if the worst happened and Jellicoe came into view. It is vital to understanding the ensuing events to stress that in no sense at all was Scheer seeking battle with the full British Grand Fleet.

At the last minute, Scheer decided to take a slightly greater risk and authorized Hipper to trail his coat as far as Norway. The British code-breakers warned the Admiralty that something was afoot and Jellicoe was already at sea when the Germans sailed in the very early hours of 31 May. Under his immediate command, coming out of their bases at Scapa and Cromarty, were 14 Super Dreadnoughts (including his flagship *Iron Duke* and two of the latest 15-inch-gun Revenges), ten 12-inch-gun Dreadnoughts and the three original battlecruisers of the Third Battle Cruiser Squadron, fresh from a week at Scapa for much-needed gunnery practice. Beatty had four 13.5-inch 'splendid cats', *Lion, Princess Royal, Queen Mary* and *Tiger*. The Second Battle Cruiser Squadron comprised two 12-inch ships, *Indefatigable* and *New Zealand*, as *Australia* was in refit. But as replacement for the Third BCS, Beatty had the four available 15-inch Queen Elizabeths of the Fifth Battle Squadron.

Beatty had long wanted these powerful and fast ships (their speed was almost that of his older battlecruisers) but, strangely, he did not consult with the Squadron Commander, Rear Admiral Hugh Evan-Thomas, during the latter's stay in Rosyth. This was a serious oversight as Beatty expected his fleet to be run on more decentralized lines than the Grand Fleet, with its voluminous books of Battle Orders.[32] This omission was but one part of a slackness that pervaded the Rosyth-based force, close to the fleshpots of Edinburgh and without a proper staff organization, despite its many highly able officers. No one was better than Beatty's flag captain, Ernle Chatfield. Chatfield had adopted – for *Lion* – safer procedures for handling ammunition, as suggested by his Warrant Officer Gunner A. C. Grant, but these were not imposed on the rest of the BCF.

Jellicoe was in a much stronger position than Scheer, who only had 16 Dreadnoughts with 12-inch or 11-inch guns, plus Hipper's similarly armed five battlecruisers. Against his better judgement, he had also brought the six pre-Dreadnoughts of the Second Squadron, which lowered his speed for no real gain in combat power.

The equivalents of the latter on the British side were the eight armoured cruisers of the First and Second Cruiser Squadrons. Deploying these modern, magnificent but obsolete ships with the Grand Fleet was unwise. As for lighter units, the two British forces had between them 26 light cruisers, 73 destroyers, five destroyer leaders and a minelaying destroyer. Beatty had *Engadine* with him for air support but, due to an error in signalling, *Campania* had been left behind at Scapa. The Germans only had 11 light cruisers between their two forces and 61 destroyers, although the latter deployed more torpedoes and were in more experienced flotillas with a more aggressive doctrine. The Grand Fleet's destroyers were in process of reorganization and in any case were seen primarily as defensive assets against German torpedo attack.

If it came to a showdown of total forces the result could hardly be in doubt. The only things Scheer could rely upon were the designed ability of his ships to take serious punishment and a tactic called 'Battle Turn Away', that would allow his fleet to melt away from danger. The best chances would come in a clash of battlecruisers, especially as the gunnery of Hipper's First Scouting Group was superior to that of Beatty's BCF. The latter had technologically more advanced equipment but it had not been designed to fight at the longer ranges at which the Jutland action would be fought. The lack of local Rosyth practice facilities was even more important.

The first serious British error was caused by misunderstandings at the Admiralty that led to Jellicoe being told that Scheer was still in harbour. Not only did this encourage the British to advance at a leisurely pace, it also meant the C.-in-C. would distrust later, correct, intelligence. Beatty's cruisers then made contact with Hipper's destroyers. As he turned to engage, Beatty made little attempt to keep Evan-Thomas in company and the battleships followed about ten miles astern. The Germans were running to the southwest to draw Beatty onto Scheer's guns. Fire was opened at 15.48 at 16,000 yards, the Germans using their full broadsides, the British only the bow guns of the leading ships. The latter overestimated the range by about a mile. Not till 16.02 were all British turrets in action. In this period, *Tiger* suffered badly from the gunfire of the battlecruiser *Moltke* and *Lion* was lucky to escape when a shell from Hipper's flagship, *Lutzow*, hit her central turret at the weak point where the left gun entered. A combination of good safety procedures and rapid flooding of the magazine saved the ship. Less lucky was *Indefatigable*. Hits in her barbettes caused catastrophic explosions in the incorrectly stowed ammunition. There were only two survivors from 1019.

The range was lengthening but Evan-Thomas came up in support and Beatty turned once more towards the enemy. By 16.19 the range was 16,000 yards and reducing. *Derfflinger* and *Seydlitz* found the range of *Queen Mary* and subjected her to a hail of rapid fire, penetrating the ammunition system and causing a huge explosion in the piles of cordite charges. Only 20 of Queen Mary's 1266 ship's company were saved. Beatty was moved to remark to Chatfield: 'There seems to be something wrong with our bloody ships today.'

The Germans then began to suffer the attentions of Evan-Thomas's Scapa-trained gunners. The rearmost German battlecruisers were hit and only superior magazine safety saved them. Then the main German battlefleet came into sight and amidst more signalling confusion the BCF and its attached battle squadron turned northwards to draw the enemy onto Jellicoe's guns. At 16.05 Jellicoe sent Rear

Admiral Sir Horace Hood's Third BCS ahead to support the BCF. It ran into the light cruisers of the Second Scouting Group. The British light cruiser *Chester* was seriously damaged before the battlecruisers disabled the light cruiser *Wiesbaden*. Hood's presence confused the enemy and was an effective cover to the British battlefleet deployment.

In the heat of the action Beatty, suffering communications problems because of damaged aerials, had not kept Jellicoe informed of the position of the High Sea Fleet. Jellicoe therefore had to take the less risky choice of deploying on the port wing, despite the fact it would delay action into the gathering darkness of the evening. As this took place the armoured cruisers closed to within 8000 yards of the High Sea Fleet to try to make their weapons effective. HMS *Defence* was hit repeatedly and blew up with all hands while *Warrior* was crippled, only being saved by the Germans being diverted by HMS *Warspite*, whose steering failed, making her describe a circle within 10,000 yards of the German fleet. *Warspite* was sent home while *Warrior* was taken in tow by *Engadine*, which had flown one sortie but which had been unable to communicate its information before rough weather made further operations impossible. *Warrior* sank the following morning.

As the fleet deployed, it passed the damaged *Wiesbaden*, which was engaged by almost every British battleship in turn but succeeded in putting a torpedo into the battleship *Marlborough*. The BCF, led by Hood, took position at the head of Jellicoe's line. This was the Battle Cruiser Fleet's finest hour, as its three oldest members put their recent gunnery training to excellent use. *Lutzow* shuddered under eight 12-inch hits from *Invincible* and *Inflexible*, two causing serious flooding that would eventually prove fatal. *Indomitable* hit both *Derfflinger* and *Seydlitz*. The Germans replied, although the stress on their stereoscopic range-finder crews caused them to be uncharacteristically late in getting the range. When they did, *Lutzow* and *Derfflinger* concentrated on *Invincible*. A hit on Q turret ignited the charges in *Invincible's* central ammunition system and then she broke in half. Six survivors from the 1027 men on board were picked up – but the damage *Invincible* had inflicted caused a slowly sinking *Lutzow* to drop out of line.

Scheer signalled 'Battle Turn Away' and the underwater threats advised against Jellicoe following Scheer into a potential trap. All he could do was remain across the German route home. Scheer then tried a premature breakthrough attempt and, briefly, the British had their prewar planned conditions, a fleet action at 10,000 yards. Scheer covered his second turn away with his ever more battered battlecruisers but it was a German destroyer attack that finally forced Jellicoe to retreat. Action eventually petered out in the gathering darkness.

By 22.30 most of the High Sea Fleet was in line, with Hipper's new flagship *Moltke* leading. She ran into the Grand Fleet's starboard column but the latter did not want to reveal its position, as night action was to be avoided. Hipper also sheered off, the lighter forces fighting a series of sharp actions in which the German cruiser *Frauenlob* was sunk. The High Sea Fleet now dropped behind Jellicoe as an escape route opened up. Tentatively, but with growing confidence, Scheer probed Jellicoe's rearguard flotillas.

The Germans were unimpressed by the tactical expertise of the British destroyers. Some showed no initiative and avoided action. When attacks were made they were made piecemeal, sometimes with insufficient blackout and with torpedoes fired at inadequate numbers at angles that were easily avoided. No amount of individual dash, notably when HMS *Spitfire* lived up to her name and rammed the battleship *Nassau*, could make up for this. The destroyer leader *Tipperary* and destroyers *Sparrowhawk, Fortune, Ardent* and *Turbulent* were sunk. The armoured cruiser *Black Prince* was blown up by repeated hits at close range from German battleships. The main British success was HMS *Onslaught* torpedoing and blowing up the German pre-Dreadnought *Pommern. Lutzow* was finally abandoned because of terminal flooding. She was given the coup de grace by a German destroyer at 01.45. Three other damaged German light cruisers, including the brave *Wiesbaden*, also sank during the night.

These losses were as nothing to Scheer's success in making his escape. Jellicoe's distrust of intelligence was a major factor, along with the failure of the Admiralty to communicate vital information to him. This was compounded by poor British enemy reporting caused by oversight, preoccupation, defective wireless and too great a concern with radio silence. It soon became clear that Scheer had slipped through the net. There was to be no new Glorious First of June. The Grand Fleet still commanded the world ocean, but it would have done that if it had not sailed at all. Jellicoe and Beatty had signally failed to wipe the High Sea Fleet from the strategic slate. All but one of the remarkably tough German battlecruisers had survived to fight another day. The lost *Lutzow*'s sister ship, *Hindenburg*, was fitting out and four larger battlecruisers were on the stocks. With a couple of 15-inch battleships about to come into commission, the loss of a German pre-Dreadnought was almost irrelevant. Over a third of the German light cruisers had indeed gone but there were better replacements on the way and for the same reasons Scheer could tolerate the loss of five destroyers.

The German fleet commander was justifiably happy: he broke out the champagne on his return. His fleet had survived, battered but unbowed. Moreover, his strategy of disproportionate attrition had been remarkably successful. Three British battlecruisers, a third of the BCF's strength, had been sunk. The loss of over a third of the British deployed armoured cruisers was their final epitaph as fleet units. Seven British destroyers and a leader had also been lost. In addition, 5672 men had been killed, 65 wounded and 177 taken prisoner; by contrast, only 2115 Germans had been killed with 80 wounded.

The British losses could also be relatively easily replaced and the Grand Fleet was in a better operational state than the High Sea Fleet in the immediate aftermath of the battle, but in no way had Scheer been put off. Jutland had shown the risks of the attrition strategy but, when his opinion that unrestricted U-boat warfare be restored was again overruled, Scheer planned another sortie as soon as his fleet was ready.

This was in August 1916 and Scheer made a virtue of the necessity posed by his only having two operational battlecruisers. The First Scouting Group was reinforced, by the first available German 15-inch gun battleship, *Bayern*, and two Kaiser-class battleships, as a force that could finish Beatty off if caught unsupported. Jellicoe, worried about the speed of the Kaisers, had decided to return the Fifth Battle Squadron to his own command but, as compensation, he had decided to operate in much closer proximity to Beatty with his entire fleet.[33] Scheer had only 15 Dreadnoughts in his main force. His plan was his original one of May: an attack on Sunderland to draw out Beatty to his doom and to demonstrate that the High Sea Fleet had not been defeated.

The summer weather made the vital German subsurface and airborne support easier, but if the two fleets came into contact, total British overall superiority was even more marked than it had been at Jutland. Jellicoe deployed 29 battleships and Beatty six battlecruisers. He also had the Harwich Force in support and a large British submarine screen for reconnaissance and attrition.

On the morning of 19 August the Grand Fleet and BCF rendezvoused off the Tay with Beatty kept on a tight leash only 30 miles ahead. Shortly afterwards the lead light cruisers were attacked by a U-boat from Scheer's northernmost line. HMS *Nottingham* was hit by three torpedoes and sank. Jellicoe suspected a minefield and turned his ships round. Only when it was clear what had really happened did he turn again to intercept the Germans reported east of the Humber. Shortly afterwards Jellicoe received the report that the submarine E23 had torpedoed the German battleship *Westfalen* earlier that morning. At 1400 the C.-in-C. read a signal from the Admiralty that the High Sea Fleet was in all likelihood only 40 miles away from Beatty. Jellicoe increased speed and signalled his fleet to expect immediate action and that he 'looked forward with entire confidence on the result'.[34]

It was an even greater opportunity than Jutland but there was no battle. Zeppelin L13, with an inexperienced reservist commander, misreported Tyrwhitt's Harwich Force as the BCF. Scheer altered course southwards to engage it, so preventing Jellicoe from bringing him to action. Scheer pursued his phantom until 14:35 when, warned by a U-boat of the Grand Fleet's presence, he retreated. The disappointed British also turned for home, losing another cruiser, *Falmouth*, to U-boats. Tyrwhitt did make contact with Scheer but decided that the brightness of the moon made a night torpedo attack impossible.

That day – 19 August 1916 – had important effects, much more important than those of 31 May. The Fleet commanders were taking the U-boat threat very seriously. On 6 September Beatty wrote that 'the old proverb that "When you are winning risk nothing" might well be applied now. And I think the North Sea South of Lat 55–30N is a very unhealthy place for Capital Ships and should be left entirely to SMs who might be able to deny the use of it to the Enemy except at grave risk.'[35] These proposals were adopted at a high-level conference in *Iron Duke* on 13 September. Only 'exceptional circumstances' would bring the Grand Fleet south of 55–30 N or east of 4 degrees E. This was approved by the Admiralty on 25 September.[36] As Fisher had prophesied, the narrow seas were best left to flotilla defence.

Scheer planned yet another sortie in September but was worsted by bad weather. The following month the German high command restarted a campaign of restricted submarine warfare against commerce. This took away Scheer's U-boats and his October sortie was limited to the centre of the North Sea east of the Dogger Bank, supporting a forward screen of destroyers and guarded by Zeppelin reconnaissance. In accordance with the new doctrine the Grand Fleet did not put to sea, but E38 torpedoed and damaged the cruiser *Munchen*. The affair demonstrated that little could be achieved without submarines and the High Sea Fleet was effectively stood down with the transfer of its destroyers to Zeebrugge to facilitate new attempts by U-boats to transit the Channel. An attempt to use larger ships to help cover a damaged U-boat coming home led to the submarine J1 torpedoing and damaging two German battleships.

Battlefleets could now only work with subsurface and air forces in a three-dimensional whole. The British were in a paradoxical position. The RNAS had over a thousand aircraft by October 1916, including some of the most capable in British service but it could not adequately support the Grand Fleet.[37] In July 1915 the Balfour–Jackson Board integrated the RNAS with the Royal Navy as a whole and on 1 September a Director of Air Services was appointed. In order to make the point, a non-airman, Rear Admiral C. L. Vaughan-Lee, was chosen, much to the chagrin of the pioneering former Director of the Air Department, Commodore Murray Sueter, who developed a strong antipathy to the Admiralty from that time.[38] The transfer of home air defence over land to the War Office was arranged and took place in early 1916. The armoured cars were a particular anomaly. Most of the RNACD squadrons were soon transferred to the War Office, except the three squadrons in Russia and 20 Squadron

RNACD that Balfour insisted remain the tank acceptance and trials organization.

All this made the RNAS more 'naval' but providing a 'fleet air arm' was still highly problematical given the state of carrier development and the lack of aircraft of sufficiently long range. Hoisting aircraft in and out was a difficult and time-consuming operation. *Campania* had been given a long flying-off deck in a major reconstruction over the winter of 1915–16. *Vindex* had commissioned with a flying-off deck. These ships could carry Bristol Scouts to intercept Zeppelins in the air. On 2 August 1916 *Vindex's* aircraft tried, but failed, to bring L17 down.[39] Early the following year the inadequate Bristols were replaced with Sopwith Pups, which first went to sea in the converted ferry *Manxman* that replaced the smaller *Engadine* in the BCF.[40] The clear utility of the Zeppelins on 19 August prompted Jellicoe to query the Admiralty about the air strength available to him. Land-based air support was still inadequate and the unsatisfactory seaplane carriers would have to do.

In the meantime, land- and carrier-based RNAS units carried out a general air offensive from Dover and Dunkirk and in the Mediterranean. Also, in the autumn of 1916, the Royal Navy initiated strategic air attacks against German industry as an extension of the blockade. No. 3 Naval (Bombing) Wing began working out of eastern France – hidden away from the RFC in the French area of operations. Attempts to rationalize Britain's air effort through an Air Committee and, later, an Air Board proved unsuccessful. Balfour used all his skill in argument to argue the case for the Navy retaining its air service.

In October 1916 German destroyer flotillas raided into the Channel. The results were very limited but the Dover Patrol under Admiral Reginald Bacon was unable to mount any defence. Balfour was moved publicly to state that there would be no repetition but such occurred on 23 November.[41] Criticism mounted and the success of the German U-boat offensive, restricted though it was, 'drove the final nail into the coffin of the Balfour–Jackson Board of Admiralty'.[42] With more German submarines at sea, monthly shipping losses doubled over the amounts lost in 1915. Countermeasures were as ineffective as ever and the very limited success of 1915, the blocking of the Channel to larger High Sea Fleet U-boats, was reversed in December. The U-boat threat caused a remarkable display of public unity between the elder naval statesmen Beresford and Fisher. The former wanted 'younger men fresh from the sea' the latter thought the U-boat menace could be 'dealt with but not by the bloody fools and Philosophic Doubters now in charge of the sea war'.[43]

In November Jackson's replacement by Jellicoe was announced. The C.-in-C. left his flagship at Scapa on 28 November and took up appointment as First Sea Lord on 4 December. Beatty inherited the Grand Fleet command. Jellicoe's appointment intensified the campaign against Balfour, and, with the fall of Asquith at the beginning of December, Sir Edward Carson became First Lord in the new Lloyd George coalition. Carson had a reputation for 'courage, decision and energy' that might assist a shake-up the naval war effort.[44]

The new Board (containing a Fifth Sea Lord responsible for the RNAS) would be faced by one of the biggest crises in the Royal Navy's history. In January 1917 the Germans decided to revert to unrestricted submarine warfare the following month. It took two months for the USA to go to war. Meanwhile shipping losses skyrocketed to a catastrophic 413 ships of almost two million tons in April. Jellicoe, the natural pessimist, went into shock. Nothing the Admiralty could do seemed to be able to stem the catastrophe. He had founded a new Anti-Submarine Division of the Staff but the British anti-U-boat patrols were still not working. The First Sea Lord argued that shortage of escorts and the inability of merchant ships to keep station meant that 'Convoy is impossible as a protection against submarines.'[45] Carson did not feel it right to overrule his professional adviser and when he called a meeting of merchant captains in February to obtain their advice it came out unanimously against convoys.

Certain critical trades were, however, beginning to be convoyed, if not, at first, in name. In mid-February, with the French economy dying from lack of power, colliers bound from western British ports to France were successfully put into 'controlled sailings' using trawler escorts. Beatty also obtained a reluctant Admiralty's permission to introduce convoys on the vulnerable Lerwick to Norway route; 20 old destroyers and 45 trawlers were allocated as escorts. Coastal convoys also operated between the Humber and Lerwick.

The latter had not had time to prove themselves before minds were changed at the Admiralty. Three factors came into play. First was the disastrous level of shipping losses. By 10 April the First Sea Lord was saying that it was impossible for Britain to go on with the war if these continued – and that there was no immediate solution to the problem. This was in conversation with Admiral William S. Sims, the US Navy's recently appointed representative in London. Sims began a campaign to get his navy's destroyers to be sent across the Atlantic to solve the perceived shortage of potential escorts. He also began to advocate convoy himself in discussions with the Prime Minister.[46]

The most important factor was, however, changing views on the Naval Staff itself. One of its most able officers, Commander R. G. H. Henderson, was in charge of the French 'controlled sailings'. From his contacts with the Ministry of Shipping he obtained figures on the actual number of ocean-going ships entering and leaving British ports. These proved that the number arriving and leaving every week was a mere 140 or so (20 a day) rather than the 5000 total movements previously estimated.

Henderson had a private line to the Prime Minister, whom he informed of the need to introduce convoys. Hankey, the Cabinet Secretary, also added his weight to the pro-convoy case. By late April Lloyd George told the War Cabinet of the 'possibility' of adopting the convoy system, quoting the support of Beatty and Sims. On the 25th April the Cabinet decided he would go to the Admiralty on the 30th April to discuss anti-submarine measures. Jellicoe, seeing the way the wind was blowing, told the War Cabinet on the 26th that convoying of ocean trade would begin when sufficient escorts were available. The same day the head of the Anti-Submarine Department, Rear Admiral A. L. Duff, submitted a key paper:

It seems to me evident that the time has arrived when we must be ready to introduce a comprehensive scheme of convoy at any moment.

The sudden and large increase in our daily losses in Merchant Ships, together with the experience we have gained of the unexpected immunity from successful submarine attack in the case of the French Coal trade afford sufficient reason for believing that we can accept the many disadvantages of large convoys with the certainty of a great reduction in our present losses.

Further the United States having come into the War eliminates some of the apparently insuperable difficulties to a comprehensive scheme of convoy.

The number of vessels roughly estimated...as the minimum necessary for escort work (45 ocean escorts and 45 destroyers for anti-submarine escorts) is large, but the necessity of safeguarding our food supply is becoming vital.[47]

The Prime Minister found he was pushing at an open door. A trial ocean convoy was already being planned. It sailed from Gibraltar with 17 ships escorted by three armed yachts and two Q ships on 10 May. As it approached the danger zone it was met on 18 May by eight destroyers and also received air escort from a flying boat based in the Scillies. It suffered no losses and it proved to a still sulky Jellicoe that the system was practicable. Nevertheless, despite shipping losses of over half a million tons monthly between May and July, convoys were only introduced slowly. Not until 24 May did a convoy sail from Hampton Roads, Virginia; two ships straggled (one of which was sunk) but the rest made it unscathed. Four more such convoys ran in June.

Sims's optimistic advocacy for more US escorts had helped stimulate the Admiralty on 15 May to decide to form a Committee to draw up a full-scale ocean convoy system. Its plans were presented on 6 June and agreed by Duff on the 11th, Jellicoe on the 14th and Carson on the 15th. Nevertheless it took another ten days to begin the setting up of a Convoy Section of the Trade Division of the Naval Staff. It is hard to disagree with Professor Marder:

The Admiralty no longer objected to convoy in principle and were prepared to see a fair trial made. But their hearts were not in it. They regarded convoys as the last shot in their lockers, were sceptical of its success, and had a lingering preference for a trade protection system based on patrolling. Besides it was argued against an extension of convoy that they could not provide escorts for a large proportion of the Atlantic trade. As a consequence of this attitude, Jellicoe and Duff were reluctant to institute a general convoy system and made no extraordinary efforts to speed up its development.[48]

In July Jellicoe opposed the redeployment of any of the 294 destroyers in home waters to convoy work. Convoy escorts were regarded as additions not substitutes to patrols. Lloyd George was getting restive. He had lost faith in his naval team.

The Admiralty War Staff had been reorganized as a result of Lloyd George's visit. Sir Eric Geddes, a forceful Scot and a dynamic railwayman who had solved the rail logistics problems in France, was appointed to the Board as 'Controller' with the honorary rank of Vice Admiral. Geddes was to run production and the Third Sea Lord design and equipment. The First Sea Lord became Chief of Naval Staff, assisted by a Deputy (DCNS) and an Assistant (ACNS), who were both Board members. The Board was now an executive body. The aim was to make the First Sea Lord, DCNS and ACNS responsible for operations, and the Controller and Third and Fourth Sea Lords for supplying *matériel*. Second Sea Lord deputized for First Sea Lord and supervised naval personnel.

In July Lloyd George appointed Geddes to replace Carson as First Lord and he took up his appointment on 20 July. He soon sacked the Admiralty Secretary, Graham Greene, and replaced him with Sir Oswyn Murray, one of the ablest civil servants of his generation, who would hold the post for almost 20 years. In September 1917 further reforms were decided upon. The Board was split into two Committees, Operations and Maintenance, both chaired by the First Lord to whom the First Sea Lord was now personally responsible for executive orders.

Against this background the convoy system was slowly implemented. Sims was the key. In June he wrote strong letters to Secretary of the Navy Daniels in Washington that caused him to overrule the anti-British Chief of Naval Operations Benson and promise co-operation in convoy. The number of US destroyers working with the Royal Navy increased from 28 at the end of June to 37 at the end of July, and their co-operation opened the way to the creation of a full-scale North Atlantic homeward-bound convoy system from Hampton Roads, New York, Sydney (Cape Breton) and Halifax. Thirteen such convoys sailed in July and only one ship out of 245 was sunk.[49]

Other ships continued to sail independently and although sinkings were not increasing they were not coming down. Jellicoe belatedly began to do 'everything possible to extend and strengthen the (convoy) system'.[50] In July inward-bound Gibraltar convoys began; in August inbound slow convoys (below 10 knots) were sailed from Dakar; and in

September fast convoys (above 10 knots) from Freetown. Outward-bound ships, now suffering severely, began to be convoyed from 11 August. By September the inbound transatlantic convoys had been split into slow (8.5–10 knots), medium (10–12.5 knots) and fast (12.5). A general convoy system to and from Port Said was introduced in October (outward) and November (inward). This step allowed the reopening of the Mediterranean to East of Suez shipping that had been routed round the Cape since March 1916. By November shipping losses had come down to less than 300,000 tons.[51]

Convoy worked for a number of reasons. Grouping ships emptied the oceans of shipping and made it more difficult for the U-boats to find targets. When they did, the submarines had the escort to contend with, a particularly formidable undertaking when an aircraft was present. If an attack was possible, only one of the ships in the group was likely to be picked off. The convoy could also be routed to avoid submarines that had given away their positions by radio.[52]

Ocean escort was provided by older cruisers, 'commissioned escort steamers', or armed merchant cruisers taken off blockade duty. This latter was now less necessary as the United States was in the war. In November 1917 the blockading 10th Cruiser Squadron, by then reduced to 17 trawlers, was stood down and its assets diverted to anti-submarine duties. Anti-submarine escort to convoys was provided by destroyers, sloops and P-boats; numbers almost doubled to 170. The advent of the US destroyers was a particular boon to Bayly at Queenstown, who would have been unable otherwise to protect ships in this vital theatre with his sloops alone. The Queenstown destroyers were probably the greatest single American contribution to winning the First World War. Nevertheless Britain provided the destroyer escort for 70 per cent of convoys.[53]

As ocean convoy was introduced, average tonnage sunk per U-boat day at sea declined from the catastrophic 18,304 tons in April to 10,268 tons in August and 6429 tons in September. The U-boats then began to concentrate on the still independently routed shipping in coastal waters and productivity improved to 8640 tons in December, when 160 British ships of 382,060 tons were lost.

There was discussion of reducing the Grand Fleet to the BCF and the Fifth Battle Squadron to release escorts but Beatty resisted this move. Major anti-submarine hunts were carried out by its flotillas in June and October 1917, supported by submarines and in the latter case trawlers equipped with hydrophones, but to little avail.[54] However futile these activities, though, Beatty was probably right in maintaining the Grand Fleet at full strength as Scheer planned to use the High Sea Fleet against the Scandinavian convoys. In October the fast German minelaying cruisers *Bremse* and *Brummer* caught a westbound convoy. They sank two escorting destroyers, *Mary Rose* and *Strongbow*, plus nine neutral merchantmen. Intelligence had given some warning and powerful cruiser and destroyer forces were at sea, but they were operating too far to the south. Beatty blamed the Operations Division and complained in person at the Admiralty.

In November 1917 a British raid was carried out into the Heligoland Bight with the aim of catching the forces protecting the minesweepers supporting the movements of the U-boats. Vice Admiral T. D. W. Napier commanded a powerful striking force of eight light cruisers and ten destroyers, supported by the 15-inch-gun cruisers *Courageous* and *Glorious*. In overall command of the operation was Vice Admiral Pakenham's BCF with five battlecruisers and nine destroyers.

Napier sighted the German destroyers and minesweepers, which retired under cover of smoke, supported by four German light cruisers. The smoke prevented the British forces having much gunnery success but Napier continued his chase as he presumed the Germans knew which areas were clear of mines. As the Germans disappeared into the smoke Napier thought it imprudent to press on until the enemy came back into view. He then took up the chase again but had lost five miles. Pakenham had sent in the shallow-draught 15-inch-gunned battlecruiser *Repulse* to provide Napier with even more muscle but eventually he signalled Napier to give up the chase. The latter turned a blind eye until he came to the edge of a dangerously mined area when he finally ordered a turn. The signal was unclear and the light cruisers continued the chase, which brought them upon two German battleships, *Kaiser* and *Kaiserin*, which opened effective fire. The cruisers *Caledon* and *Calypso* were hit and seriously damaged and *Repulse* covered the British withdrawal.

The British guns had scored only one serious blow, a 15-inch round that damaged the funnels and boiler room of the light cruiser

Konigsberg. The engagement had been beyond the capabilities of the British fire-control systems, especially given the zigzag courses of both sides' ships and the smoke screens that prevented fall of shot being spotted. To quote Marder, 'That the failure of 17th November occurred nearly 18 months after Jutland had revealed serious deficiencies in staff work, co-ordinated action and gunnery caused many to look askance at the Admiralty.'[55] To add insult to injury, four German destroyers annihilated a Scandinavian convoy on 12 December and there were also problems over the highly porous Dover Straits barrage, with disagreements between the Plans Division and the Dover Patrol commander about its conduct.

The grumbling aviation problem also contributed to undermining Geddes' confidence in Jellicoe. The provision of a fleet air arm did make some progress in 1917. Beatty's new Grand Fleet Aeronautical Committee recommended the replacement of seaplanes by higher performance landplanes. Two more converted ferries, *Nairana* and *Pegasus*, appeared for use with the BCF and the last large light cruiser, *Furious*, was commissioned as a partial aircraft carrier with a hangar and large flying-off deck instead of her forward 18-inch gun. No sooner had the latter joined the fleet in July than a pioneering deck landing was carried out on 2 August by Squadron Commander E. H. Dunning, who flew his Sopwith Pup around the central superstructure with the ship at full speed, effectively hovering over the deck onto which he was pulled down. Attempting to repeat this dangerous procedure cost Dunning his life but *Furious* was taken into the yards to have a flying-on deck added aft. Aircraft were also being added as 'one-shot weapons' mounted on platforms in normal warships and in August HMS *Yarmouth* of the Harwich Force launched a Sopwith Pup that shot down Zeppelin L23. In October the first experimental flight of a Pup fighter from a platform on the turret of the battlecruiser *Repulse* took place.

Yet just as the Royal Navy began to integrate aircraft more effectively with the fleet, it was decided to take them away from its control. Pressure from the Army saw the allocation in 1917 of more RNAS fighter squadrons to support the Western Front (the first had been sent in October 1916) and in March 1917 the withdrawal of the strategic bombing force for similar duties. It was becoming ever harder to sustain the existence of two air forces. The Air Board was given much wider powers and, after the bombing of London by German bombers seemed to reveal serious weaknesses in Britain's air power, a committee of the War Cabinet, chaired by General Smuts, reported on 17 August that a single 'Royal Air Force' should be created under an 'Air Ministry'. Jellicoe opposed this move but the First Lord asked Beatty's advice. The latter, frustrated at the Admiralty's apparent low priority for aircraft for fleet work, could see no reason why much of what the RNAS did could not be given to a separate air force. The new Air Ministry might actually be more forthcoming with a fleet air arm.[56] The C.-in-C. would live to regret his enthusiasm for the new service.

By the end of the year this disagreement, the reverses at sea and Jellicoe's support for Bacon at Dover finally decided Geddes to tell the Prime Minister it was either him or Jellicoe. Lloyd George approved the First Sea Lord's dismissal and on Christmas Eve Jellicoe got an unwelcome present in the form of a letter informing him that he was to be replaced by his erstwhile deputy Rosslyn Wemyss. The new Board took up office on 10 January 1918.

There was much doubt in the Service about both the dismissal of Jellicoe and the manner of his going, but the new First Sea Lord was

an officer of good judgement and common sense, and one who in times of crisis never got rattled or even worried... his great moral courage was well known: he would take risks and never hesitate to assume full responsibility for everything that was done. He made every possible use of the brains of the Naval Staff, instituting regular and formal morning Staff meetings for a discussion of the general situation and the planning in outline of schemes and operations.[57]

Wemyss supervised the general direction of operations, the Deputy First Sea Lord, Rear Admiral George Hope, taking over much of the day-to-day administration as well as primary responsibility for foreign operations. DCNS had responsibility under the First Sea Lord for home operations while ACNS looked after trade defence and anti-submarine warfare. It was generally agreed that the new arrangements were a great improvement.[58]

Convoy continued to work well, where it was applied. The only reason the U-boats scored what successes they did was the unwillingness to use it in British coastal waters. British mercantile losses to U-boats in the first half of 1918 remained around 200,000 tons. As coastal convoy was introduced from June to cover most shipping in the North and Irish seas losses fell. The air effort was diverted from patrolling to escorting these convoys with great effect. In August British shipping losses were 146,000 tons, in September 137,000, in October only 55,000.[59]

It was reducing losses rather than sinking U-boats that marked the British victory. Depth charges were, however, beginning to make their mark, 21 U-boats being sunk in 1918 by this means; only mines killed more that year. Convoy escorts were by far the most efficient U-boat killers. Between February 1917 and November 1918 21 submarines were sunk by escorts and the same number by hunting forces and patrols. Only 393 merchant ships were, however, sunk in convoy against 2936 independently routed ships. The convoy U-boat:merchant ship exchange ratio was thus 1:19 as against 1:140 for independents.[60] Remarkably, only a limited number of ships were actually engaged primarily in convoy escort – 257 in October 1918 (5.1 per cent of the 5018 warships in commission). Even if ships sometimes used are added, the number only rises to about 15 per cent of total strength. Hunting and patrol operations went on, indeed the Admiralty actually reduced escorts in the spring to enhance patrols.

Another anti-U-boat measure was to try to attack them in their bases. This was equally ineffective. Brave attempts by the Dover Patrol to block Zeebrugge and Ostend in April 1918, under the dashing leadership of Vice Admiral Roger Keyes, Bacon's replacement, won gallantry medals but no strategic advantage. Keyes was more successful in his operations using patrols and illumination to replace the net barrage in the straits. German destroyers struck at the patrols, with some success in February, but in that month the High Sea Fleet U-boats again gave up the Channel passage.

In April 1918, to universal rejoicing, the long-heralded movement of the Grand Fleet (since December 1917 reinforced by the American Sixth Battle Squadron) to Rosyth took place. That month Scheer came out for an attack on the Scandinavian convoy but was forced to turn back by a breakdown in the battlecruiser *Moltke*. The submarine E42 put a torpedo into the crippled German vessel but it was a last missed opportunity for a fleet action, One doubts if *Australia, Indomitable, Inflexible* and *New Zealand* in immediate support of the convoy would have stood much of a chance against Scheer's full strength, but equally Scheer was facing annihilation if caught by Beatty's full forces, which included 31 battleships (four from the US Navy).

The Grand Fleet was by now a fully three-dimensional force. The fast steam-powered fleet submarines of the 'K' class delivered in 1917 proved tricky to operate in close proximity with surface ships, notably when two were sunk in the unfortunate 'Battle of May Island' at the end of January 1918, but they impressed many who saw them for their speed and seaworthiness and they might have provided a surprise for Scheer.

At its creation in April 1918 the RAF took over 2949 seaplanes and aeroplanes from the RNAS and over 55,000 personnel. Most were airmen who regarded themselves already as members of the 'Air Service' and saw little future in the Royal Navy. Beatty's expectations were met in an enormous addition of air strength to the fleet at sea. By the end of the war, over 100 RAF aircraft were being carried by battleships, battlecruisers and cruisers, as well as carriers. *Furious* rejoined the fleet in March but could not use her landing deck operationally. Nevertheless she carried out offensive sweeps, her Sopwith Camels forcing down a German seaplane in June and bombing and destroying two naval Zeppelins in their sheds at Tondern in July. Only in October did the first fully flush deck carrier, capable of landings as well as take-offs, join the fleet: HMS *Argus*, a converted liner. She carried Sopwith Cuckoo torpedo bombers, to which Beatty had long been looking forward for their capacity to lay their eggs in other peoples' nests, the German fleet anchorage. The war was too far advanced for this experiment to be tried.

In August Tyrwhitt used his air capabilities in a sweep of the Heligoland Bight exits. His four light cruisers and 13 destroyers were towing two lighters carrying Camels and three carrying flying boats; there were also six of the torpedo-armed coastal motor boats

(CMB) delivered since 1916. The CMBs were wiped out by German seaplanes, but Tyrwhitt had his revenge when Zeppelin L53 was shot down by a pontoon-launched Camel.

In the summer and autumn of 1918 the allied armies, sustained by British sea power, defeated the German army on the Western Front. The Royal Navy was not just an enabler, however. The Royal Naval Division, with an Army brigade under command, had been on the Western Front since May 1916. It continued to distinguish itself to the Armistice.[61] Until 31 October 1918 the Division suffered 32,631 casualties, mainly wounded, but 7939 killed. This was an interesting comparison with the 39,766 casualties suffered by the rest of the Navy over the whole war, 33,361 of those, however, being dead.[62]

As for material assets the Royal Navy in the First World War lost: 13 battleships; 3 battlecruisers; 2 aircraft carriers; 25 cruisers; 17 armed merchant cruisers; 63 destroyers and destroyer leaders; 10 torpedo boats; 52 submarines; 5 monitors; 7 gunboats; 2 minelayers; 18 sloops; a P-boat; 13 armed boarding steamers; and 442 auxiliaries (257 of them trawlers).[63]

Despite these losses, the Navy grew enormously during the First World War period from 658 units of over 2.5 million tons to over 5000 of about 4.5 million. The number of light cruisers increased from 64 to 89 and destroyers and leaders almost doubled from 222 to 430. From 1914 a standard two-funnelled light cruiser evolved from the Cambrian and Centaur classes, commissioned in 1915–16, through the Caledon and Ceres classes to the Capetowns and larger Danaes under construction at the war's end. Twenty-eight of these ships were completed in all. There were also five 10,000 ton 7.5-inch-gun armed ships laid down, the prototype of the later 'heavy cruisers' of the interwar period. The first, however, was rushed to completion as an aircraft carrier – a mini-*Furious*. She commissioned as HMS *Vindictive* with the Grand Fleet in October 1918.

The year 1916 had seen the initiation of both a programme of 1500–1600 ton destroyer leaders to match feared new German large destroyers and the initiation of a class of 1100 ton standard destroyers of the 'V' and 'W' classes. No less than 46 were built before the war's end and they were to be important and long-lived assets. A more heavily armed modified 'W' class was ordered in quantity – 54 boats – in early 1918 but most were later cancelled. Smaller destroyers were also reverted to in 1917, some 57 'S' class being ordered in 1917. Only two were cancelled but they became obsolete more quickly than their larger contemporaries.

The Royal Navy increased in personnel strength over the war period. In July 1914 regular strength had stood at 145,318. By September 1918 this had increased to 265,277. To these must be added the 8268 retired officers and pensioners recalled to service and the 19,626 of the Royal Fleet Reserve, 25,072 RNRs, 51,588 RNVRs, 37,374 RNR (Trawlermen) and 1792 Colonial Reserves, making a grand total of 408,997. Most extra ratings were obtained by temporary 'hostilities only' admissions to the reserves. The shortage of personnel was such that women were recruited to take up shore billets. The Womens Royal Naval Service was founded in 1917 and by November 1918 it boasted a strength of 4821.

It had all been a strategic success story but there had been no great successful fleet action. Convoy had eventually protected shipping while command of the sea – and poor German rationing – had enforced a pitiless blockade that had made the defeats of the German army so corrosive of national morale. When, following the 11 November Armistice, the best ships of the High Sea Fleet surrendered to the Grand Fleet off the Firth of Forth, the ebullient Beatty made the most of it. Nevertheless, a rather sensitive Admiralty felt it necessary, at the end of 1918, to produce a secret memorandum which, in the first paragraph of the section 'Command of the Sea', states the Admiralty's perspective on what it had achieved thus:

The war has been fought and the final decision reached on land; but the land campaign was rendered possible only by reinforcements and supply from overseas. The armies of the Western Front, where the main offensive lay, have to a great extent been transported thither across the seas. The passage of the allied troops to the Dardanelles, Salonika, Egypt, Palestine, and Mesopotamia depended entirely on the security of our sea communications. The campaigns of East Africa, Samoa, New Guinea, South West Africa and the Cameroons, and of Archangel in the far north rested on the same foundation. All these depended mainly on the supremacy of the allies at sea – guaranteed by the Grand Fleet – and on the carrying power of the British Mercantile marine. The Navy and Mercantile Marine of Great Britain have, in fact, been the spearshaft of which the Allied armies have been the point.[64]

6 The Interwar Period

The prevailing sense of postwar pacifism coupled with Britain's weak economic condition provided a difficult environment for the Admiralty. On 15 August 1919 the Cabinet decided that no major war would take place for ten years and that service estimates should be revised accordingly. This was in the context of a paper presented to the Cabinet three days earlier by the First Lord. The latter was now Walter Long, who had replaced Geddes the previous January. The paper had pointed to the burgeoning strength of the United States Navy, 'the only navy for which we need have regard', and in respect of which the Admiralty required a decision of the Government as to whether it should be the standard against which the British fleet should be built. Japan, still Britain's ally, could be 'put aside for the moment whether as an individual opponent or as a partner in any possible combination against us'.[1]

The Cabinet responded by ordering the Admiralty to revert to the prewar standard of one power plus 60 per cent, excluding the USA as before the war. The Admiralty responded by arguing that it was only the USA's distance that had prevented it being counted 'as one of the two principal powers against whose possible combination we were providing'.[2] The Admiralty continued to hold out for a one-power standard based on the USA. The latter was in the process of a major build-up following the commitment made in 1916 to a US Navy 'second to none'.

The only capital ship under construction for the Royal Navy was the mighty HMS *Hood*, a huge battlecruiser that combined battleship protection and armament (12-inch belt and eight 15-inch guns) on a displacement of over 40,000 tons and speed of 31 knots. She had been laid down in 1916 as a counter to the large German battlecruisers under construction and planned and her design had been completed before the lessons of Jutland were fully digested. Extra armour was added but the design was not considered fully up to date either defensively or offensively; *Hood*'s three sisters, laid down in 1916–17, were cancelled on the slips in October 1918. Despite her defects, however, *Hood* herself, on commissioning in May 1920, was the finest capital ship in the world. She was better protected than the American battlecruisers being laid down that year and her guns were in new mountings with greater elevation for longer range. Any subsequent capital ships, however, would need at least 16-inch guns, as about to be deployed by the Americans and Japanese.

Could, however, such vessels be afforded? Along with its declaration of the 'ten-year rule', the Cabinet in August 1919 called for the Naval Estimates of 1920–1 to be only £60 million as against naval expenditure of £154 million for 1919–20. The Admiralty eventually presented Estimates of £84 million for 1920–21, basing its request on an acknowledgement of the one-power standard, including the USA. Long stated, from the Government front bench on 17 March 1920, that 'our Navy should not be inferior in strength to the Navy of any other power, and to this principle the present government firmly adheres... That is the foundation of the Naval policy of His Majesty's government'.[3]

As Christopher Bell argues, this was 'a substantial victory' for Long and his new First Sea Lord, Earl Beatty, who had replaced Wemyss in November 1919. Against formidable opposition, the Admiralty 'had secured a naval standard relative to the United States, a power it freely admitted Britain was unlikely to face in war; it obtained the only standard which might conceivably allow it to resume construction of capital ships in the near future; and it received a public commitment to this standard, which no future cabinet could renounce without risking political and public protest'.[4]

There were enough cruisers, destroyers and submarines left over from wartime programmes to meet requirements. Three classes of new light cruiser were under construction, the four remaining large 7.5-inch-gun Hawkins class, eight 6-inch 'D' class (four of which had been cancelled following the armistice) and two fast Es (a third of which was cancelled). These ships were commissioned between

1918 and 1926. Thirty-eight 4.7-inch armed modified 'W' class destroyers were cancelled in 1918–19, leaving 18 to be completed to add to the 46 war-built 4-inch armed V/Ws. The 57 smaller 'S' class destroyers were also largely completed postwar, only two being cancelled. Some 33 submarines were cancelled in 1918–19 but 40 were completed. In order to obtain experience with large cruiser-type submarines, one 2500 ton example, equipped with two twin 5.2-inch-gun mountings, was laid down in 1921. As X1 she was commissioned in 1925.

Considerable importance was placed on improving the situation with aircraft carriers. A pair were under construction at Armstrongs on the Tyne, HMS *Hermes*, the first carrier built as such from the keel up, and HMS *Eagle*, converted from the incomplete Chilean battleship *Almirante Cochrane*. To clear the yard, the two hulls were removed incomplete and they were finished in Royal Dockyards as funding allowed in 1923–4. It was also planned to reconstruct *Furious* as a flush-decked carrier although work could not begin until 1922.

By mid-1920 the Admiralty was considering its plans for capital ships, as the increasingly 'fused' battleships and battlecruisers were now generically known. Four such ships were to be laid down in 1921 and four more in 1922. The four 1921 ships were magnificent, if rather odd-looking, fast 'Super Hoods' of over 48,000 tons with modern armour protection and triple 16-inch guns all mounted forward. Together with the existing three 15-inch battlecruisers, these would balance the six new battlecruisers building in the USA. To reinforce the 13.5- and 15-inch gun ships of the main battlefleet against the ten new 16-inch American battleships being built, four ships of similar size to the 'Super Hoods' but slower and more heavily armoured were intended for 1922, armed with three triple 18-inch guns also mounted forward.

These plans, essential to maintain the announced naval standard, were opposed by the Treasury. The Committee of Imperial Defence formed a high-powered subcommittee chaired by Bonar Law to investigate the case for the capital ship. The strategic framework was war against the United States.[5] The committee split; half of it, led by Bonar Law, reported that, although capital ships were not obsolete, self-styled 'progressive' naval officers, notably Rear Admiral Herbert

Richmond, had convinced it that new examples should not be built. Beatty obtained the support of Churchill, now Minister for War and Air, to call for the immediate laying down of the 'Super Hoods', if for no other reason than to give the British Empire something to trade in a possible agreement with the USA.

During the Bonar Law committee's deliberations, Long's health broke down and Lord Lee of Fareham succeeded him as First Lord. Lee and Beatty were able to defend the Estimates from a serious attack by the Cabinet's Finance Committee, which wanted to uphold the £60 million figure for 1921–2. The Admiralty were able to get over £80 million, including £2.5 million for replacement of obsolete ships but the number of capital ships in commission was reduced to 16 from 20. The design of the 'Super Hoods' was completed and the ships actually ordered on Trafalgar Day 1921.

A month later, however, work was suspended. The reason was the sensational opening in November of the conference in Washington, called by the new Harding Administration to discuss both naval and Far Eastern affairs. The British delegation was led by Arthur Balfour, with technical advice from Beatty himself and Chatfield, now Rear Admiral and Assistant Chief of a reformed and unprecedentedly effective Naval Staff. Beatty and Chatfield were flabbergasted to hear the dramatic initial speech by US Secretary of State Hughes that proposed the mutual abandonment of new capital ship-building programmes, scrapping 15 ships under construction in the USA, the four projected British battlecruisers and 15 Japanese ships building and projected. Older ships should also be scrapped to achieve an agreed ratio of strength; broad parity between Britain and the US, with Japan having three-fifths of that strength; other types of ship would be maintained in proportion. There should be a ten-year 'holiday' in new capital ship construction and future ships were to be limited to 35,000 tons.

Britain emerged well from these proposals, although the Admiralty were worried about the industrial effects of the 'holiday' and their need for more cruisers than the other naval powers, given Britain's imperial responsibilities and dependence on overseas trade. The British were able skilfully to use the Japanese desire to complete the almost finished battleship *Mutsu* to obtain a compromise by which the

Americans also retained two more 16-inch-gun ships, *Colorado* and *West Virginia*, and Britain was allowed to build two completely new 35,000 ton 16-inch-gun capital ships, the 23-knot battleships *Nelson* and *Rodney*. The 5:5:3 ratio was also applied to aircraft carriers with an individual limit of 27,000 tons, except for two larger vessels converted from incomplete capital ships. The USA had pressed for the latter provision so they could convert two of their incomplete battlecruisers to carriers. Japan also converted two redundant capital ship hulls. Britain eventually chose not to build such large ships but to proceed with the conversion of the light battlecruisers *Glorious* and *Courageous* into 22,500-ton fleet carriers. This allowed more tonnage for an extra carrier if desired.

Beatty had to return home early, leaving the technical work of the British delegation in the hands of Chatfield. The latter was not able to undermine tonnage as the basis of the agreed ratios but he was able to get a more satisfactory definition of it – 'standard displacement' – and he helped prevent the ratio system being applied to other types of warship. The only agreed limitation was 10,000 tons and 8-inch guns which effectively defined the new 'light cruiser' (as opposed to 'battlecruiser').

The 'Treaty for the Limitation of Naval Armament' was signed in Washington on 6 February 1922. The British had come out of it better than any other naval power with permission to build two new capital ships. America's lack of battlecruisers was considered to be a major disadvantage by contemporary wargamers at the US Naval War College, who considered the British would have a real advantage in a fleet action.[6] The two new battleships and the larger cruisers required to meet the Washington standard would help keep the British warship industrial infrastructure in business. The major drawback from the British point of view in the Washington settlement was the replacement of the Anglo-Japanese Alliance by the Four Power Pact of 13 December 1921. This confirmed Japan as a potential enemy against which the Admiralty had to plan more seriously.

The possibility of war with Japan required a fleet base in the Far East. As early as 1919 the Admiralty had considered the construction of such a facility at Singapore, as the Admiralty thought the Anglo-Japanese alliance might not survive. In 1921 the Admiralty proposed that a base be built in the Johore Strait and in June the proposals were approved by the Cabinet. A committee to decide on the measures necessary was set up in November.

Simultaneously with these developments, the former First Lord, Sir Eric Geddes, began to chair his Committee on National Expenditure in August. It was intended to come up with proposals for deep cuts in government spending. It was to defend the Admiralty from Geddes that Beatty returned early from Washington. Beatty defended his corner ably, especially when his old friend Churchill was given the task of chairing a committee to review Geddes' proposals as they affected the armed services. In his report, Churchill defended both the one-power standard and the Singapore base. Although cuts were to be made in shore establishments and the Naval Estimates were to be only £2 million more than Geddes' £60 million, Churchill recommended a smaller reduction in naval personnel, to around 100,000 rather than Geddes' 88,000. A compulsory retirement scheme was, however, introduced for lieutenants, which forced 350 to leave – the infamous 'Geddes Axe'. As Roskill points out, it had been 'a mistake to swell the list of permanent officers during the war so greatly, when much of the necessary expansion could have been accomplished by the wider granting of temporary commissions...it is worth recording that in the Second World War the same mistake was not repeated'.[7]

The Admiralty's Estimates for 1922–3 were only slightly increased to almost £65 million but important improvements in capability were taking place. The year 1922 saw the establishment of a new Anti-Submarine Branch. Anti-submarine warfare in the Royal Navy had been transformed by the advent of active sonar (Asdic as it was called in the Royal Navy).[8] Britain led the world in this technology, which was applied first to the specialist P and PC boats of the First Anti-Submarine Flotilla based at Portland for training and then to fleet destroyers. The conviction began to grow – encouraged by anti-submarine officers anxious to increase the stature of their infant branch – that the threat of the submarine had been mastered. Chatfield was more circumspect: 'We have got to the stage when the hitherto "undetectable craft" is detectable...the time is coming when we shall have to rebalance our theories as to the tactical use of submarines'.[9]

Major unfinished operational business in this immediate postwar period had been the intervention against the Bolsheviks in the former Russian Empire. In November 1918 a force led by five C-class light cruisers was sent to the Baltic, under Rear Admiral Alexander-Sinclair, to 'show the flag and support British policy as circumstances might dictate'.[10] It was later signalled that Bolshevist warships operating off the coast of the Baltic should be assumed to be doing so with hostile intent and treated as such. Two more cruisers were sent, which was a wise precaution as one of the original ships suffered underwater damage and another, *Calypso*, struck a mine and sank. Alexander-Sinclair landed arms to help the Estonians who were fighting for their independence and evacuated refugees from Riga. He then withdrew to Copenhagen.

The Cabinet decided to relieve Alexander-Sinclair with a new force, which was under Rear Admiral Sir Walter Cowan, primarily to help defend Estonia and Latvia from the Bolsheviks. Cowan was reinforced but was prevented for the time being from taking the offensive against the Bolshevik fleet. There were, however, clashes when Bolshevik ships came out and the new submarine L55 was lost to Bolshevik patrol craft. A means of attacking the enemy fleet at anchor was provided by a pair of coastal motor boats deployed for running agents in and out of Petrograd and which were not directly under Cowan's orders. The commander of the pair, Lt. A. W. S Agar, began his own private offensive that eventually bore fruit on the night of 17–18 June when, in CMB 4, he torpedoed and sank the cruiser *Oleg*, at anchor to the south of Kotlin Island. Wemyss, the First Sea Lord, used this to attempt to obtain more robust action against the Bolsheviks. The carrier *Vindictive* and eight larger 55-ft. CMBs were deployed (one was lost being towed across the North Sea). The carrier grounded but her aircraft could operate from shore bases. Cowan planned to use them to cover a night CMB attack on the Bolshevik fleet at Kronstadt. It attacked in the early hours of 18 August, under the command of Commander C. C. Dobson, who had received the voluntary reinforcement of Agar in CMB7 to bring his flotilla back up to eight boats. CMB79 torpedoed and sank the submarine depot ship *Pamiat Azova*. Two battleships, the Dreadnought *Petropavlovsk* and the pre-Dreadnought *Andrei Pervosvanny*, were also hit and disabled. Three CMBs were lost but the Bolshevik surface fleet had been virtually neutralized in the most effective use of fast attack craft in the Royal Navy's history.

The Bolsheviks hit back on 1 September when their submarine *Pantera* sank the destroyer *Vittoria*. Three days later mines, which had already claimed the minesweepers *Myrtle* and *Gentian* in July, sank the destroyer *Verulam*. The Reds were, however, not the only targets. By October focus had shifted to the German forces of General von der Golz and his Russian puppet General Bermondt, who were refusing to evacuate the Baltic states. The cruisers *Cleopatra* and *Dragon* fought a sharp action with the fort commanding the entrance to Riga. *Dragon* was hit and suffered the last casualties at the hands of the Germans in the war of 1914–19, but the Germans and their supporters were forced to withdraw. The following month Bermondt's forces tried to take Libau but were repulsed with the assistance of the 15-inch guns of the monitor HMS *Erebus*.

Service in the Baltic against the Bolsheviks was unpopular with many of the ratings, especially those who had joined up for war service. In October, a hundred members of the ships' companies of destroyers at Rosyth about to be sent back the Baltic left their ships. The following month there was a mutiny in the carrier *Vindictive* and minesweeper crews refused duty. In December there was even trouble in Cowan's flagship, the cruiser *Delhi*. Pay had been generously increased in 1919 to help keep sailors (who had been the vanguard of the revolution in Russia and Germany) loyal. As the situation in the Baltic stabilized with the withdrawal of the Germans and the conclusion of treaties recognizing the independence of the Baltic states, the British squadron, which had done much to ensure this outcome, was reduced and in 1921 eventually withdrawn.

The Royal Navy was also involved in intervention operations in other areas of the Russian Empire, notably on the Caspian, where a considerable flotilla of two seaplane carriers, nine armed merchantmen, 12 CMBs and two CMB carriers was built up. This gained control of the sea for a period before the vessels were handed over to the Whites. Another unusual unit was Commander J. Woolfe-Murray's Naval Mission to Siberia, an armoured train created by the armoured cruiser *Suffolk* at Vladivostok to support Czech forces in central Siberia.

As Roskill says of its operations near Omsk: 'it seems unlikely that naval officers and men have ever before been in action so far from salt water'.[11] Its equipment eventually took to the water again in a force of 21 river steamers manned largely from *Suffolk*'s replacement, HMS *Kent*, which fought Bolshevik craft until withdrawal was ordered in July 1919.

The Grand Fleet ceased to exist on 7 April 1919, being replaced by the Atlantic and Home Fleets. The Atlantic contained the First Battle Squadron (the Rs), the Second Battle Squadron (the Queen Elizabeths), the Battle Cruiser Squadron (*Lion, Princess Royal, Renown, Repulse* and *Tiger*), the First Light Cruiser Squadron, the first three Destroyer Flotillas and six Submarine Flotillas. The Home Fleet of older ships only had a brief life as an active force, its units being placed in reserve in November 1919. Strength in the Mediterranean was increased with *Iron Duke* (flagship), *Marlborough, Benbow, Emperor of India, Centurion* and *Ajax*, the Third Light Cruiser Squadron of C-class ships, the Sixth Destroyer Flotilla and Fourth Submarine Flotilla. It became inceasingly preoccupied by the need for a naval presence in Turkish ports as nationalists, led by Kemal, were challenging the official government. At the beginning of 1920 the First Battle Squadron was sent east to reinforce the Mediterranean Fleet. By March there were seven battleships off Constantinople, *Revenge, Ramillies, Royal Sovereign, Royal Oak, Ajax, Marlborough* and *Benbow*, along with the seaplane carrier *Ark Royal*. Under the cover of the big ships seamen and Royal Marines were landed as *Ark Royal*'s aircraft reconnoitred overhead. This temporarily reinforced the Sultan's authority but there was little the ships and their landing parties could do to prevent Kemal consolidating his power in Asia Minor. As he put it, 'battleships cannot climb over mountains'.[12]

The terms proposed for the draconian Treaty of Sèvres further strengthened the Kemalist position. The Allies supported the Greek invasion of Asia Minor and men from *Revenge* and *Royal Sovereign*, supported by the seaplane carrier *Pegasus* and two destroyers, occupied Mudania. A battleship-supported landing in eastern Thrace helped force the hapless Ottoman regime to sign the Treaty of Sèvres and the First Battle Squadron was sent home.

In mid-1922 the Greeks became the targets of gunboat diplomacy, when, contrary to the wishes of the other allies, they threatened Constantinople. A major naval concentration was assembled to deter action and support the French forces defending the city. All six of Sir Osmund Brock's Mediterranean Fleet battleships (HMS *King George V* having replaced *Emperor of India*) were deployed, with the seaplane carrier *Pegasus*, destroyer depot ship *Diligence* and nine S-class destroyers. Brock was later reinforced by Tyrwhitt's Third Light Cruiser Squadron and two more destroyers. The overawed Greeks, aware of the vulnerability of their forces in Asia Minor to maritime interdiction, reassured their erstwhile allies that they would not occupy Constantinople without their consent.

Another threat to the Greeks came from Kemal, who had declared his government the only legitimate Turkish regime on 30 January 1922. By September the the Greeks were being driven out through Smyrna. Admiral Brock appeared off the port in *Iron Duke*, to be joined by HMS *King George V* and *Ajax*, the cruiser *Cardiff* and destroyers. Merchant ships were commandeered to evacuate British nationals. The British were the most powerful part of a force that included French, Italian and American ships. Brock's attempts to obtain an orderly surrender were prevented by the outbreak of fire and the Royal Navy ships present were caught up in the evacuation of as many Greek and Armenian refugees as possible.

Kemal now menaced the neutral zone created by the treaty of Sèvres on the eastern shore of the Dardanelles. The British feared him acting as a stalking horse for Bolshevik Russia, allowing it to gain control of the Straits. Brock was told Kemal was to be stopped and he received powerful reinforcement, including, once more, four 15-inch battleships from the First Battle Squadron. When Turkish forces entered the neutral zone at Chanak war threatened. Brock's warships provided cover for the outnumbered ground forces ashore, which were reinforced by some 6-inch guns taken from HMS *Benbow*. A flotilla of ships' boats and other small craft, backed by destroyers, prevented Turkish movement across the Straits. Despite considerable tension at times – the destroyer *Speedy* was sunk in collision with an unlit tug and Turkish guns fired at another RN destroyer – careful diplomacy on the spot prevented conflict and the

Turks withdrew. A new peace treaty was eventually concluded at Lausanne in 1923, after which the fleet was finally withdrawn from the Straits. After five years a 'heavy, tedious and often anxious commitment' had come to an end.[13]

The1922 crisis marked the breakdown of the Lloyd George coalition and a new Conservative Government came to power at the end of October with Leo Amery, the previous Parliamentary Secretary, as First Lord. His Estimates, introduced in March 1923, were at £58,000 a reduction on the previous year's figure. New construction money was to cover the battleships laid down the previous December, the cruiser minelayer *Adventure*, laid down in November, and preliminary work on a 1300-ton submarine designed primarily for Far Eastern service. Work was going on within the Admiralty, however, on ambitious new plans for 17 10,000-ton 8-inch cruisers, eight to be laid down in 1924. Japan was already building new cruisers to the Washington limits and Britain was short of the target of 70 cruisers deemed necessary to cover both fleet and trade defence duties. To replace over-age destroyers two flotillas (18 vessels in all) would be required annually from 1927–8. Seven of the new overseas submarines were required annually from 1925–6. The Chancellor, Neville Chamberlain, approved some immediate orders as an anti-unemployment measure and Estimates of £62.25 million were informally agreed for 1924–5.

Such was not to be, however, as the Government went to the country on the question of imperial preference. The Conservatives did not do well and the Liberals decided to support the Labour Party, which entered government for the first time. The new First Lord was Lord Chelmsford, a former Viceroy of India and a non-party peer of generally progressive views, who took the job on condition that the fleet be 'adequately maintained'.[14] Beatty and the other sea lords found that relations with the new Government were much more cordial than expected. The main bone of contention was a Treasury attempt to reduce the pay of officers and men to reflect reductions in the cost of living. Reluctantly, the Admiralty agreed that personnel joining after 1 July 1924 be paid at reduced rates, the burden falling most heavily on the lowest ranks.

The new Government indulged the pacifist instincts of Prime Minister Ramsay McDonald in announcing the cessation of work on the Singapore base. It saw, however, the advantages of continuing naval shipbuilding to create jobs and the eight new cruisers were only cut by three. *Kent, Suffolk, Berwick, Cornwall* and *Cumberland* were duly laid down in 1924. Indeed, the extent of the programme led to a debate in the Commons in which the Conservatives supported the Government against the Liberals and the dissident Labour left. Two experimental new destroyers, one each from Thornycroft (*Amazon*) and Yarrow (*Ambuscade*), were also put into the programme to explore the best type for future construction. The Estimates were, however, less than the previous year's, at £55.8 million.

The year 1924 also saw a compromise solution to the problem of naval aviation, which had become an interdepartmental running sore in Whitehall. The creation of the Royal Air Force put a component of the fleet that the Navy considered to be vital under the control of another service with a very different outlook. The new RAF had inherited the Admiralty's wartime ideas about the utility of attack on the enemy homeland. This was now the centrepiece of its strategic doctrine. Also, the junior service's bureaucratic weakness had seen it suffer the most swingeing postwar cuts. It was most reluctant therefore to put a high priority either on aircraft or training for operations with the fleet. The RAF was willing to have a limited number of specialized units to work with the Navy ('Coastal Area' was set up for this purpose in September 1919) and it was willing to accept naval officers for general RAF service. But the Air Ministry was unable to go along with Admiralty requests that maritime units should be manned wholly by naval personnel, seeing this as the thin end of a wedge that would lead to a future partition. In November 1919 the Chief of the Air Staff, Sir Hugh Trenchard, asked Beatty for a two- to three-year period of 'tranquillity and freedom from criticism' before a definitive settlement on the basis of specialist portions of the RAF being paid for by the older services.[15] In announcing the permanent organization of the new service in December, Churchill, the Minister for War and Air, even spoke of these specialist portions becoming 'an arm of the older services'.[16]

When the Admiralty pressed for this solution it was rebuffed. Reports from sea made clear the inadequacy in quantity and quality of RAF contingents working with the fleet. The advent as ACNS of

Chatfield, convinced that aircraft were essential to the fighting efficiency of the fleet, added to the Admiralty's aggressiveness on this issue. On Chatfield's recommendation an Air Section of the Naval Staff was formed, which was boycotted by the Air Ministry. The Admiralty kept up the pressure for secondment of officers for purely naval work and succeeded in 1921 in achieving the creation of a branch of air observers within the Royal Navy. The following year, pressed by Chatfield, Beatty took the opportunity of the Geddes Committee to join with the Army in calling for an examination of the financial extravagance of a third service. Both Geddes and the Government continued to back an independent RAF, but it was announced that a committee would be set up to examine naval–air co-operation.

As a first step, Churchill sent both Beatty and Trenchard a paper setting out the basis of a compromise. The Admiralty would define the roles and quantities of aircraft required to work with the fleet in battle, pay for them and control them when employed on naval purposes. The Air Ministry was to act as a 'shop' for material and the RAF would continue to be the 'parent service for all airmen' in order to preserve the 'general unity of the Air Service', although interchange of personnel between the services was to be encouraged.[17]

The 1922 political crisis delayed the creation of the committee until March 1923 when it met as a subgroup, chaired by Lord Balfour, of Lord Salisbury's general investigation into inter-service co-operation. The Balfour subcommittee reported in July 1923 and generally went along with Churchill's compromise, specifying that the Air Ministry should provide all the material the Admiralty demanded for its 'Fleet Air Arm' and that that FAA aircraft could not be removed for other purposes without Cabinet approval. Naval officers would be seconded to the RAF but at least 30 per cent of officers in carriers would be light blue. Fleet reconnaissance as well as spotting would be carried out by RN personnel.

Negotiations on the implementation of the Balfour compromise went on into 1924. The two relevant ministers requested yet another committee to adjudicate. This was chaired by Haldane, the Lord Chancellor, and was composed of Trenchard and Keyes, now Deputy Chief of Naval Staff. The two officers were married to sisters and

were left by Haldane to hammer out an agreed interpretation of the
Balfour recommendations.

The Trenchard–Keyes Agreement was forwarded to Haldane in
July 1924 and the Cabinet approved it. It created the 'Fleet Air Arm
of the Royal Air Force' made up of aircraft whose performance and
numbers would be specified by the Admiralty but whose specifications would be drawn up by the Air Ministry, which was also responsible for procuring the machines. Shore facilities would be provided
by the RAF, who would carry out training to Admiralty requirements.
Naval ratings would replace RAF personnel on carriers in various
grades and would provide telegraphist air gunners in aircrew. Up to
70 per cent of FAA pilots were to be attached RN or Royal Marines
personnel with dual rank in both their original service and the RAF
(in fact a reversion to RNAS practice when air service ranks were not
necessarily the same as RN). The RN's own Observer branch would
carry out all reconnaissance and spotting.

As the medium-term organization of the Fleet Air Arm was being
decided, the Air Ministry was delivering the second postwar generation of carrier aircraft. The Fairey Flycatcher fleet fighter was
replacing the Nightjar and the Plover, the Bison and the Blackburn
were replacing the Westland Walrus in fleet spotter flights, and the
Fairey IIID the Parnall Panther and the unsatisfactory Seagull
amphibian in fleet reconnaissance flights. Single-seat Blackburn Darts
equipped new fleet torpedo flights. Although numbers were limited,
these were specialist naval aircraft that fulfilled the Admiralty's needs.
Indeed, in the Bison and the Blackburn the enclosed accommodation
for the naval observers was verging on the luxurious!

In the autumn of 1924 the minority Labour Government fell and
the Conservatives won the ensuing General Election. Almost immediately the work on the Singapore base was restarted. The Treasury,
now under the dynamic leadership of Winston Churchill, whom
Baldwin had picked out of the political gutter after his fall with the
Lloyd George coalition, was out to control naval expenditure. Churchill
was Janus-faced on defence expenditure. In his make-up there was a
dichotomy between his enthusiasm for weapons and armed forces on
the one hand and, on the other, his fixation with his father, who had
resigned on the question of high defence expenditure. He oscillated

between the two and now firmly wished to follow in his father's footsteps, to allow room for tax cuts and social reform, and to improve his new party's electoral prospects. In Cabinet he called for the extension of the ten-year rule and a review of the Admiralty's cruiser programme. The Admiralty hoped for Estimates of £65 million for 1925–6, partly to cover the new costs of the Fleet Air Arm.

Churchill strongly attacked the proposals, denying the likelihood of a war with Japan and the need for any new construction programme except for new submarines. The First Lord, W. C. Bridgeman, a former Conservative Home Secretary and an honest and quietly able politician who won and kept the confidence of his Admiralty colleagues, countered the Chancellor. A compromise was agreed. When the Estimates were presented, they were only £60.5 million, almost what Churchill wanted, but funds for new construction were held over for more discussion. During these deliberations, the Chancellor obtained an official assessment that there was no likelihood of war with Japan for the next ten years (an interesting extension of the ten-year rule with regard to the most likely opponent). Pressure for Beatty to give was intense but he was prepared to resign over the issue and the Admiralty was not without friends in the ruling party. The Whips told the Prime Minister there was more political danger in backing the Treasury than the Admiralty and at the last minute, in July, Baldwin put forward his own proposals. These were that seven cruisers were to be laid down: four in 1925–6 and three in 1926–7. In the event this programme moved a little to the right, given continued pressure on the Naval Estimates. Also, the Australians agreed to build two Kents, *Australia* and *Canberra*, laid down in mid-1925. The first two British ships, *London* and *Devonshire*, built to a slightly modified design, were not laid down until 1926 and the other pair, *Sussex* and *Shropshire*, not until 1927. The three 1926–7 cruisers followed in mid-1928, the full-size *Dorsetshire* and *Norfolk* and, to please the Treasury, a new smaller class with only six guns, HMS *York*. The first six new overseas submarines based on the prototype *Oberon* were also in the 1926–7 programme although they were not begun until 1927. More cruisers, submarines and the beginning of destroyer replacement were planned for 1927–8.

As Bell puts it, 'The Cabinet accepted that the Japanese threat was sufficiently remote that it did not necessitate immediate naval preparations, but also that the Admiralty's long-term projects could continue as a means of insuring against this danger in the more distant future.'[18] A new definition of the one-power standard was endorsed by the Cabinet in May 1925:

The requirements of a one-Power standard are satisfied if our fleet, wherever situated, is equal to the fleet of any other nation, wherever situated, provided that arrangements are made from time to time in different parts of the world, according as the international situation requires, to enable the local naval forces to maintain the situation against vital and irreparable damage pending the arrival of the main fleet, and to give the main fleet on arrival sufficient mobility.

Pressure on the Estimates did not slacken, however. No sooner were the new plans announced than the Treasury set up a Fighting Services Economy Committee, chaired by Lord Colwyn. This tempted the Admiralty to reopen the campaign for a naval air arm, carrier and land-based, under its full control. This did not go down well with Colwyn, who supported the Air Ministry and called for substantial reductions in the Navy Estimates. The Treasury was satisfied with the 1926–7 Estimates coming down to just over £58 million.

With such financial pressure on both estimates Chatfield, now Third Sea Lord, suggested at the end of 1926 that another naval arms-control treaty, extending limitations to smaller types of ship and extending the life of capital ships, might be in the British Empire's interest. In February 1927 President Coolidge told Congress that he had suggested the delegates to the Preparatory Commission for the Disarmament Conference at Geneva be empowered to begin negotiations on the further limitation of naval armament. The Conference opened in June with the First Lord leading the British delegation. The Americans duly suggested 5:5:3 ratios for cruisers, destroyers and submarines. The British suggested reductions in the sizes of ships, notably battleships to 30,000 tons with 13.5-inch guns and cruisers to 7500 tons and 6-inch guns. A 5:5:3 ratio would be accepted on 8-inch-gunned cruisers but the British insisted that she have 70 cruisers in total. The Americans insisted on overall cruiser parity on the basis of a common tonnage limit much less than that which would allow 70 British ships. They also demanded the right to make all their ships 8-inch. The impasse reflected the American ideological fixation with 'a navy second to none' (Congress would never sanction cruisers up to British total tonnage requirements) and the difference in role for the cruiser in both navies. The US Navy saw their future cruisers as small battlecruisers operating with the main fleet, the British saw the majority of theirs (45 to 25) as trade defence assets. The Americans remained adamant and the Conference broke down in mutual recrimination.

In July 1927, with the Geneva Conference in session, Beatty stepped down after his extended term of office as First Sea Lord. During his old chief's run-down period, Chatfield had borne the brunt of maintaining the Admiralty's position in London, being willing to see Baldwin personally when it seemed too many concessions might be made at Geneva.[19] Beatty had requested he be succeeded by Jellicoe's old Chief of Staff, Sir Charles Madden, to help heal the split between Beatty's and Jellicoe's supporters in the controversy that had arisen within the service over the Battle of Jutland. Madden was an intelligent and highly experienced officer, respected by his political masters, but lacking the charisma and force of character of his predecessor. Chatfield remained as Third Sea Lord until November 1928, when he assumed command of the Home Fleet.

Given the failure of Geneva, the Admiralty pressed on with its cruiser programme, which called for three more new ships per year. The First Lord suggested the British go for 6-inch ships but Chatfield and the Naval Staff insisted that the least they could accept for the 1927 ships were smaller 8-inch cruisers of a modified York type. Churchill wanted cancellation of all cruiser construction and the Admiralty, in difficulties making its expenditure fit the £58 million of the 1927–8 Estimates, cancelled two of the projected cruisers, leaving only one, *Exeter*, to be laid down in 1928. The first flotilla of A-class destroyers was also laid down, eight vessels plus a slightly larger leader, *Codrington*. Another six overseas submarines, the Parthian class, were also started. Churchill, however, was on the warpath and at the beginning of 1928 demanded a reduction of the 1928–9

Estimates below the requested £61 million. That figure was duly reduced (to just over £57 million) but it was decided that the two cruisers built in that year's programme – *Northumberland* and *Surrey* – would be full 10,000-ton ships. The second B-class destroyer flotilla would go ahead (albeit with a less expensive flotilla leader), as would an R-class flotilla of six overseas submarines, intended for the Mediterranean.

The formidable Chancellor was determined to cap defence expenditure and in June wrote to the Committee of Imperial Defence that the ten-year rule should be deemed to be in force until it was decided to alter it. This was accepted a little reluctantly the following month and gave Churchill excellent grounds to attack the 1929–30 Estimates. Another reason for economy was the higher level of operational expenditure, primarily caused by events in China. The three-cornered conflict there between Nationalists, Communists and warlords, as a concurrent anti-foreign campaign, provided much work for the vessels of the China Station protecting British interests and nationals. The construction of the powerful Insect-class river gunboats, for work on the Danube during the war, had provided a welcome re-equipment for the China riverine forces. There were 14 river gunboats in service in China by 1922, over half of them Insects. The total force was increased to 17 by 1930, 13 on the Yangtze and four on the West River. Four new gunboats were launched in 1927–8. Larger ships backed up these forces as required, e.g. when the cruiser *Emerald* bombarded antiforeign elements in Nanking in March 1927. The China Station was also a primary deployment area for the impressive new 10,000-ton cruisers and five Counties were on station by 1930, backed up by the aircraft carrier *Hermes*.

Despite this increased activity, the 1929–30 Estimates were kept down to below £56 million. It was hoped that significant building would continue; three cruisers (of which it was later decided that one would be a new 6-inch design), a third new destroyer flotilla and six submarines (two large and fast boats designed for operations with the main fleet and four relatively small S-class built for patrol operations in European waters). In announcing the Estimates Bridgeman stated that the Fleet Air Arm would be 153 aircraft strong by the end of the year. In the financial circumstances it was understandable that air provision would not be lavish. Indeed, Dudley Pound as ACNS had reduced the eventual intended planned build-up of aircraft from 346 to 251. The new carrier that had been programmed to take up Britain's spare Washington tonnage was postponed in order to obtain more experience of *Glorious* and *Courageous* (which were only just coming into service).

The trend towards cuts was enhanced by Labour's return to power after becoming the largest single party in the election of May 1929. A. V. Alexander became First Lord. A much-underrated man, Alexander combined an appreciation of political realities with an ability to display considerable mettle in his departmental interest. Drawdown in the existing programmes could not be prevented. As a first step, all units not yet begun – the cruisers *Northumberland* and *Surrey* and the submarines *Royalist* and *Rupert* – were suspended and later cancelled, and at the end of the year the 1929 Programme was reduced to the single 6-inch cruiser, a reduced flotilla of five C-class destroyers, one fleet submarine and a pair of S-class submarines.

Both Prime Minister Macdonald and President Hoover were committed to the cause of arms limitation. The economic climate deteriorated with the Wall Street Crash, paving the way to achieving what had failed at Geneva in 1927. A new naval conference opened in London in January 1930. The two leaders had decided in principle on delaying capital ship construction for five years and on cruiser parity based on 50 ships. The Admiralty reluctantly accepted that they might tolerate the cruiser figure if it was clearly accepted to be only a five-year measure, and that a steady building programme of three new ships a year was safeguarded. It took until April for the Treaty to be agreed between Britain, the USA and Japan. Despite the Admiralty's severe misgivings about its industrial consequences, the capital ship building holiday was extended until 1937. The oldest ships, which would have merited replacement, were to be scrapped or, in one case, converted to demilitarized training ships, leaving Britain and America each with 15 capital ships and Japan 9. The British ships doomed by this were all the 13.5-inch coal burners: the battleships *Iron Duke* (demilitarized as the training ship), *Marlborough, Emperor of India* and *Benbow* and the battlecruiser *Tiger*. On the vexed cruiser question the type was now divided into two categories by gun size: 'heavy' with 8-inch guns and 'light' with 6-inch. Agreement was reached on 15 heavy cruisers for Britain, 18 for the USA (no more than 15 of which would be built before 1935) and 12 heavy cruisers for Japan. Britain would be allowed 192,200 tons of 6-inch light cruisers, the USA 143,500 tons and the Japanese 100,450. Britain and the USA would have 150,000 tons of destroyers each, Japan 105,500 and the three powers would have parity in submarines at 52,700 tons.

The London Treaty has been heavily criticized. John Ferris sees it as a key factor in undermining the naval supremacy that had been maintained throughout the 1920s.[20] As the Admiralty feared, the non-construction of capital ships did lead to further reduction in capacity for armour plate, by over a half, but it is far from certain, as Ferris himself concedes, that such construction would have taken place even if the Treaty had not been in place. The economic crisis that hit Europe in 1931, coupled with doubts over the continued viability of the battleship among leading politicians, might well have prevented new construction, as it did of aircraft carriers. It must also be remembered that the Admiralty strongly supported the extension of battleship life, which implied delay in replacement and helped create the logic of the capital ship measures adopted.

The Treaty probably helped the Admiralty in its negotiations over new construction with the Government. The tonnage limit for cruisers was used as an imperative to build 90,000 tons of new light cruisers. Three more 7000-ton 6-inch ships were put into the 1930 Programme, sisters of *Leander* of the 1929 Programme, laid down in September 1930. It was planned to split construction of the remaining ships over the following three years between pairs of the Leander type and a new smaller 5000-ton Arethusa-class cruiser designed primarily for fleet work. A full destroyer flotilla would be programmed each year, as would three submarines, a mix of three new design minelayers, two large fleets, and seven S-class.

Madden had the first part of the building programme in place when he stepped down at the end of July 1930. His term of office had been extended for another year in order to keep out his originally intended successor Sir Roger Keyes. Keyes was a controversial figure, especially after the Royal Oak Affair of 1928, caused by the clash of personalities on board that battleship and the subsequent courts martial, a situation in which he as Mediterranean Fleet C.-in C. had been involved and which he had done nothing to ameliorate, indeed the opposite. This confirmed a lack of political sophistication – a serious matter in a First Sea Lord in a time of naval disarmament. As Roskill puts it, 'one can understand the reluctance of ministers to accept a First Sea Lord who was likely to prove highly intractable on such issues'. Roskill also doubted 'whether Keyes, in spite of his panache, his gallantry and his magnetic personality, was well equipped either by character or by intellect to hold the highest office his service had to offer'.[21]

Madden's successor was Sir Frederick Field. Roskill is very critical of him, regarding him as 'the most colourless First Sea Lord' of the period. His health was indeed uncertain but Field had distinguished himself as a naval diplomat on the flag-showing world cruise carried out by *Hood* and *Repulse* in 1923–4. It was understandable that Alexander should regard him as safe.

In 1931 Field and the Board of Admiralty were caught up in the financial and political cataclysm of that summer. In August Macdonald formed a National Government with Conservative support. Austen Chamberlain replaced Alexander as First Lord. Cuts were being demanded in naval pay, notably the abolition of the favourable 1919 rates, which over 70 per cent of junior rates and no less than 94 per cent of senior rates were being paid. The Admiralty acquiesced in these demands and did not present the news well to the fleets – the result was considerable unrest on the lower deck. On 15 September, at Invergordon, which the Atlantic Fleet was using as a base for exercises, the ships' companies of four capital ships, first *Valiant* and then *Rodney, Nelson* and *Hood*, went on strike. The cruiser *Norfolk* and minelaying cruiser *Adventure* also mutinied. Vice Admiral Tomkinson of the Battlecruiser Squadron, acting fleet commander because of the illness of the C.-in-C., cancelled the exercises. Some normality was restored in *Hood* and *Nelson* and mutiny was nipped in the bud in *Dorsetshire* but the following day *Hood* had another strike and the cruiser *York* mutinied also. That afternoon the fleet was ordered to return to home ports where cases of hardship would be investigated; order was eventually restored in all ships.

The mutiny completed the process of destroying confidence in the pound and Britain was forced to leave the Gold Standard. On 21 September the Prime Minister announced that cuts would be limited to 10 per cent on the 1919 rates. Chamberlain had offered a complete amnesty but 121 men were sent to barracks, of which 24 were discharged, services no longer required. There were no courts martial but those officers involved in the affair, including members of the Board who were not thought to have advised Chamberlain adequately (notably Frederic Dreyer, DCNS), had their careers blighted. The reconstruction of the Cabinet following the 1931 election saw Chamberlain replaced by Sir Bolton Eyres-Monsell. Monsell was a former naval officer himself and this experience, coupled with what Roskill calls his 'parliamentary skill, tact and patience', put him in a good position to restore the service's prestige.[22]

This began in earnest when the infirm Field was finally replaced on 21 January 1933 by the greatest naval officer of his age, Admiral Sir Ernle Chatfield. Beatty's former flag captain had a wealth of experience at the Admiralty as Fourth and Third Sea Lord and as ACNS. He had just commanded the Atlantic and Mediterranean Fleets, in the latter post successfully preventing any outbreaks similar to Invergordon. In correspondence with Eyres-Monsell, Chatfield had insisted that until 'the Sea Lords connected with the events of 1931 have all left it will be impossible to get criticism stopped and take the strong action that should and must be taken regardless of persons, to establish the dignity, authority and prestige of the Board without fear or favour'.[23] Chatfield's appointment was the finishing touch to a new set of Sea Lords who had just taken up appointment; Dudley Pound, Charles Forbes and Geoffrey Blake, with Vice Admiral J. C. Little replacing Dreyer as DCNS.

Chatfield's vigour and authority was soon demonstrated in his overruling the other Sea Lords to cancel a plan to introduce sail training for ratings. Chatfield knew from his early days that sailing ships were dangerous and he recognized that the technically orientated ratings of the 1930s would hardly benefit from such an enforced obligation. He was not, however, generally overbearing and allowed the other Sea Lords to operate without undue interference. Pound was replaced by former submarine 'ace' Martin Dunbar-Nasmith in 1935; Forbes by Reginald Henderson in 1934. The latter was to have a particularly important role, staying in post as Controller until March 1939, when his health collapsed with the strain of masterminding naval rearmament. With the vision of Jutland before him Chatfield was also determined that future British ships should always be adequately protected and the skills of the Royal Navy crews, in which he always had the greatest confidence, should be allowed to assert their advantage.

Chatfield wanted to diminish the perceived gap between the Admiralty and the fleet. Members of the Board of Admiralty normally wore morning dress on official occasions as befitting their membership of a civilian body. Chatfield insisted, however, that naval members of the Board wear uniform when visiting ships and Monsell went along with this by adopting a nautical civilian rig with yachting cap. The worst grievances on pay and pensions were also resolved.[24]

Little could be done about the battlefleet until the building holiday expired but there was some urgency in revising the cruiser programme. The Japanese had exploited a loophole in the London Treaty to build large 'light' cruisers of similar size to the 8-inch heavies but armed with six-inch guns. The first two were laid down in 1931 and two more were programmed. The 1931 and 1932 British Programmes had each included two 7000-ton light cruisers and a 5000-ton ship. In early 1932 the Board had ordered that a large light cruiser with triple 6-inch mountings be designed. In 1933, with the USA following Japan down the large light cruiser route, the Admiralty decided to alter the two larger cruisers of the year's programme to the new 9100-ton design. Originally called Minotaurs, the new ships were eventually named after cities, the first two being *Newcastle* and *Southampton*, laid down in October and November 1934. Three more were programmed for 1934, along with the last Arethusa, the annual destroyer flotilla (eight H-class plus leader) and the long-awaited large, purpose-built, modern aircraft carrier allowed under treaty limits.

The Naval Estimates had, understandably, reached a nadir in 1932–3 of £50.5 million but there was an increase in Chatfield's first year to £53.6 million and to £56.6 million in 1934–5. The upward trend could not be avoided as the Government faced the dangers of the increasingly darkening international horizon. The Japanese had invaded Manchuria in 1931 and Hitler came to power in Germany at the beginning of 1933. The ten-year rule was abandoned that year, at the end of which it was agreed that a Defence Requirements Committee (DRC; the Chiefs of Staff and the Permanent Secretaries of the Foreign Office and the Treasury, chaired by Sir Maurice Hankey the Cabinet Secretary) be set up to prepare a programme to meet the worst defence deficiencies. The committee responded with a five-year programme that included capital ship modernization, improving the Fleet Air Arm and funds for the Singapore base (although the largest individual headings were fuel and personnel). The Cabinet, however, wished to emphasize air rearmament against Germany rather than naval security against Japan and the DRC's recommendations were rebalanced accordingly, much to the chagrin of Monsell and Chatfield, who emphasized the fleet's unpreparedness for war in Cabinet discussion.

Chatfield's submission to the DRC reflected his anxiety that, although new battleships could not be laid down until the beginning of 1937, existing capital ships should be given better protection and greater anti-aircraft (AA) armament. The Queen Elizabeths had both the best development potential and the most suspect machinery. In 1934, therefore, two were taken in hand for reconstruction, with *Warspite* getting completely new machinery and guns of increased elevation and *Malaya* getting a less extensive modernization that was limited to protection and AA armament. The two older, lightly protected, battlecruisers were also important candidates for modernization to maintain a fast squadron, a major edge for the British battlefleet. *Repulse* had a lighter scale of rebuild with better armour in 1933–6. On completion of this work, *Renown* was taken in hand for a more extensive rebuild with new machinery.

The Admiralty managed to squeeze just over £60 million out of the Treasury for 1935–6. The numbers of men voted were increased to almost 94,500 (from a low point of less than 90,000 actually borne in 1932–4) and a normal building programme was announced of three large 6-inch cruisers (*Liverpool, Manchester* and *Gloucester*), another standard flotilla of destroyers and three submarines. The latter were a minelayer, an S and a prototype T-class patrol submarine of only

1100 tons, the better to fit the London limits. Later an extra flotilla of seven surface ships was added to the programme. These were large destroyer-type vessels armed with eight 4.7-inch guns, developed as answers to the 2000-ton Japanese 'Special Type' destroyer. The new super destroyers challenged the existing ship nomenclature system and a new classification, corvette, was considered. Eventually it was decided instead just to name them out of the existing flotilla series; thus was the Tribal-class destroyer born.

During 1935 the international situation deteriorated further. Hitler denounced the military clauses of the Treaty of Versailles and Italy, a valuable ally against Germany, was becoming alienated over its ambitions towards Abyssinia. In July the DRC was reconstituted and Chatfield reopened his campaign to obtain approval of a two-power standard, to give security both against Japan and the strongest European naval power. He scored only a partial success. A stronger definition of the one-power standard was confirmed: Britain should be able to:

send to the Far East a fleet sufficient to provide 'cover' against the Japanese Fleet; we should have sufficient additional forces behind this shield for the protection of our territories and mercantile marine against Japanese attack; at the same time we should be able to retain in European waters a force sufficient to act as a deterrent and to prevent the strongest European naval power from obtaining control of our vital home terminal areas while we make the necessary redispositions.[25]

This, the Admiralty now argued, was insufficient. They wanted a 'new naval standard' that would enable Britain to place a fleet in the Far East 'fully adequate to act on the defensive and to serve as a strong deterrent', while allowing the maintenance in home waters of a force able to 'meet the requirements of a war with Germany at the same time'.[26] Although this was endorsed by the DRC, if the new naval conference ended without quantitative limits the Committee's immediate recommendations were based on the revised one-power formula, which became known as the 'DRC Standard'. This implied an impressive enough fleet: 15 capital ships, ten aircraft carriers, 70 cruisers, 16 flotillas of destroyers and 55 submarines. A programme of new construction was proposed between Estimates years 1936–7 and 1942–3. Two new battleships would be laid down in the first year, three in the second, two each in the succeeding two years and one each in the following three; over this period four new carriers would be built along with five new cruisers per year. For destroyer types, another flotilla of nine Tribals was to be built in 1936–7 with a flotilla of more normal destroyers in alternate years thereafter. The production rate of submarines would continue at three a year. The Fleet Air Arm would be increased from 190 in 1935, to 357 in 1939, and 504 in 1942.

The Admiralty had clearly seen the advantages of arms control in the 1920s and now saw it as a natural solution to the problem of a revived German Navy. If Germany was determined to rearm, the best solution was to get her to accept some limits that were within the boundaries of practical British naval policy to counter, a 35 per cent ratio. Hitler offered such a deal and it was a very attractive one. As Maiolo puts it:

the 35% ratio equalled in the Admiralty's view the maximum tonnage level for any European fleet; second, the Admiralty rightly concluded that Germany would likely aim to expand its naval forces to that level by about 1942; and third, the Admiralty's knowledge of the details of German warship construction before June 1935 was quite accurate. The Admiralty was not being hustled into an ill-considered position by Nazi diplomacy or compromised by poor intelligence, but was using armaments diplomacy to advance its long range strategic programme.[27]

The Anglo-German Naval Agreement was concluded by an exchange of notes in June 1935.

A full-scale Naval Conference was in preparation at London. In December 1934 the Japanese had given notice of their intention to terminate the Washington Treaty at the end of 1936. The Japanese claimed parity with the other two major naval powers, and a willingness to reduce strength to such a level, including the abolition of capital ships and aircraft carriers. The Conference opened at the Foreign Office in London in December 1935 with a speech by Stanley Baldwin, who had been Prime Minister since June. The British wanted a reduction in the size of ships (notably capital ships to 25,000 tons with no guns bigger than 12-inch), and agreed tonnage limits, but were determined, at Chatfield's insistence, to return to 70 cruisers. The Americans wanted overall reductions on the basis of the existing ratios. The Japanese insisted on their proposals and left the Conference in January. This opened the way for a limited agreement on qualitative limitation for capital ships (35,000 tons and 14-inch guns), aircraft carriers (23,000 tons), cruisers (8000 tons and 6.1-inch guns) and destroyers (2000 tons and 5.1-inch guns). There was an escalation clause that allowed capital ships to be armed with 16-inch guns, should a Washington Treaty power not agree to the lower calibre. Britain and the Dominions, the USA and France signed the Treaty on 25 March 1936. This Second London Treaty was an attempt to limit the costs of rearmament by restricting the size and cost of the ships of the other naval powers to those the British felt affordable. In that it had little success although, as Roskill argues, it did have some positive impact in finally allaying Anglo-American naval rivalry.

Italy did not sign up to London as she was at daggers drawn with Britain and France over Abyssinia. In 1935, as war threatened between Italy and the African state, it was decided to send major reinforcements from home and distant stations to the Mediterranean and Red Sea. Dudley Pound was due to take over from Admiral Sir William W. Fisher as C.-in-C. Mediterranean but it was decided that, in order to retain the latter's local knowledge, 'WW' should remain, with Pound as his Chief of Staff. The reinforcement was carried out relatively quietly so as not to provoke the Italians, and the Battlecruiser Squadron (*Hood* and *Renown*), together with the four Leanders of the Second Cruiser Squadron and the Sixth Destroyer Flotilla, were kept at Gibraltar rather than sent to reinforce Fisher directly.

Chatfield was highly frustrated at the situation. It was 'a disaster that our statesmen have got us into this quarrel with Italy, who ought to be our best friend because her position in the Mediterranean is a dominant one'. Collective security had 'run away with all our traditional interests and policies' and meant that the Empire had to be prepared to 'fight any nation in the world at any moment'.[28]

Understandably, as the Chief of Naval Staff of a great imperial power with many African holdings, Chatfield had no objection to Italy taking Abyssinia – indeed he welcomed it as it put Britain in a more favourable strategic position, with a pressure point on Mussolini. It was certainly unwise, at a time when it was far from clear that Britain could deal with both Japan and Germany, to throw Italy into enemy arms. Although Fisher and his men were rightly confident of their capabilities against the Italians, losses in a conflict with Italy would weaken Britain vis-à-vis Japan, whom it was anticipated would take advantage of the situation.

In October Italian forces invaded Abyssinia. Baldwin stated that the British did not contemplate military action but economic sanctions were imposed. Oil was not included, partly because of the problems of making it effective, given American non-membership of the League, and partly because of the danger of armed retaliation by the Italians. The attempt by the Foreign Ministers of France and Britain to come to a compromise territorial solution failed because of domestic opposition in both countries and the conflict escalated into a full-scale Italo-Abyssinian war at the beginning of 1936. The strength of the Mediterranean Fleet stood at five battleships (the three Queen Elizabeths not in dock and two 'R's), a carrier, 36 destroyers and 12 submarines.

If war had broken out, Fisher intended to use his ships to dominate the central Mediterranean between Italy, Tripoli and Greece, attacking the enemy at sea and in harbour. A carrier strike on the Italian Fleet at Taranto was planned. In the event, no conflict arose. Fisher came home in March and in June 1936 the readiness of the fleet was reduced. Italy conquered Abyssinia; relations between Mussolini and Britain and France were permanently soured. The feelings of Chatfield and his colleagues, who were pleading with the politicians to reduce rather than increase the number of Britain's enemies, can be readily imagined.

The Abyssinian Crisis did, however, provide a suitable atmosphere for the Admiralty to increase the building programme beyond original DRC plans. The official logic was acceleration, obtaining the DRC Fleet by the end of financial year 1938–9; the reality was to move towards the New Standard as quickly as possible.[29] In July 1936 an increased programme was announced. There would now be seven cruisers, two 10,000-ton enlarged Southamptons (*Belfast* and *Edinburgh* – the London Treaty only came into force in 1937) and five of the new 5600-ton Dido-class cruisers, armed with ten 5.25-inch guns, which could help protect the fleet from aircraft. The destroyer flotillas were increased by adding to the second group of Tribals an extra flotilla of eight 1700-ton J class vessels. These were not so large, but a considerable increase in capability over the previous fleet standard. Two aircraft carriers would be laid down immediately rather than one, and eight submarines would be built, a last minelayer, four Ts and the first three of the new small 540-ton U-class, built for training and short-range patrol work.

Although things were going Chatfield's way, there still remained considerable hostility in certain quarters to a resumption of capital ship building. The air enthusiasts were claiming that their bombers could sink capital ships at a fraction of the cost of a large gun-armed armoured warship. A committee was therefore set up under the chairmanship of Sir Thomas Inskip, the newly appointed Minister for the Co-ordination of Defence, to investigate the question of the vulnerability of capital ships (VCS) to air attack. The VCS Committee established more realistic comparative costings between bombers and battleships and Chatfield successfully got over his basic point that if the airmen were right and battleships proved unduly vulnerable to bombing attack, money would have been wasted on the new ships; if bombers could not sink battleships and the enemies of the British Empire had them, then that Empire would be lost.[30] It was as well that he did. Until the invention of guided armour-piercing bombs, high-level bombers, upon which the enemies of the battleship were basing their claims, were of little use against manoeuvring warships. Chatfield clearly regarded the report of the VCS Committee at the end of July 1936 as a significant prelude to the rebuilding of the battlefleet.

The Admiralty clearly recognized that dive-bombing was a much more effective anti-ship tactic, but the Air Ministry did not agree. It stolidly refused to develop a suitable sight. This was but one of the differences that continued to poison relations between it and the Admiralty on the Fleet Air Arm question.

It was not that the Air Ministry did not provide adequate aircraft designs, even to unlikely Admiralty aircraft requirements, such as the three tiny Parnall Peto reconnaissance seaplanes, designed for the experimental aircraft-carrying submarine M2 that operated them from 1928 until the boat was accidentally lost in 1932. Progressive modernization of the FAA had continued. The late 1920s had seen the Fairey IIIF take over a combined spotter-reconnaissance role and a new two-seat Blackburn Ripon torpedo bomber enter service. Excellent new Hawker fighters, the single-seat Nimrod and two-seat Osprey appeared in the early 1930s, as did the Fairey Seal spotter-reconnaissance aircraft and Blackburn Baffin torpedo bomber.

A more general move to multi-purpose aircraft was recommended in a paper written by aircrew in HMS *Courageous* in 1930 and enthusiastically taken up by the Admiralty's Air Division – against the better judgement of the Air Ministry.[31] The results were specifications issued by the Air Ministry in 1933 for combined torpedo spotter-reconnaissance (TSR) biplanes and in 1934 for a fighter-dive-bomber. The results of the former was an unsuccessful Blackburn design, the Shark (let down by an unsuitable engine), replaced by the Fairey Swordfish which was the standard TSR in front-line squadrons by the end of 1937.

It seems clear that in the 1930s, high aerodynamic performance became less of a priority in Admiralty requirements for Fleet Air Arm aircraft. The Air Division of the Naval Staff acted on some very questionable assumptions, notably that all aircraft designed for operation over the sea were of inherently low performance because they had to be multi-seat for navigational reasons (a natural prejudice of the naval observers who were dominant over the dual-rank pilots). This requirement for passengers made the aircraft the more suitable for multi-purpose duties to squeeze maximum capability out of a limited size fleet. When the Blackburn Skua, designed for the fighter-reconnaissance-dive bomber role, ran into development problems, the Admiralty insisted that an existing two-seater light bomber design be developed into a fighter-reconnaissance aircraft as a fall-back (the eventual Fairey Fulmar). The Admiralty eventually produced a three-seat spotter-fighter requirement, a machine the Air Ministry thought unrealistic. No wonder the Air Minister complained that 'The Naval Staff had the tendency to ask for machines which would do the impossible.'[32]

The complaint from the Admiralty that it was not getting the right aircraft needs to be put into this context. Yet the situation did reflect the dual-control system up to a point. The Admiralty's lack of appreciation of the potential of an aviation world caught up in a technological transformation was a reflection of the lack of mid-grade naval pilots suitable for staff appointments. Making one's career subordinate to another service's promotion was not a pathway to be encouraged in young officers of potential. Eight years after the Trenchard–Keyes agreement there were no FAA officers with RAF rank higher than Flight Lieutenant. The creation in 1933 of a new squadron structure rather than flights was produced in part to provide posts for 16 new Naval squadron leaders. There were ten of the new squadrons, 800–3 (fighter), 810–12 (torpedo bomber) and 820–4 (spotter-reconnaissance).

The shortage of naval volunteers for the FAA, which continued after 1933, meant that the FAA remained small, even if more aircraft could have been afforded. The Admiralty would not countenance diluting the 70 per cent of FAA pilots with more RAF personnel and the Air Ministry would not allow RN ratings to be considered as pilots. This was just about acceptable in the era of the ten-year rule, but the expansion of the FAA planned in the naval rearmament plans made dual control untenable. Chatfield had always been aggressive on the Fleet Air Arm question and was determined that dual control should not stand in the way of providing the fleet with an air arm of sufficient size and with the required capability (however idiosyncratic). It was his hardest struggle, 'the only one which gave me real anxiety', as he later put it.[33]

The Admiralty were able to mitigate their observer problems by training ratings and warrant officers for the task. To solve the pilot question, Inskip was tasked with an enquiry into manning. Just before the investigation began, Sir Samuel Hoare, still smarting from his enforced resignation as Foreign Secretary over the Ethiopia affair, replaced Monsell on 6 June 1936. Although welcome to Chatfield and his colleagues for the clarity and realism of his strategic vision, Hoare had been Air Minister in the 1920s and he could not be expected to press the Admiralty's FAA case as strongly as his pre-decessor. Nevertheless, when Chatfield responded strongly to Inskip's very limited suggestions by calling in the strongest possible terms for the transfer of control in order to ensure the efficiency of the fleet, the First Lord sent Chatfield's protest on to Baldwin with a supportive note.

Inskip left open the possibility of a further enquiry on the whole question of control. The issue was becoming political – even Churchill, reversing his usual position on naval aviation in order to embarrass the Government, publicly supported Chatfield, who provided the rebel back-bencher with supporting documentation. In a personal conver-sation with Baldwin at the beginning of 1937, Chatfield hinted at resignation if an investigation was not held. Terms of reference for the wider enquiry were drawn up and the First Lord briefed the Sea Lords not to ask for too much. Because of pressure from Lord Weir (the former Air Minister and member of the Balfour subcommittee, now acting as an important adviser to the Government), the investi-gation was carried out by the Chiefs of Staff, chaired by Inskip. No consensus was possible, but Inskip said he would make his own appreciation and present it to a small ministerial committee for a decision.

Political events now intervened. At the end of May 1937 Baldwin was replaced by Neville Chamberlain and Hoare by Duff Cooper. The ministerial committee was due to meet in July but, in June, Inskip, under pressure, told Chatfield it would not. The First Sea Lord now openly threatened resignation and it was decided that Inskip must settle the issue himself. Pressed by Chatfield, Inskip gave his decision to Chamberlain on 21 July. He recommended that the Fleet Air Arm be passed to full Admiralty administrative control but that Coastal Command (as it now was) of land-based maritime aircraft would remain light blue. The feeling in the Cabinet was that the FAA was no longer necessary to the integrity of a massively rearming RAF, and the Air Minister's opposition was muted. It was agreed that the change would be announced on 30 July.

The vexed FAA issue was finally settled in principle but the Inskip Award could not be put into effect immediately. New air-maintenance ratings and rating and warrant officer aircrew had to be trained and short-service aircrew officers recruited. RAF personnel willing to transfer were allowed to do so. The naval air organization at the Admiralty was greatly expanded with the recreation of the Air Division of the Naval Staff and the setting up in 1938 of departments for Air Personnel, Materiel and Maintenance and Repair. ACNS (Air) was replaced by a Fifth Sea Lord and Chief of Naval Air Services.

Not until 1939 was the take-over finally put into effect. In March the Admiralty set up an aviation branch; the following month four airfields, Lee-on-Solent, Ford, Worthy Down and Donibristle, were transferred from the RAF. On 24 May 1939 administrative control of the FAA was formally taken over by the Admiralty.

In November 1938 the new 22,000-ton carrier *Ark Royal* was commissioned. She was, as planned, able to carry no less than six squadrons, two of fighters and four TSR. She provided the Home Fleet's carrier, *Courageous* becoming a training carrier. *Glorious*, with one squadron of fighters and three TSRs, was in the Mediterranean and *Eagle*, with two squadrons of TSRs, was in China. All TSR carrier squadrons had been equipped with Swordfish since late 1937. The fighter situation was more fluid, with the long-lasting Osprey/Nimrod combination being replaced from late 1938 by the Skua, supplemented in 1939 by the related Roc turret fighters. After development problems with the Blackburn aircraft, the RAF had offered surplus Gladiators to provide fleet fighters. Despite Admiralty doubts about the utility of single-seaters, *Glorious*'s 802 Squadron was equipped with these aircraft from May 1939. The pilots revelled in the performance of what were, in comparison to other fleet types, high-performance aircraft and the ship asked for a complete Gladiator squadron rather than one with a flight of Skuas.[34]

At about the time full control of the Fleet Air Arm was assumed, one can detect a downgrading of fighters in Admiralty operational doctrine. Chatfield put some emphasis on them but in late 1938 the Home Fleet clearly regarded them as only being of use to aid spotting. The new, heavier, anti-aircraft gun armaments of ships would make air attack of fleets 'uneconomical' and be the primary defence.[35] Given the lack of radar and means of fighter control, these views were understandable.

The tendency to regard passive armour protection and AA guns as primary protection from the air was dramatically reflected in the new fleet carriers, *Illustrious* and *Victorious*, of the 1936 Programme. They had an aircraft complement only half that of *Ark Royal* but 4.5-inch armoured hangars. In original concept, the plan was to operate up to three of these ships together with an FAA depot ship support carrier. This would have mitigated the effect on the low individual aircraft complements.[36]

In further steps of acceleration of the DRC programme, the two remaining carriers of this type, *Formidable* and *Indomitable*, were in the 1937 building programme. The former was laid down early in June 1937 to the same design as the other two but the latter, laid down in November, was altered while under construction, with an extra half hangar to allow a fourth squadron to be carried.

The first two battleships of the DRC programme, *King George V* and *Prince of Wales*, had been laid down on 1 January 1937, the day the Treaties expired. They were built to the Second London Treaty limitations of 35,000 tons and 14-inch guns. Ten of the latter weapons were mounted, two guns of the original design being sacrificed at Chatfield's insistence so the ships could receive maximum armour protection.[37] The need for speedy capital ship replacement meant that the next three ships of the 1937 programme had to be generally similar. Laid down early in May–July 1937, they were originally to have been named *Anson, Jellicoe* and *Beatty* but were commissioned as *Duke of York, Anson* and *Howe*. The year 1937 also saw *Valiant* and *Queen Elizabeth* taken in hand for major conversion.

It was hoped that the cruisers of the 1937 programme would be 8000-ton vessels armed with 5.25-inch guns, but production facilities for the latter mountings were limited and the seven ships were built as Fiji-class diminutives of the Southamptons, with twelve 6-inch guns and better ammunition arrangements for the 4-inch AA armament. Two more flotillas of the larger fleet destroyers were also ordered, as were seven submarines, all of them T-class.

By any standards this was an ambitious programme, fully compatible with the New Standard, and in April 1937 the Admiralty unveiled their ambitions to the Cabinet. The New Standard fleet meant 20 capital ships against 15, 15 carriers against ten, one hundred cruisers against 70, 22 flotillas against 16 and 82 flotillas against 55. Accept-ance of these plans was impossible. Indeed, much against the Admiralty's will, the Cabinet fixed an annual 'ration' of £1500 million for all Britain's services. Chatfield railed against rationing and suggested the Government reduce its enemies if it could not afford to confront them. Damage to his plans was, however, limited. The 1938 programme was still larger than a DRC standard programme: two new battleships, *Lion* and *Temeraire* (with 16-inch guns), an armoured hangar carrier, *Implacable* (with still further increased aircraft capacity), a mix of seven Fiji and Arethusa cruisers, three submarines and three very fast minelayers of new design. The addition of the latter necessitated cancelling destroyers, but these could not have been built for some time and were blatantly surplus to the DRC requirement.

Chatfield stood down in August 1938. The Chamberlain Govern-ment took his advice shortly afterwards and prevented a premature outbreak of war over Czechoslovakia. Despite the realism of the new First Sea Lord, Admiral Sir Roger Backhouse, and the other Chiefs of Staff who advised strongly against war, Duff Cooper found this hard to swallow and resigned, being replaced by Earl Stanhope. Stanhope was an ally of Chamberlain but his knowledge of naval affairs was limited and the Sea Lords remained highly influential in naval policy. Backhouse received very useful support by the appointment of Rear Admiral Andrew Cunningham as DCNS in November1938. This dynamic officer had more than usual influence because of the First Sea Lord's failing health.

The 1938 crisis led to a reorientation of British maritime strategy. Although in November 1938 Backhouse personally promised the Australian High Commissioner that the two Nelsons and five 'R's would be sent to Singapore in a crisis, he was, in fact, pushing a Mediterranean strategic emphasis, going for Italy first in any war with the expected German–Italian–Japanese coalition. In Backhouse's words: 'If we struck Italy a series of hard blows at the start of hostilities she might be counted out and the whole war turn in our favour.'[38] Japan would be contained by a small Flying Squadron based around two capital ships and a carrier.[39]

Chatfield, appointed Minister for the Co-ordination of Defence in January 1939, was more reluctant to accept the new strategic emphasis and the Committee set up in early 1939 to review strategy left the situation open. It would be 'for the Government of the day...to decide on the redistribution of Naval forces required to meet the situation'.[40] The Australians were informed that although the British still intended to send a fleet to Singapore, its size 'would be determined at the time'.[41] The Tientsin crisis of 1939 made the prospect of sending a fleet east a very real one and the Naval Staff rejected the Flying Squadron, favouring instead as large a force of capital ships as possible. It was no coincidence that Cunningham, sent out to the Mediterranean to implement the plans he and his chief had made, was almost immediately reined in by the new First Sea Lord, Admiral Sir Dudley Pound, who replaced the ailing Backhouse in June 1939.

Pound's previous responsibility had been the Mediterranean Fleet, which had led an active life under his command. Civil war in Spain had broken out in July 1936. Units of Pound's fleet were ordered to go to Spanish ports to evacuate refugees; units of the Home Fleet carried out similar duties in the Bay of Biscay. The Nationalists attempted to blockade the Biscay coast but the ineffectiveness of this was eventually demonstrated when HMS *Hood* saw off the cruiser *Almirante Cervera*. The British naval leadership, unhappy with the situation, wished to grant both sides belligerent rights in order to prevent incidents, but when Bilbao eventually fell the battleship *Royal Oak* covered the evacuation of Republicans by sea.[42]

In May 1937 the destroyer *Hunter* was mined off Almeira. At the end of August, her sister *Havock* was attacked by the Italian submarine *Iride*, which was herself counterattacked. The Italians had begun a submarine campaign against Republican seaborne logistics. At Nyon, in September, an international agreement set out anti-submarine patrol areas and 36 British destroyers were deployed. By this time intelligence had revealed that the Italians had given up using their submarines illegally but the patrols helped check any resurgence of activity. As the war ended, British ships reverted to their original role of refugee evacuation.

The need to protect merchant shipping from submarine and air attack was reflected in the naval building programme. In 1938–9 Backhouse pushed the construction of new types of vessel intended for escort and anti-submarine operations. As George Franklin has pointed out, the Admiralty had developed techniques and equipment for defence of trade against submarines. It was planned that convoys be introduced if an enemy began an unrestricted attack on seaborne trade.[43] This would require escort forces made up both of older fleet destroyers, kept in reserve for the purpose, and new specialist escort vessels.

A limited number of sloops had been built from 1927 onwards, four a year from 1928, but these were intended primarily for use as overseas gunboats and minesweepers rather than as escorts. In the early 1930s more attention was given to the escort role and eight sloops of the Grimsby class were built to a more heavily armed design, more suited to escort duties. They were still too slow, however, to keep up with Atlantic convoys so, in 1932, work began on an 18-knot ocean sloop primarily designed for such work. Thus was the 1200-ton Enchantress class born, named after the ship of the first batch of three completed as an Admiral's dispatch vessel (a major problem of escort-vessel building was obtaining Treasury support for ships with primarily a wartime role). In parallel, a 570-ton sloop was developed for anti-submarine operations in coastal waters, the Kingfisher class. The largest number with which the Admiralty had thought it could get away with were 17 coastal and ten convoy sloops. *Enchantress* and *Kingfisher* were among the five sloops in the 1933 programme. By 1939 eight convoy sloops (redesignated 'escort vessels' were in commission or launched, along with nine coastals. Two more convoy sloops were in the 1939 programme to complete the requirement of ten such assets.

Although excellent ships, especially with their latest armament of 6–8 dual-purpose 4-inch guns, the convoy sloops were considered to be too slow by Backhouse. Already conversion had begun of older V and W-class destroyers into specialist escort vessels with modern twin 4-inch AA guns. This the First Sea Lord saw as a better way forward. Instead of sloops, 20 escort vessels, new 1000-ton 28-knot destroyer-type ships appeared in the 1939 programme. These Hunt-class escort destroyers were a flawed concept: they were over-armed for their size and did not have the range for Atlantic work. During the war the original convoy sloop design was reverted to but the Hunts, as modified, proved useful in coastal waters and the Mediterranean.

The Hunts reflected an emphasis on limited-range escort work, in coastal waters, and in the nearer western approaches. No one expected France to fall and provide Germany with forward Atlantic bases. In this context it was particularly unfortunate that the existing coastal sloops were proving to be unsuitable for mass production, with their turbine power plants. So, at the beginning of 1939, the Admiralty became interested in a mass-produced 1000-ton whalecatcher design for coastal anti-submarine work. Doubts were expressed about its low speed and lack of subdivision but Backhouse emphasized that 'we must have numbers'.[44] Thus was born the Flower-class 'corvette' of which 56 were ordered. They were not perfect ships but they proved adequate when pressed into ocean escort duties in the forthcoming war.

The emphasis on escort vessels meant that the next two 16-inch battleships had to be dropped from the 1939 programme, along with two of the four projected Fiji-class cruisers. Two more flotillas of fleet destroyers were ordered, the Ms and the Ns, along with another fast minelayer. Another large-capacity armoured carrier was also to be built, *Indefatigable*.

The 1939 programme has a modern look to it, with emphasis on smaller combatants, carriers and no battleships but the Naval Staff still considered the gun-armed capital ship its key striking asset and considered plans to expedite new construction by combining new hulls with existing 15-inch mountings. Thinking about the use of capital ships had not ossified in any way. Moretz has shown Roskill was wrong to argue that the Royal Navy was only trying to refight the battle of Jutland. There was much tactical innovation, notably the move to emphasize night action.[45] By the end of the 1930s the Royal Navy's tactical skills were second only to those of the Japanese, although both the Japanese and the Americans, unhampered by the national priority for strategic air warfare, were pulling ahead in the quantity and quality of their naval air arms.

During 1939, as the political situation moved through the occupation of Bohemia to confrontation with the Germans over Poland, Chatfield chaired a Committee on the Acceleration of Defence Programmes. The Navy did not obtain all its perceived needs; the sheer capacity of the country to rearm at sea was being strained.

Ships were being constructed in quantities beyond the capacity to produce guns and mountings to match. Indeed, Britain was rearming at sea as fast as it could. When war did eventually break out, a powerful fleet was available to confront Germany, abandoned by its allies because of its entente with the Soviet Union. As the conflict developed, however, the prewar nightmare of overcommitment would become all too real. The Royal Navy's abilities and resources would be strained to the maximum.

7 The Second World War

The strategic situation at the outbreak of the war was much more favourable than that expected in the nightmares of the 1930s.[1] The Royal Navy's sole opponent was Germany, who had 21 larger U-boats at sea in the Atlantic and the Channel. Their orders were not to sink unarmed merchantmen without warning. U30, however, mistook the liner *Athenia* for an armed merchant cruiser and sank her without warning. The 112 passengers and crew lost convinced the Admiralty that the Germans had indeed begun unrestricted submarine warfare. It was therefore decided to put into effect the plan to introduce ocean convoys in the western approaches. This did much to neutralize the U-boats. The ill-considered policy of hunting them with fleet carriers was abandoned after *Ark Royal* had a lucky escape and *Courageous* was sunk. Although outward-bound convoys were only escorted to 15° west, the convoy system was able to reduce losses from 41 ships in the first month of war to 21 in November. By the end of 1939, nine U-boats had been sunk, three by escorting destroyers, two by patrolling destroyers, one by a British submarine, and three by the Royal Navy's mine barrage in the Straits of Dover – which stopped Germans using that path to the Atlantic.

In November and December 1939 German mines posed the main threat to British shipping. Fields of magnetic mines were laid off the east coast and the port of London was almost closed. In December 33 ships were sunk by mines. The threat then receded, first because the Germans temporarily ran out of mines, then because of British countermeasures. In late November a magnetic mine was successfully dismantled and examined and in March 1940 minesweeping trawlers with special LL magnetic sweeps began work. Ships were also fitted as rapidly as possible with degaussing coils that rendered the mines' firing mechanisms ineffective. The anti-mine campaign continued throughout the war with each German design, such as the acoustic mine introduced in 1940, being met with an adequate countermeasure. Royal Navy personnel also distinguished themselves by defusing unexploded sea mines used as blast bombs in attacks on Britain's cities.

The final prong of the German trident aimed at Britain's maritime trade comprised the German surface fleet. Two 11-inch-gun 'Panzerschiffe' (colloquially known as 'pocket battleships') were at sea at the outbreak of war, *Deutschland* in the North Atlantic and *Admiral Graf Spee* in the South Atlantic and Indian Ocean. Both had orders to avoid British warships, which limited their impact as they could not attack convoys. *Graf Spee*, however, decided to disobey instructions and win a significant naval action by sinking an escorted convoy expected off the River Plate. This sealed her fate. *Graf Spee* found not a convoy but Commodore Henry Harwood's raider-hunting group, the heavy cruiser *Exeter* and two light cruisers, *Ajax* and *Achilles*. Harwood, who had taught anti-panzerschiff tactics in the 1930s and who had been in command on this station for several years, had guessed the mystery raider might be drawn to the Plate. He handled his ships brilliantly and the German ship was so badly damaged that she entered Montevideo for repairs. Harwood was reinforced by his fourth cruiser *Cumberland* and still heavier ships were on their way. Even if *Graf Spee* had broken out, she was low on ammunition and her chances of escaping were slim. Langsdorff, *Graf Spee*'s commander, very conscious of his personal responsibility for this débâcle, had little choice but to scuttle his ship and commit suicide. Harwood was knighted and promoted Rear Admiral, and full propaganda value was garnered from the truly famous victory of the River Plate.[2] Surface raiders sank only 15 ships of 6337 tons in the first four months of war.

On 3 September 1939 the Admiralty signalled to the fleet, 'Winston is back', marking Churchill's return as First Lord of the Admiralty. This news may have buoyed up the morale of the junior ranks, as it suggested the prospect of decisive action, but senior officers had rather different memories. To them, the signal was a warning. Churchill's restless energy always yearned for the offensive and he was far from satisfied with a policy of defending shipping and a renewed distant blockade. This was especially so as the Germans took the opportunity to make raids on the blockaders both at sea and in harbour. In the early hours of 14 October the battleship *Royal Oak* was sunk by Gunther Prien's U47 in Scapa Flow. Then the following month the armed merchant cruiser *Rawalpindi* was sunk by the German battleships *Scharnhorst* and *Gneisenau*.

There has been much controversy about the ability of Sir Dudley Pound to mitigate the First Lord's overenthusiastic meddling in operations.[3] Much work went into dissuading Churchill from Operation Catherine, forcing the Baltic and cutting Germany off from her vital Scandinavian iron ore supplies. This plan, which would have risked serious losses, was replaced by one to capture the Swedish iron ore mines, or at least cut the supply line down the Norwegian coast. In effect, a race for Norway began between the Allies and the Germans, which the latter narrowly won. On 9 April 1940 a series of German landings took place at every major Norwegian port from Oslo to Narvik.

On 8 April the Royal Navy had begun minelaying in Norwegian waters. In the Clyde, cruisers were ready with troops in case this provoked German reaction, but these forces were disembarked by Admiralty order when German movements were misconstrued as an attempted break-out by heavy ships into the Atlantic. The forces covering the minelayers clashed with the enemy off the Norwegian coast. The destroyer *Glowworm* came across the heavy cruiser *Hipper* and rammed her, causing her considerable damage. Admiral Whitworth, Vice Admiral of the Battlecruiser Squadron in the modernized *Renown*, fought a successful running battle with the two 11-inch-gun German fast battleships *Scharnhorst* and *Gneisenau*, which were forced to use their superior speed to get away. The Germans did succeed, however, in getting their troops ashore, even at Narvik, where eight destroyers slipped undetected into Vestfiord. The Admiralty had unwittingly uncovered the entrance by its misconceived orders.

This whole adventure should still have been strategic suicide for the Germans with their inferior fleet, but for one factor: Fliegerkorps X of the Luftwaffe. This was specially trained in maritime operations and was rapidly deployed to Norwegian airfields. The Admiralty prevented Admiral Sir Charles Forbes, the Commander-in-Chief, Home Fleet, mounting an immediate attack on Bergen before Fliegerkorps X arrived, and events on the afternoon of 9 April showed that it was already too late. In an all too accurate bombing attack on the Home Fleet, the Tribal-class destroyer *Gurkha* was sunk. Other ships were hit but not seriously damaged. The attack persuaded Forbes that waters covered by bombers were too dangerous for his fleet. Even if the capital ships were safe, his cruisers and destroyers were not. Forbes decided to withdraw northwards, leaving the main German maritime supply lines to submarines.

The Royal Navy was finding that its prewar faith in anti-aircraft guns against any air threat was misplaced. Roskill blamed the High Angle Control System (HACS), a relatively crude device that only estimated the enemy aircraft's course and speed rather than measured it. The Naval Staff thought that the stabilized platform required by a full tachymetric system was beyond its suppliers' capabilities. Putting the blame on HACS was, however, questionable. Even more advanced tachymetric systems proved ineffective until the development of radar proximity fuses, later in the war. The difficulty of accurately setting the time fuses of AA shells to explode close to a fast-moving target were probably insuperable.[4]

The Royal Navy also used its own aircraft to strike back. Skua dive-bombers from Orkney sank the cruiser *Konigsberg* in Bergen on 10 April – the first large warship ever to be sunk from the air. The main British successes, however, were in the north where Fliegerkorps X was still unknown. On the same day *Konigsberg* was sunk, the five H-class destroyers of the Second Flotilla, led by Captain Warburton-Lee, an aggressively-minded destroyer commander nurtured by interwar exercises, made an attack on the German destroyers at Narvik. Two German ships were sunk, including the flagship, and three damaged. Six merchant ships were also sunk, including the supply ship for the troops ashore. Sadly, however, the attack had gone in unsupported because of more Admiralty-originated confusion and Warburton-Lee was caught by the five remaining German ships on his way out. His more heavily armed leader *Hardy* was hit and the Captain killed. *Hardy* had to be run aground and the destroyer *Hunter* was also lost, colliding, before she sank, with her sister *Hotspur*. The latter was able to get away with the other two ships, but the award of a posthumous Victoria Cross to the heroic Warburton-Lee could not wipe out the sour taste of an operation that could have gone better. Whitworth, blaming himself for not having used more initiative to go against the orders from London, led an overwhelming force up the fiord on 13 April to finish the job. This consisted of the battleship *Warspite* and nine destroyers, which annihilated the eight remaining German destroyers.

The two battles of Narvik were a disaster for the German navy, involving the loss of the backbone of its destroyer force. They were, however, the only bright spots in an otherwise dismal record for the Royal Navy. In mid-April troops were landed under naval escort at Harstad near Narvik, but nowhere was the Navy able to make much progress against the twin enemies of German air power and a disastrous combination of overenthusiastic First Lord and overcentralizing First Sea Lord. British aircraft carriers without, as yet, the means of radar fighter control, were incapable of using their own aircraft to interfere with German air attacks. From early May, these were being carried out by the formidable Stuka dive-bomber, which proved its anti-ship potential by sinking both a French destroyer and HMS *Afridi* during the evacuation of Namsos at the beginning of May. In the end, Narvik was briefly taken, only to be evacuated again as a result of the opening of a life-and-death struggle in France and Flanders. It was the final overflow of misfortune that yet another valuable fleet carrier, HMS *Glorious*, was lost during the evacuation when it was caught by *Scharnhorst* and *Gneisenau*. The escorting destroyers were, however, able to score a damaging torpedo hit on *Scharnhorst*.

The German conquest of France in May–June 1940 had a fundamental impact on the Royal Navy. First, it had to evacuate the British Army from the ports and beaches of mainland Europe, notably from Dunkirk. Contrary to popular legend, the small craft mobilized by the navy to assist in the evacuation carried very few troops all the way back to Britain. Of the 338,226 troops lifted by Operation Dynamo, half were lifted by warships and many other ships and craft were Royal Navy manned. The entire operation was organized by the Flag Officer Dover, Admiral Sir Bertram Ramsay, ably assisted by Rear Admiral W. E. Wake-Walker and Captain W. G. Tennant.

The Royal Navy then had the distasteful task of neutralizing the French fleet. A new Gibraltar-based squadron, Force H, was formed under Vice Admiral Sir James Somerville, to relieve the French of responsibility for the western Mediterranean. Its first task was to be ordered by Churchill, now Prime Minister and Minister of Defence, to bombard the erstwhile allies at Mers-el-Kebir near Oran. One French battleship was destroyed and a newer battlecruiser disabled, but another battlecruiser, *Strasbourg*, a major target of the operation, escaped to Toulon, avoiding an attack by *Ark Royal*'s slow Swordfish. At Alexandria the Commander-in-Chief, Mediterranean Fleet, Admiral Sir Andrew Cunningham, incurred considerable Churchillian displeasure by his slow but statesmanlike attitude which obtained the disarming of the French ships there without bloodshed. French feelings were understandably outraged by the Mers-el-Kebir attack and an attempt in September to use most of Force H plus units of the Home Fleet and South Atlantic Station to cover a Free French landing at Dakar was driven off, with damage to the battleship *Resolution* and cruiser *Cumberland*.

September 1940, however, saw the Royal Navy succeed in one of its main and most unsung achievements of the war – the deterrence of a German invasion of the United Kingdom itself. The arrival of the German army in northwestern France and the Low Countries led the Admiralty to fill the ports on the east and southeast coasts of England with warships to guard against the threat of invasion. By early September 1940, Admiral Sir Reginald Plunkett-Ernle-Erle-Drax's Nore Command had 38 destroyers and seven coastal sloops based at Immingham, Harwich and Sheerness, waiting to fall on any German invasion force ill-advised enough to try a Channel crossing. These were backed up by the cruisers *Manchester, Birmingham* and *Southampton* at Immingham, and *Galatea* and *Aurora* at Sheerness. On the other flank of the invasion, Commander-in-Chief, Portsmouth, deployed another nine destroyers and five Free French torpedo boats backed up by the old cruiser *Cardiff* and battleship *Revenge*. No fewer than 700 smaller craft were also deployed, with 200–300 at sea at all times from the Wash to Sussex to provide early warning.[5]

The battered German Navy was in no position to provide an effective screen and even the Luftwaffe would have faced serious problems preventing a flotilla of this size from a massacre of the Wehrmacht in its improvised invasion barges. The Luftwaffe itself thought it had an alternative to 'Seelowe' ('Sealion'), the invasion plan – the 'Adlerangriff' ('Eagle Attack'), an attempt to gain air superiority over southern England and then systematically destroy London in a few days. The Luftwaffe had little interest in merely supporting the other two services. The Adlerangriff, the Germans' only credible strategy against a Britain that still commanded the narrow seas, foundered on the rocks of RAF Fighter Command's highly advanced air defence system, a belated vindication of the creation of a separate air service in 1918 and the priority given to the RAF in prewar rearmament.

The deployment of valuable escort vessels to anti-invasion duties helped tilt the Battle of the Atlantic in Germany's favour. More importantly, Germany's possession of the Biscay ports was a force multiplier of the utmost importance for the U-boats. These were circumstances that no prewar planner could have contemplated. On 17 August, Hitler declared a total blockade of the British Isles; all shipping of whatever nationality was to be sunk on sight. German U-boat commanders called the period from July to October 1940 the 'Happy Time'. Two hundred and seventeen merchantmen fell victim to the U-boats, whose captains made their reputations picking off individual, unescorted ships as they passed outward bound beyond the convoy dispersal point, straggled from the convoys, or sailed their lonely independent courses. By September and October the Germans even began to inflict serious attrition on convoyed shipping, using wolf-pack night attacks.

The escorts were both insufficient in numbers and unprepared for the scale and nature of the night attacks. There were no proper communications between the ships beyond signal lamps and the different vessels often arrived unbriefed about tactics or even the nature of the convoys. The commanders did not know each other and operated as uncoordinated individuals. With the invasion threat reduced, more ships could be allocated to escort tasks, and at the end of October the close escort line was moved further westward. Escort groups began to be formed and better training began to be given to new anti-submarine crews, notably by the terrifying Commodore

'Monkey' Stephenson at HMS *Western Isles* at Tobermory. Radio telephones allowed effective tactical co-operation and the standard depth-charge pattern was doubled in size.

Losses to U-boats increased to a new peak of 61 ships in June 1941, but the tide was already turning. The situation improved for the British for four main reasons. First, more escorts became available, which allowed convoys to be extended. Fifty old destroyers, obtained from the USA too late to be added to the anti-invasion forces, came into service in the escort role. They were later supplemented by former US Coastguard Cutters. The Royal Navy began to get the vital assistance of a fast-growing Royal Canadian Navy and forward basing in Iceland extended reach. From April 1941 convoy anti-submarine surface escort was extended to 35° West. Then, in May, the first convoys were given escort all the way across the Atlantic, and, in mid-July, convoys were finally extended to Sierra Leone.

Secondly, better equipment was developed for the escorts. The problem of U-boat attack on the surface at night was solved by fitting radar to escorts, first the metric wave 286 and then the revolutionary centimetric 271 that had sufficient resolution to detect reliably the low silhouette of a surfaced U-boat. When starshell proved ineffective at illumination, it was replaced by brighter 'snowflake'. Wolf-pack tactics meant much radio indiscretion by U-boats and their commanders, and Royal Navy escorts began to be fitted with High Frequency Direction Finders (HFDF).

Thirdly, the Admiralty developed an efficient submarine-tracking system. Originally this was based on radio direction finding alone, but in 1941 the coded messages began to reveal their secrets. Between March and June the U-boat code was effectively broken by the government cryptanalysis centre at Bletchley Park. German signals could usually be read within 36 hours, sometimes immediately. Convoys could thus often be routed away from known enemies.

Fourthly, co-operation with RAF Coastal Command improved. It was placed under Admiralty operational control and joint area headquarters were created, notably for Western Approaches Command and 15 Group at Derby House, Liverpool. For all these reasons, U-boat productivity slumped permanently and the 'aces' began to disappear. In March 1941 three notable U-boat captains,

Prien, Schepke and Kretschmer, were all killed or captured in attacks on convoys. The cutting edge in these significant successes were the First World War V/W-class destroyers, a vindication of the Admiralty's decision to retain sufficient of these valuable ships in reserve with the role of convoy escort in mind.

The Royal Navy continued to contain the surface threat. In October 1940, Captain E. S. Fogarty Fegen, of the armed merchant cruiser *Jervis Bay*, earned a posthumous Victoria Cross by covering the scattering of convoy HX 84 when it was attacked by the pocket battleship *Admiral Scheer*. On Christmas Day 1940, the cruiser *Admiral Hipper* was driven away from the Middle East troop convoy WS 5A by the strong escort, the cruisers *Berwick, Bonaventure* and *Dunedin*, supported by the carrier *Furious*. Early in 1941, in Operation Berlin, *Scharnhorst* and *Gneisenau* were able to cruise the North Atlantic for almost two months, but on the two occasions they found convoys they were deterred from attacking by the old 15-inch-gun battleships which the British used as ocean escorts with this eventuality in mind. Some of Germany's disguised merchant raiders were also brought to book. In May 1941, the heavy cruiser *Cornwall* destroyed the *Pinguin* in the Indian Ocean, and in November the particularly successful *Atlantis* finally succumbed to the cruiser *Devonshire*.

In May 1941 Germany's first full-sized battleship, *Bismarck*, broke out into the Atlantic. With the cruiser *Prinz Eugen*, she attempted to pass through the Denmark Strait. The Commander-in-Chief, Home Fleet, Admiral Sir John Tovey, who had replaced Forbes in December 1940, was covering this passage with Vice Admiral Holland's Battlecruiser Squadron, HMS *Hood*, accompanied by the fast battleship *Prince of Wales*. This looked a more powerful pair than it was. The mighty *Hood*, largest capital ship in the fleet and pride of the interwar navy, was well protected in weight of armour, but was vulnerable to long-range fire. *Prince of Wales* was so new that she was not yet fully worked up and still had civilian workmen on board to deal with teething troubles. The Germans, with typically accurate opening salvoes, were able to exploit these weaknesses to annihilate *Hood* and drive off *Prince of Wales*, but not before the latter had scored damaging hits that forced the Germans to abort their mission. Tovey tried to use his available fleet carrier, *Victorious*, to slow the Germans down but she was also new and ill-prepared and her strike was ineffective. Then, to add to Tovey's woes, the Germans were able to shake off the shadowing cruisers. *Bismarck* attempted to make for France but poor radio discipline, a little cryptanalysis, and an RAF flying boat brought the battleship back into contact. She was then attacked by Somerville's Gibraltar-based Force H in the shape of a strike of Swordfish torpedo bombers. Despite an initial mistaken attack on the cruiser *Sheffield*, the Swordfish eventually crippled *Bismarck* with a hit in the stern. Unable to steer, she was closed by Tovey in his flagship *King George V*, supplemented by HMS *Rodney*, which had been diverted from a voyage to America to begin a refit. The two British capital ships pounded the one German into a wreck that eventually sank with very heavy loss of life. Attempts to save survivors had to be curtailed because of the U-boat threat.

The *Bismarck* affair demonstrated how thinly spread was the Royal Navy in the spring of 1941. Shortage of battleships was becoming a real problem and it was decided to build one of the projected 15-inch-gun ships to utilize existing mountings. HMS *Vanguard* was duly laid down at John Brown's yard on the Clyde on 2 October 1941. She was to be the last of her line.

Cunningham, in the Mediterranean, had been forced to take a back seat in the opening months of the war, but as soon as Italy entered the conflict he had every intention of handling his fleet as aggressively as possible. Malta was held to be untenable because of its proximity to Sicilian air bases and the Commander-in-Chief moved his main base to Alexandria. In July 1940 both the Mediterranean Fleet and the Italian fleet were at sea, covering convoys in the central Mediterranean, and they came into contact off Calabria. The British had three capital ships to the Italians' two and Cunningham's fleet flagship, the modernized *Warspite*, was able to hit the Italian *Giulio Cesare* at disturbingly long range, causing the Italians to withdraw. Sadly, however, the old carrier, *Eagle*, had great difficulty in slowing the enemy down with its small number of Swordfish. Nevertheless, Cunningham had succeeded in asserting an important moral ascendancy.

Both sides increased their strength in the succeeding months. Cunningham received a second modernized battleship, *Valiant*, and the first of the new fleet carriers, *Illustrious*. The Italians tripled their battleship strength to six ships, including two new 15-inch-gun units, *Littorio* and *Vittorio Veneto*. Cunningham therefore decided to make the long-promised air strike on an enemy fleet in its main base. On the night of 11 November, 21 Swordfish from *Illustrious* attacked Taranto and succeeded in torpedoing three Italian battleships. At a stroke, Italian strength was halved and the surviving members of the fleet withdrew to less exposed bases.

The success of Taranto allowed the British to begin passing convoys through the Mediterranean once more, covered by Force H in the west and Cunningham in the east. The Italians sent out two of their surviving battleships against the first of these, but *Ark Royal*'s Swordfish were less effective against the fast-moving Italians by day than *Illustrious*'s similar aircraft had been against anchored opponents at night and Somerville had to break off the pursuit.

Much worse was to follow, however. As Mussolini faced strategic failure everywhere, Hitler was forced to come to his aid. Fliegerkorps X was deployed to Italy at the beginning of 1941. It immediately registered its appearance by disabling *Illustrious* in a heavy Stuka attack on 10 January and sinking the cruiser *Southampton* the following day. The decision of Taranto had been reversed. The Germans also opened the first air siege of Malta, which struggled with increasing difficulty to keep up some pressure with air and submarine forces on Axis supply-lines to North Africa.

As Cunningham campaigned for better anti-air warfare capability and improved shore-based air cover, his preoccupation shifted to the deployment of British troops to Greece which began in March 1941. The Germans prevailed upon the Italians to use their still-powerful surface fleet to interdict this movement, and the result was the Battle of Cape Matapan at the end of the month. Cunningham had been reinforced via the Cape with the carrier *Formidable*, whose Albacore torpedo biplanes hit the battleship *Vittorio Veneto*, slowing her down for a time. She was eventually able to get away but the Italian heavy cruiser *Pola* was damaged in a second air strike. The Italian commander sent back her two sisters, *Zara* and *Fiume*, to assist, and this sealed the fate of all three, which were sent to the bottom by gun and torpedo fire in a night surface action. The Italians were totally unprepared for such night encounters, for which the Mediterranean Fleet had been training for a decade.

This success at sea was soon overshadowed by failure ashore. The Germans swept through Greece and Cunningham was faced with the need to cover evacuation. Over 50,000 men were evacuated for the loss to air attack of four transports and two destroyers. Then Churchill insisted that an emergency convoy, Tiger, be fought through the Mediterranean to reinforce both Malta and Egypt. This operation was successfully carried out and Cunningham received a valuable new battleship, HMS *Queen Elizabeth*, but *Formidable* suffered significant losses to her small complement of Fulmar fighters. This was to create problems, as the Mediterranean Fleet's greatest travails from the air were about to begin.

The Germans wished to complete their occupation of Greece by taking Crete through combined airborne and seaborne attack. The Royal Navy was able to massacre the seaborne component of this attack but the paratroops, at great loss, forced yet another evacuation. Crete was covered by Fliegerkorps VIII, whose aircraft soon cut their teeth all too effectively in the anti-shipping role. Fliegerkorps X also joined in from North African bases. In the operations around Crete, Cunningham lost two light cruisers, an AA cruiser and six destroyers. Three battleships (including *Warspite*, which had to go to the United States for repairs), five cruisers, another AA cruiser, and seven more destroyers were damaged, as was *Formidable*, crippled by the same air forces that had smashed her sister. The Mediterranean Fleet approached breaking-point as it repeatedly ran the air gauntlet, but over half of the garrison of 32,000 was transported from Crete to Egypt. The Commander-in-Chief's powers of leadership were strained as tautly as the fleet itself, but Cunningham was able to gain an extraordinary response to his appeal not to let the army down.

Only the diversion of much of the Luftwaffe to the Eastern Front took the pressure off the Mediterranean in the second half of 1941. The Luftwaffe remained strongest in the eastern basin and Malta had to be supplied from the west. Repeated carrier operations flew in fighters while two major convoys were run, covered by Force H, reinforced from the Home Fleet. More developed techniques of radar fighter control allowed *Ark Royal* to provide effective air cover. Thus sustained, Malta began to be a more important submarine and air base. The small boats of the U-class based there were established formally as the 10 Flotilla in September 1941, but, despite much heroism and considerable success, notably by Lieutenant Commander M. D. Wanklyn in *Upholder*, who sank two Italian liners in a pack attack on a convoy, the pressure was marginal at best. There were more supplies reaching Axis North African harbours than could be transported by truck to the front.[6] Only surface forces could really cut the Axis jugular, and in October Force K was sent there, composed of the small light cruisers *Aurora* and *Penelope* and two destroyers. Force K was able to annihilate supply convoys located by code-breaking and the Axis supply crisis finally became real. Force K was reinforced by Force B of similar size and the Axis disasters continued. A destroyer force on passage to reinforce Cunningham added to Axis woes by sinking two Italian fast light cruisers trying to rush fuel to Tripoli.

The Germans were forced to react and in October Hitler decided to send U-boats to the Mediterranean. This had the useful side-effect of reducing the pressure in the Atlantic, but the increased threat in the Mediterranean soon took its toll. On 13 November, while returning from yet another reinforcement of Malta's air strength, *Ark Royal* was torpedoed and sunk. Eleven days later, U331 penetrated the screen of the Mediterranean Fleet and sank the battleship *Barham*. British troubles continued in December. Although the Italian fleet was kept from the fast supply ship, *Breconshire*, off Sirte, by a cruiser force from both Malta and Alexandria, when the Malta cruisers sailed immediately afterwards to attack another convoy they ran into a minefield, losing the cruiser *Neptune* and a destroyer sunk, and another cruiser damaged. The Malta striking-force was effectively neutralized. In Alexandria harbour itself the remaining Mediterranean Fleet battleships *Queen Elizabeth* and *Valiant* were sunk at their moorings by Italian Maiale human torpedoes. Within a few days the main Royal Navy striking potential in the Mediterranean had been destroyed. Finally, in December, Fliegerkorps II was deployed to Sicily to reopen the air siege of Malta.

The Mediterranean campaign thus meant that when American pressure looked as if it might drive Japan to war in late 1941 the concept of a full-scale fleet based on Singapore was a dead letter. The Admiralty produced plans for a fleet based in the Indian Ocean, but Churchill insisted that a small but fast deterrent force be sent all the way to Singapore. This was a reversion to the rejected prewar idea of a 'Flying Squadron'. The Prime Minister browbeat Pound into sending *Prince of Wales* to join *Repulse*, which was already in the Indian Ocean. The new carrier *Indomitable* was also to be sent when she had completed trials. In fact she would not have been available when the Japanese offensive began, even if she had not been damaged in a grounding accident in the West Indies.[7]

Force Z was nevertheless formed around the two capital ships, commanded by Admiral Sir Tom Phillips, a gifted staff officer and VCNS since June 1939 but who had fallen foul of Churchill. A sea command was a good way to get Phillips away from London but he had no recent operational experience. His force was an unbalanced one, with no organic air cover, no cruisers and only four destroyers, of which half were First World War veterans. This was not the fleet bristling with AA guns considered prewar. When the Japanese invaded Malaya on 8 December Phillips sailed to interfere with the landings at Singora. He seems to have misinterpreted the information that fighter cover was not available in the north as meaning that no fighter cover was available anywhere. He never subsequently asked for air cover, despite the provision of a fighter squadron at Singapore especially for the purpose. Abandoning his original plans because of being spotted by Japanese reconnaissance aircraft, he was misled into closing the coast at Kuantan, thinking that landings had taken place there. Force Z was then spotted by a striking force of Japanese navy land-based Mitsubishi long-range strike aircraft. Torpedo bombers first disabled the flagship and then sank *Repulse*, despite excellent ship handling by Captain Tennant, the hero of Dunkirk. *Prince of Wales* then succumbed to extensive flooding.[8] The Singapore base itself fell with the rest of the island two months later.

The remnants of the Royal Navy in the Far East became a contribution to an Allied force of cruisers and destroyers which, under Dutch command, fought vainly to defend the Dutch East Indies. Without the basics of Allied tactical co-operation, such as a common signalling system, the combined force was outfought in the Java Sea by a Japanese navy that had developed surface torpedo warfare to perhaps an all-time peak. Among the losses was HMS *Exeter*, hero of the River Plate.

In order to protect India, the Admiralty reverted to its policy of building up as powerful an Eastern Fleet in the Indian Ocean as possible. By the end of March, all four surviving R-class battleships and the repaired *Warspite*, flying Somerville's flag, were based in Ceylon and at Addu Atoll in the Maldives. With the battleships were three carriers, the armoured-hangar *Indomitable* and *Formidable* and the old *Hermes*. Between them, these ships carried only 90 aircraft – Albacore and Swordfish biplanes and a mixed bag of fighters. These were soon to be faced by virtually the entire carrier fleet that had attacked Pearl Harbor – five carriers with 300 modern, high-performance fighters and strike aircraft, screened by four fast battleships and a dozen smaller escorts. Somerville, newly arrived in the theatre, had warning of the Japanese approach and planned to try to manoeuvre into a position where he might use his unique ability to fly at night together with a supposed – and misplaced – superiority in night surface action to bring on an engagement in darkness. He knew he could not fight the Japanese carriers by day.

In the end the British were lucky that the two fleets missed each other. The Japanese attacked Colombo and Trincomalee but only sank detached portions of Somerville's forces, notably the cruisers *Cornwall* and *Dorsetshire* and the carrier *Hermes*. The Japanese, on a raiding expedition to protect their western flank before trying conclusions with the Americans in the Pacific, withdrew. Yet Churchill was right to call this 'the most dangerous moment' of the war. If the Japanese had put more effort into an Indian Ocean offensive to cut Allied supply lines, Somerville's fleet would have been doomed. His 'fleet in being' policy was exactly the right one. A major defeat in the Indian Ocean, with the loss of perhaps all four of the old and vulnerable Rs, each one a potential *Hood*, would have been a blow from which British prestige, and the Churchill Government, would have found it hard to recover. All that could be done was to rely on the US fleet to defeat Japan in the Pacific while safeguarding as far as possible communications in the western Indian Ocean. Madagascar was occupied in a well-executed amphibious operation in early May.

Early 1942 was not a good time for the overstretched Royal Navy. In February the battleships *Scharnhorst* and *Gneisenau*, with *Prinz Eugen*, carried out the daring Channel dash to return home from Brest up the Channel. The limited surface and Fleet Air Arm forces available in the area were unable to prevent this débâcle, despite much heroism. Mines were, however, able to damage the German ships, one of the many successes of the joint Admiralty–Air Ministry air mining campaign. The Royal Navy supplied the weapons and Coastal and Bomber Commands the delivery aircraft.

Minelaying was also a role for coastal forces. A new generation of motor torpedo boats (MTBs) had been built from the late 1930s and the Fall of France had given such assets greater relevance to the Royal Navy. Heavily armed German motor torpedo boats (E-boats) preyed on coastal convoys, and motor gunboats (MGBs) were developed from unsuccessful motor anti-submarine boats to act as countermeasures. British MTBs of improved design attacked German coastal convoys by night, while Fairmile motor launches (MLs) were used for escort and patrol duties. The latter design was also evolved into a powerful MGB. By November 1942, 90 MGBs, 101 MTBs, and 263 MLs were deployed round Britain's coasts. In October 1942, they scored a major success when the disguised raider *Komet* was sunk by MTB 236 as it moved down-channel. Coastal forces played a significant role until the end of the war, in the Mediterranean as well as the narrow seas. Over the whole war they sank 40 enemy merchantmen and 70 warships.

Since the late summer of 1941 maritime supplies for the Soviet Union had been a major commitment for the Home Fleet. The Arctic convoys were as much a political gesture as a real logistical link. Over the war as a whole three-quarters of the Anglo-American supplies to Russia went via the Pacific or the southern route via Iran. Nevertheless, in 1941–2 the Arctic route was dominant in terms of supplies delivered: at a time when there were few Anglo-American troops in action, no better proof of commitment could exist than the efforts made to fight the merchant ships through to Archangel and Murmansk against some of the bitterest resistance and in the worst weather conditions faced by seamen in any theatre in any war.

In early 1942, the Germans built up their surface forces in Norway. *Tirpitz, Bismarck*'s sister ship, arrived in January and in early March, escorted by three destroyers, she put to sea to intercept PQ 12. Code-breaking allowed Tovey to sail to intercept with *King George V, Duke of York* and *Renown*. All depended on the ability of the carrier *Victorious* to slow *Tirpitz* down, but her Albacores could not score any hits. It was a disappointment but not a complete failure. The Germans decided to be still more cautious, especially if a British carrier was in the vicinity.

Three German destroyers were used to attack PQ 13, which sailed at the end of March. The Germans were, however, caught by the covering force, the British cruiser *Trinidad* and the destroyers *Fury* and *Eclipse*. The weather conditions were especially vile, with a heavy snowstorm blowing and freezing spray. The heavily armed but top-heavy German ships were at a disadvantage and Z26 was sunk. Unfortunately *Trinidad* suffered the indignity of being hit by one of her own torpedoes which reversed course in the extreme cold. She was given temporary repairs in Russia but was bombed and sunk on the way home in May.

As the spring days rapidly lengthened in the far north, Pound warned the Cabinet of the dangers of running Arctic convoys in these conditions. A major loss was the cruiser *Edinburgh*, torpedoed by U456, hit again by three German destroyers (one of which was sunk), and finally given a coup de grace by the British destroyer *Foresight*. The convoys were, however, able to get through in both directions, with remarkably little loss considering the circumstances.

In June 1942, therefore, the Germans determined to strike the next convoy in force. The target was PQ 17, of 35 merchantmen which came together in Hvalfiord in late June. The close escort was six destroyers, four corvettes, three minesweepers, four armed trawlers, and two AA ships. The covering force was made up of the heavy cruisers HMS *London*, HMS *Norfolk*, USS *Tuscaloosa*, USS *Wichita*, and three destroyers. In support, and hoping for a major fleet action, was the main body of Tovey's Home Fleet, the battleships HMS *Duke of York* and USS *Washington*, aircraft carrier HMS *Victorious*, two more cruisers, and eight destroyers. PQ 17 had become the bait in a trial of strength between the Allied and German navies.

As long as the convoy kept together, it was safe from the air and submarine threats, but on 4 July, mistakenly believing the German heavy units to be at sea, Pound personally decided to scatter the convoy. The escort and covering forces concentrated, expecting imminent action. They were not to know that at that time the Germans were still at Altenfiord. There was no need for valuable surface forces to be risked and, after a brief foray, they were recalled. In all, U-boats and aircraft sank 22 merchant ships from PQ 17, taking to the bottom 430 tanks, 210 aircraft, 3350 other vehicles, and almost 200,000 tons of cargo. Pound had committed one of the worst professional errors of the war against the best intelligence advice.

The year 1942 saw Malta, in Correlli Barnett's brilliant phrase, become 'the Verdun of the naval war', an island largely neutralized by Axis air power, acting as a kind of strategic black hole sucking in aircraft, merchantmen and warships. The only silver lining to this strategic cloud was the skill and courage shown by the Royal Navy in fighting through the Malta convoys. The year opened with one of the finest actions in the entire history of the service, the Second Battle of Sirte, when Rear Admiral Philip Vian used the Mediterranean Fleet's remaining cruisers to drive off a powerful Italian surface force composed of a battleship, three cruisers and ten destroyers. The threat of torpedo attack was skilfully used to keep the enemy at arm's length. Sadly, it was all for nothing: Fliegerkorps II sank all four ships of the convoy, including the naval supply ship *Breconshire*. Only 20 per cent of the convoy's supplies were landed.

This was Cunningham's last major action before he was sent to the United States as Pound's representative on the combined Chiefs of Staff in Washington. His successor was Harwood, whose first major operation was the convoy Vigorous, to Malta from Alexandria. After heavy attacks by Axis aircraft and German E-boats, the convoy, threatened by the Italian fleet, was ordered to turn back with the loss of a cruiser, three destroyers and two merchantmen sunk, and two more cruisers damaged. At the same time another convoy, Harpoon, approached Malta from the west. The two old carriers *Eagle* and *Argus* had difficulty putting up effective fighter cover and an Italian surface force drew even this off. Only two of the six merchant ships arrived, for the loss of two destroyers and serious damage to a cruiser, three destroyers and a minesweeper.

The only solution was the largest convoy yet from the west. Other fleet operations and the Arctic convoys ceased as a huge force, including two battleships, seven cruisers, and 24 destroyers, was put together for Operation Pedestal. *Victorious, Indomitable* and *Eagle*, equipped with 72 fighters and excellent radar direction systems, worked up before the operation into the most effective carrier fighter force yet deployed by the Royal Navy. The carrier *Furious* was to fly in more fighters to Malta. *Eagle* was sunk by U-boat attack, *Indomitable* was put out of action by bombing, and the destroyer *Foresight* was sunk by a torpedo bomber. After the main covering force withdrew, the convoy was attacked by mutually supporting submarines, E-boats (both German and Italian) and aircraft. The AA cruiser *Cairo* was sunk and the light cruiser *Manchester* scuttled after being torpedoed. In the end only five out of 14 merchant ships got through but it was just enough: Malta did not fall. Moreover, Malta's air defences, made more effective by changes in doctrine and sustained by Pedestal, allowed the island's forces to prevent Axis shipping being sent directly to Tobruk, so helping starve Rommel's forces at Alamein of supplies and contributing to his defeat.

The maritime focus now shifted to French North Africa, where Churchill had persuaded the Americans to mount the first major Allied amphibious landing of the war to help open both the Mediterranean sea route and offensive opportunities against southern Europe. The Royal Navy had progressively improved its techniques of combined operations. A Combined Training Centre was set up at Inveraray at which increasing numbers of crew were trained for the proliferating array of landing craft. In 1942 there were two contrasting major raids across the Channel: the successful destruction of the Normandie dock at St Nazaire, and the costly raid on Dieppe. Dieppe demonstrated the need for proper planning, bombardment and headquarters ships.

The Royal Navy took prime responsibility for ensuring the success of the Mediterranean landings. Cunningham returned as Allied Naval Commander Expeditionary Force. His deputy was Ramsay, who would become the Royal Navy's greatest exponent of the painstaking and complex staff work required for major amphibious operations. One hundred and sixty Royal Navy warships were assembled with two battleships, a battlecruiser and seven carriers, including three of the new escort carriers. Direct attempts to capture Algiers and Oran proved costly, with the loss of a destroyer and two former American coastguard cutters, but a counterattack by French destroyers was beaten off by HMS *Aurora*. The Italian fleet did not intervene. Only the Germans' rapid reinforcement of Tunisia prevented the full strategic benefit being reaped.

The advance of the Eighth Army in the east opened the road to Malta. The last convoy to be opposed was Stoneage in November; by the end of the year the Malta surface striking force, Force K, had been reconstituted, together with a companion force at Bone, Force Q. Together with submarines, aircraft, and later MTBs, these forces inflicted heavy losses on Axis shipping. The Royal Navy locked the Axis force in and with their surrender in large numbers the full fruits of the Mediterranean strategy could at last be enjoyed. Through-Mediterranean convoys made a considerable saving in shipping.

Spring 1943 also saw the major turning point in the Atlantic. The heavy shipping losses in the first half of 1942 had been the responsibility of the US Navy as the U-boats were able to slaughter unescorted shipping off the American coast. Few ships were sunk in the convoys in mid-Atlantic. The success of the better-organized and -equipped Atlantic escorts in 1942 was in spite of the intelligence loss that occurred in February 1942 when the Germans introduced a fourth wheel into their coding machines. Until December, the skilled plotters in the Submarine Tracking Room at the Admiralty lost their major insight into Donitz's activities, but the experience of the preceding months and other intelligence sources combined to mitigate the situation. Only towards the end of 1942, with a full-scale convoy system created in the western Atlantic, were the U-boats regrouped for their climactic assault on the Atlantic convoys.

In January 1942 there were only 91 U-boats operational and fewer than a dozen at any one time were doing serious damage to Atlantic shipping. By July there were 140 operational boats, by October 196, and by April 1943 no fewer than 240. These concentrated their efforts where the escorts were at their weakest – the gap or 'black hole', south of Greenland, where air cover was still not available. In December, Bletchley Park was able to break the new U-boat code, but decrypts were not always immediately available and there were so many U-boats at sea by March 1943, about 70, that evasive routing was virtually impossible.[9]

In the first 20 days of March 1943 54 merchant ships were sunk, two-thirds in convoy (of which 21 were lost from the especially hard-pressed SC 122 and HX 229). The large convoy proportion was partly due to the smaller number of ships being sailed independently, but it led the Admiralty to reconsider its whole convoy strategy. Yet, if the British thought they were losing in March 1943, the Germans did not think they were winning. Every ship sunk had to be paid for in hours of fruitless attacks worsted by the ever more efficient escorts. If Allied aircraft were present, the situation for the U-boats became almost impossible. The straw that finally broke Donitz's back, therefore, was the closing of the black hole in mid-Atlantic where air cover was not available.

The Admiralty had to fight a long and bitter struggle with the RAF, the US Navy and Churchill to obtain sufficient aircraft with the range to plug the mid-Atlantic gap. Barely sufficient Liberators were only available in the spring of 1943. Escort carriers were equally late in appearing. The first, HMS *Audacity*, was used successfully in late 1941 but was sunk escorting convoy HG 76. American-built replacements were supplied to the Royal Navy in 1942, but they were deployed to higher priority tasks – the North African landings and Russian convoys. Only in April 1943 were the first escort carriers, HMS *Attacker* and HMS *Biter*, deployed to defend convoys. The following month the first merchant aircraft carriers sailed with convoys. These were cargo ships fitted with flight decks and a small complement of Fleet Air Arm Swordfish anti-submarine aircraft.

Escort carriers were used in some of the Support Groups, which were escort groups added to convoys that intelligence had revealed as threatened, to hunt attacking submarines to destruction. There were now many more escorts available. The Flower-class corvette had been put into mass production and a 1400-ton ocean-going twin-screw development created and produced was given the title 'frigate'. This name was also applied to American destroyer escorts provided under lend-lease. The excellent prewar convoy sloop was also put back into limited production. As the new wartime programmes of fleet destroyers were delivered, beginning with the O-class in 1942, older destroyer classes were modified to improve their escort capabilities and added to escort groups. Fleet destroyer flotillas were also released for escort work, especially after Arctic convoys were suspended in March 1943.

In April shipping losses were halved and the escorts claimed a U-boat for every ship sunk in convoy. For the first time U-boats failed to press home attacks; it was simply getting too dangerous. The turning point came with Convoy ONS 5; its close escort was the B7 group which consisted of two destroyers, a frigate, four corvettes, and two rescue trawlers. It was supported by two support groups – the First Escort Group composed of a sloop, three frigates, and an ex-US coastguard cutter, and the Third Escort Group, with five destroyers transferred from fleet work. Land-based air cover was provided, including very long-range Liberators. No fewer than 42 U-boats were deployed against ONS 5, of which six were sunk and five damaged seriously. A dozen merchantmen sunk was poor reward for such a concentration of force by the Germans, especially when combined with such losses. The Germans were now smashing themselves against a convoy escort system of ships and aircraft that for the first time in the war had no loopholes to be exploited.

Admiral Sir Max Horton, the distinguished submariner and Commander-in-Chief, Western Approaches, sensed victory. The remaining convoys in May had better weather and more air cover from escort carriers and Liberators. Convoy attacks never again reached ONS 5's level of intensity. SC 129 lost two ships, but its escort sank a U-boat and a pack of ten boats was driven off. In May, the exchange ratio, once running at 100,000 tons of merchant ships per U-boat sunk, came down to 10,000 tons per boat. Forty-one submarines were sunk, 14 by convoy surface escorts and 11 by air escorts. With losses at such unbearable heights Donitz felt he had little alternative but to call off his wolves to lick their wounds.

The news was little better for the Germans in the north. After the PQ 17 disaster, Tovey had decided to give the next Arctic convoy an exceptionally powerful destroyer escort to help keep German surface ships at bay without either scattering the convoy or risking his heavy ships. To defend against the air threat, the new escort carrier *Avenger* was assigned. The convoy sailed in September 1942 and was heavily attacked by aircraft and submarines. It lost 13 ships, but this cost the Germans three U-boats and 22 aircraft.

Apart from one homeward-bound convoy, there was now a pause in Arctic convoys while Operation Torch consumed the lion's share of Allied naval forces. When they resumed in December they were recoded: convoys to Russia were now JW and those in the opposite direction RA. In the Arctic twilight of the last day of 1942 JW 51B was attacked by the cruiser *Hipper* and pocket battleship *Lutzow*, escorted by six destroyers. Captain Sherbrooke's escort of six destroyers, supported by Rear Admiral Burnett's covering force of HMS *Sheffield* and *Jamaica* and two more destroyers, sank the destroyer *Friedrich Eckholdt* and kept the rest of the German battle group at bay for the loss of the minesweeper *Bramble* and destroyer *Achates*. Sherbrooke lost an eye when his ship HMS *Onslow* was hit by four 8-inch shells but he won the Victoria Cross for a well-conducted action that became known as the Battle of the Barents Sea.

Hitler was incensed and ordered the decommissioning of the German major surface units. Raeder resigned to be replaced by Donitz, who was able to obtain a reversal of the scrapping order in order to keep a fleet in being, tying down Royal Navy assets. *Tirpitz* emerged from self-maintenance in January and *Scharnhorst* arrived in March. The Admiralty tried to neutralize the threat by using new midget submarines called X-Craft in a daring attack in September 1943. The explosion of the side charges laid by these boats caused grievous damage to *Tirpitz*. The ship's armament and equipment was severely shaken and put out of action and she was immovable and unsteerable. Repairs would take a long time.

Scharnhorst escaped damage in this attack but met her nemesis in December when she attacked convoy JW 55B (convoys had restarted the previous month). This was supported by Sir Bruce Fraser, the new Commander-in-Chief of the Home Fleet, with his flagship, the battleship *Duke of York*, accompanied by the cruiser *Jamaica* and four destroyers. Burnett's cruiser covering force comprised *Sheffield,*

Belfast and *Norfolk. Scharnhorst*'s signals were being read by the British and was kept wrong-footed throughout. She was surprised by Burnett's cruisers on the morning of 26 December and hit by two 8-inch shells which knocked out her forward radar. Partially blinded, *Scharnhorst* made off into the Arctic darkness. She tried once more to find the convoy but was again caught by the British cruisers. Burnett shadowed on radar and homed in Fraser. When *Duke of York* and *Jamaica* opened fire, *Scharnhorst* tried to get away and a chase developed. She might have escaped, but a shell penetrating her engine room almost brought her to a standstill. The delay was enough for Fraser's destroyers to attack with torpedoes. They hit the German ship four times, slowing her down again and allowing Fraser and Burnett to catch up. *Scharnhorst* was finished off by multiple torpedoes fired by *Jamaica, Belfast*, and returning convoy RA 55A's destroyer escort. The Battle of the North Cape was the last battle between big-gun battleships in the history of the Royal Navy.

Only *Tirpitz* remained. Informed by Enigma intercepts when she would be ready for trials, the British planned a major carrier air strike, Operation Tungsten, for early April 1944. Fraser was sufficiently well informed to make his attack just as the battleship was about to leave her anchorage for sea trials, on 3 April. Two fleet carriers were used, *Victorious* and *Furious*, together with an escort carrier force of four ships. These carried the monoplane Fairey Barracuda torpedo bomber reconnaissance aircraft, introduced the previous year, 40 of which were launched, escorted by 79 fighters. *Tirpitz* was hit or near-missed 16 times and knocked out once more. The bombs were dropped too low for most to penetrate her main armour (one that did failed to explode) but *Tirpitz*'s design made her vulnerable to damage above her armour; also, her engines were disabled by shock damage. Attempts to mount subsequent carrier strikes were foiled by smoke screens and AA defences, and the final destruction of *Tirpitz* was left to RAF Bomber Command.

Late 1943 saw the U-boats attempt a counterattack in the Atlantic. They were armed with new homing torpedoes to take on the escorts and heavier anti-aircraft armaments to take on Coastal Command and the Fleet Air Arm. In the first of the new convoy battles, in September, ON 202 and ONS 18 were attacked. Warned by intelligence derived from code-breaking, the convoys were concentrated with a combined escort and a Canadian support group. A merchant aircraft ship (MAC) was with the convoy and Liberators gave additional air support. Three escorts and six merchant ships were sunk, all when flying was impossible. The Germans lost two U-boats and two more were damaged. This was the best the Germans could do before the escorts acquired Foxer decoys to combat the homing torpedoes. In October, the Germans lost no fewer than 23 U-boats attacking convoys. SC 143 was typical: one merchant ship out of 39 ships in the convoy and one escort sunk, in exchange for three U-boats.

In early 1944 the U-boats concentrated in the Western Approaches. Here support groups such as Captain Johnny Walker's Second Escort group of six sloops were able to hunt them to destruction around the convoys. In February, Walker's group alone sank over half the total of 11 U-boats destroyed in operations to the west of Ireland. Escort groups such as Walker's were by now superbly well-trained teams that could operate with the minimum of signalling and on the basis of mutual confidence. The Germans gave up attacks on convoys in March 1944. U-boats concentrated on covert, submerged patrols, utilizing the schnorkel to stay submerged as long as possible. Until the end of the war, British coastal waters witnessed a dangerous game of cat and mouse with submarines stalking their prey and ships equipped with sophisticated anti-submarine weapons such as the Squid ahead-throwing mortar hunting them down. In January 1945, there were about 335 Royal Navy destroyers, frigates, sloops and corvettes deployed in the anti-U-boat role around Britain's coast, escorting convoys and patrolling focal areas. An improved class of frigate, the Loch, was produced, as were improved Castle-class corvettes in yards that could not build the larger vessels.

The U-boats were unable to prevent the great amphibious landings of 1943–4 which re-established Allied military power on the European continent and caused considerable German strategic concern. The Mediterranean offensive continued in 1943 with the invasion of Sicily in July. This had an enomous effect on Hitler, who called off his great Citadel offensive in Russia.[10] Ramsay masterminded the Husky plan for Sicily, which was covered by six British battleships and two RN fleet carriers. The Salerno landings, on mainland Italy in September, saw another display of the Royal Navy's strength, with fleet and escort carriers providing vital air cover. Italy had capitulated the day before and, in scenes reminiscent of 1918, her fleet surrendered itself at Malta. The strategy conceived in 1939 had finally been consummated and it was a suitable point for Cunningham to return to London to replace Pound, dead from a brain tumour. During the Salerno landings the Germans introduced guided anti-ship missiles, one of which damaged *Warspite*. When the Anzio landings took place in January, the cruiser *Spartan* was sunk by missile attack. This was not quite the last major Royal Navy warship loss of the war as *Penelope* was sunk by U410 in the Mediteranean in February 1944.

The greatest amphibious operation of all was Operation Neptune, the landings in Normandy, in June 1944. This was fundamentally a Royal Navy affair which provided the Allied Naval Commander, Ramsay, with the lion's share of naval assets, from bombardment, covering and escort forces to landing ships and craft. Of the 2468 major landing vessels in the two Task Forces deployed on 6 June, only 346 were American. Of the 23 cruisers covering the landings 17 belonged to the Royal Navy. With Rear Admiral Tennant in command, the Royal Navy also developed the innovative prefabricated Mulberry harbours to be built off the beaches. Corelli Barnett well described Neptune as a 'never surpassed masterpiece of planning' which demonstrated that the Royal Navy's capacity for detailed staff work was greater than often estimated. The landings saw considerable naval activity beyond shore bombardment, extensive and crucial though that was. Clandestine surveys by Combined Operations Pilotage Parties, and a huge minesweeping operation using 255 minesweepers and danlayers, prepared the way for the invasion armada. Meanwhile, escort groups acted as an effective U-boat barrier on both flanks. On 8 June a sharp destroyer action disposed of the main surface threat, when four British and two Canadian destroyers with two Polish destroyers sank two German destroyers, ZH1 and Z32, and heavily damaged Z24. A campaign then had to be waged against manned torpedoes, E-boats, and explosives-laden motor boats. Losses were signficant, for example the Hunt-class destroyer *Quorn* was sunk by a manned torpedo, with heavy loss of life, on 3 August. Once the Allied armies began their advance, naval parties cleared captured ports.

The Home Fleet covered the Arctic convoys, which continued to run with powerful escorts to draw out and destroy Norwegian-based U-boats. Using both surface action groups and escort carrier forces, forward offensive operations were carried out against German sea communications and bases along the Norwegian coast. These culminated in a successful sortie, commanded by Rear Admiral Rhoderick McGrigor, in May 1945 by three escort carriers, two cruisers and seven destroyers, to destroy the German U-boat infrastructure in Vestfiord.

The end of the Italian and German fleets allowed the Royal Navy to begin recovering its position in the Far East. Many major offensives were planned by Mountbatten's Southeast Asia Command, but resources for implementation were never available. By the spring of 1944, however, Somerville's Eastern Fleet was built up sufficiently to go over to the offensive. In April, the carrier *Illustrious*, together with the USS *Saratoga*, struck Sabang and Soerabaya. Two more British carriers arrived in July and Somerville mounted another attack on Sabang, supplemented by shore bombardment and a destroyer torpedo raid.

It had been decided at the Cairo summit in November 1943 that Britain would send a fleet to the Pacific. In this theatre the key weapons had been carriers and their aircraft, and American aid assisted in creating sufficiently powerful forces. The Americans supplied both aircraft and flying training and US techniques of carrier operation were adopted. HMS *Victorious* was deployed to reinforce the temporarily hard-pressed Americans in the Pacific in 1943 and obtained useful experience. Using deck parks, it was possible eventually to increase the size of carrier air groups to 45 in *Illustrious, Formidable* and *Victorious*, 63 in *Indomitable* and 78 in *Implacable* and *Indefatigable*.[11]

The quality of Fleet Air Arm aircraft greatly improved. As a first step, fighter squadrons had been re-equipped with higher-performance single-seat fighters, American-built Wildcats (designated Martlet for a time) and navalized versions of the Hurricane and Spitfire. The Seafire was never a fully satisfactory carrier aircraft in terms of its strength of construction, range and landing charateristics but it was widely deployed in various improved variants and would live on in the first line long after the war. The two-seater fighter reconnaissance aircraft was not abandoned and a better Fairey design, the Firefly, provided a long-lived Fulmar replacement.

In order to improve the situation still further, the improved American Hellcat single-seat fleet fighter was supplied, as was the even higher-performance Corsair, which the Americans were initially unwilling to operate from their own carriers. The Corsair required high hangars and could only be handled by the original Illustrious class. *Indomitable* carried Hellcats while *Implacable* and *Indefatigable* had to make do with Seafires and Fireflies. The much superior American Grumman Avenger took over the topedo bomber reconnaissance role in all the fleet carriers.

In 1942 the Admiralty embarked on a major wartime carrier construction programme. Three 37,000-ton Audacious-class armoured carriers with high double hangars were laid down in 1942–4 and four 47,000-ton Gibraltar-class ships were ordered in June 1943. Significantly, the latter abandoned the closed armoured hangar concept in order to allow engines to be run up in the hangar and the launching of very large strikes of piston-engined aircraft. Both these classes would have been able to operate the 100-aircraft air groups of the Americans. None, however, were launched by the war's end and the Maltas were never even laid down. To allow more rapid construction, a small 13,000–14,000-ton light fleet carrier design was developed, of which two batches, the Colossus and Majestic classes, were laid down in 1942–3. Non-armoured, they were designed to carry 24 aircraft but were deployed with 36 Barracudas and Corsairs. Four rather larger 18,000-ton light fleets, the Hermes class, were laid down in 1944–5 to operate heavier aircraft and four more were ordered.[12]

Commanded by Sir Bruce Fraser, the British Pacific Fleet (BPF) – the carriers *Indomitable, Victorious, Indefatigable* and *Illustrious*, together with the battleships *King George V* and *Howe*, 6-inch cruisers *Swiftsure* (a new modified variant of a Colony) and *Gambia*, the Didos *Black Prince, Argonaut* and *Euryalus* and 14 of the latest fleet destroyers of the Q, U and W flotillas – arrived on station in March 1945. As in prewar plans *Unicorn* was in the fleet train as repair and maintenance carrier. Two more fleet carriers, *Formidable* and *Implacable*, joined later, as did many other ships, including, just before the end, one of the new large heavily armed Battle-class destroyers. It was a brave show and the BPF was given Task Force status (TF 57 or 37 depending on which US admiral, Spruance or Halsey, was in command) but in reality it was only a single Task Group's worth in terms of the gigantic fleet deployed by the Americans. The roles were reversed from the situation at Scapa in 1918, when an American battle squadron had formed a part of the British Grand Fleet. Much had to be learned about distant fleet support, fleet train, and replenishment at sea, lessons that would stand the Navy in good stead in the postwar era. The British Pacific Fleet saw considerable action, not least off Okinawa, where its armoured hangar carriers proved resilient under kamikaze suicide attack, but the Americans made sure that it was never in the forefront of the final defeat of the Japanese navy. It did, however, participate in the final bombardment of the Japanese home islands and its battleships were the last British gun-armed capital ships to fire their guns in anger. The very last occasion was late on the foggy night of 28 July, when HMS *King George V* fired 265 rounds of 14-inch at the 'Japanese Musical Instrument Works' which made aircraft propellers.[13]

In the Indian Ocean, surface, escort carrier and submarine forces kept up a maritime offensive. In May 1945, in an operation that combined the traditions of surface torpedo attack with the new action information organization necessitated by three-dimensional sensors, the Twenty-Sixth Destroyer Flotilla sank the Japanese cruiser *Haguro*. The following month another cruiser, *Ashigara*, was sunk by the submarine *Trenchant*, and, at the end of July, in a daring midget submarine attack, *Takao* was sent to the bottom of her anchorage by charges laid by XE3 and XE1.

On 2 September 1945 Admiral Sir Bruce Fraser signed the Japanese surrender, on behalf of the United Kingdom, in Tokyo Bay. The following day Penang was reoccupied by Royal Marines from HMS *London*. On the 5th, the destroyer *Rotherham* began the reoccupation of the Singapore naval base. On 9 September, the landings to reoccupy Malaya took place. Southeast Asia Command had to reoccupy and maintain order in the former French and Dutch empires as well as Britain's own. The first of the new light fleet carriers, *Colossus, Glory Venerable* and *Vengeance*, helped cover the reoccupation of Allied territory.

The Second World War had cost the Royal Navy dear. Some 224 major surface ships of corvette size and above had been sunk; 139 destroyers were sunk, 31 more than had been in service in 1939. A total of 1525 British warships of all types were lost, of over two million tons. Over 50,000 naval personnel lost their lives, many of them members of the Royal Naval Reserve and Royal Naval Volunteer Reserve. The service had fought well, much better than in the First World War, and if not all of its initial capabilities had been proved adequate, its capacity to learn from experience and apply new technology had been second to none.

The Royal Navy had also grown enormously both in size and scope. The strength of the fleet had increased from almost 400 major combatants (of which over one-third were in reserve) to almost 900. In terms of personnel, the growth was even greater, from a prewar strength of 129,000 to 863,500 by mid-1944.[14] Of this last figure, 72,000 were members of the Women's Royal Naval Service (WRNS) who carried out a wide range of shore roles, from mine modification to general administration. Women in uniform had become an essential and permanent feature of naval life.

The increased demand for personnel reflected the extent to which the wartime navy was based ashore. Developments in technology required training, research and support facilities that had never before been necessary. The Fleet Air Arm required a major shore organization as well as aircrew serving at sea, and other new types of naval forces such as landing craft and coastal forces added to demands for personnel. The Admiralty itself had grown into a huge organization, with major outstations at Bath and Taunton. This increased the problems of those who planned demobilization and the size of the postwar fleet. Like their predecessors in every previous period of peace, they would be forced into difficult choices.

8 The Postwar Navy

The nuclear bombs that ended the war promised to make obsolete long wars in which sea power had been most relevant. Nevertheless, the Naval Staff at the Admiralty could console itself that it would be some time before nuclear weapons would wreak their strategic revolution in full. Even when they did, naval forces would play a part in their delivery (or threatened delivery). Moreover, there would be 'conflicts between small nations...and threats to our own territory which may be settled without the use of atomic weapons and in which a more or less normal navy would play its usual part'.[1] This was the key to the Navy's survival strategy for the postwar period.

Strategic worries were, however, the least of the Royal Navy's immediate concerns in the aftermath of war. Service personnel needed to be returned home, prisoners repatriated, mines swept and British authority restored both in the Empire (as most naval officers still thought of it) and elsewhere.[2] Never had British power been so widely dispersed as in 1945, and never had its foundations been weaker. The Attlee administration had the enormous problem of reviving an economy bankrupted by war, constructing a new, more equitable domestic social order, and deciding on an appropriate level of military strength. Ambitious plans for the postwar Navy remained dormant. In the Cabinet's initial discussions on Britain's postwar defence posture, the Prime Minister conceded American supremacy on the seas. Dogged attempts by A. V. Alexander, the First Lord of the Admiralty, to put strategic priorities rather than resource allocations as the main parameters in the defence policy equation, fell on stony ground. In Ernest Bevin's homely metaphor, 'we must cut our coat according to our cloth'.[3]

There was no question of completing wartime construction plans. Plans to restart the Lion-class battleships to a revised design and build the large fleet carriers on order were abandoned and a new programme of six large cruisers postponed indefinitely. The fleet carrier and light fleet carrier programmes that were already under construction were cut back also. Only two of the large armoured hangar ships, *Eagle* (as *Audacious* was renamed) and *Ark Royal*, and four of the Hermes-class ships, *Albion, Bulwark, Centaur* and *Hermes*, survived in the yards, to be completed as soon as practicable. This was a minimum force capable of operating the heavier and faster aircraft types planned for the future. The existing carrier fleet made up of armoured hangar carriers of prewar conception and the still incomplete programme of light fleet carriers built for Second World War aircraft had only limited development potential, although the cancellation of most of the final generation of piston-engined naval aircraft planned for 1946–7 helped solve the problem temporarily. The six Majestics were also suspended and none saw service with the Royal Navy. The immediate operational postwar carrier force was provided by the six economical Colossus-class light fleets *Glory, Ocean, Vengeance, Theseus, Triumph* and *Warrior*.

Britain had more than enough ships left over from the war: the problems were deciding which to continue running in the operational fleet, how many to place in reserve, and how many to dispose of. Those vessels that were so old and worn-out were soon scrapped. Many others were decommissioned and filled British dockyards and harbours, poised to be mobilized in any future, traditional conflict. But, if these ships were to be used in the future, they required refit and maintenance facilities – a drain on the active fleet and manpower-intensive.

It was decided, after some haggling between the Admiralty and the Treasury, that the Royal Navy would be the smallest of the postwar services, with a regular strength of 144,000 (compared with 135,000 in 1939). The Admiralty hoped to retain 225,000 men at the end of March 1947, but Hugh Dalton, the Chancellor, demanded the maximum demobilization possible to get British industry working once again in order to gain the export earnings that would maintain, among other things, the future Navy. The economic threat to Britain's security was paramount. Risks would have to be taken elsewhere.

In February 1946 it was decided by the Cabinet's Defence Committee that there would be no war in the next two or three years

and that no hostile fleet would exist for the next few years. Attempts
to conjure up the spectre of a Soviet naval threat had only limited
effect. No naval building programme was drawn up for 1946 and
the planned Naval Estimates and manpower ceilings were reduced.
The Prime Minister remained dissatisfied. Why, he asked in July
1946, were 182,000 male naval personnel (the figure conceded to
the Admiralty by the Treasury) required in 1947 when 119,000
had been sufficient to man a much larger fleet in 1938? The Admiralty's
reply shows the different requirements of the more complex
postwar Navy.

The introduction of the large carrier, the heavy increase in anti-aircraft
guns, the immense growth in technical equipment, the development of radar
and W/T, the speed of the modern commerce destroying submarine, the
advent of combined operations and the introduction of short term conscription
have substantially changed the situation and their cumulative effect has
been largely to increase the number of men required to maintain a given
number of naval ships, units and training depots and schools.[4]

Much debate went on in the Navy over the utility of having
national servicemen who required 10,000 extra men to train them.
But the need to be prepared for rapid mobilization, plus a persistent
shortage of regulars, forced the Admiralty to use conscripts to maintain
the operational fleet. In 1949 some 11 per cent of the total personnel
strength of 144,500 were conscripted.

The Navy was not an attractive career in the late 1940s. Old-
fashioned ships and conditions of service, and inadequate financial
rewards versus the promise of opportunities and extra security in
Welfare State Britain created an unfavourable situation. Not only had
few sailors joined as regulars during the war, but those who had showed
little inclination to re-enlist. In 1948 only 22 per cent of seamen ratings
were re-enlisting (compared to 61 per cent in 1938). In some categories,
the lower ranks of stoker and mechanician, the retention rate was
negligible, some 4 per cent. This not only meant that there were
fewer men than necessary to man ships, but also meant a greatly
enhanced training load to deal with recruits and retraining men in
specializations of which there was a shortage. An almost entirely new

postwar regular Navy was being created; in the meantime it was extremely difficult to keep ships running.

The year 1947 began quite well for the Navy, with attempts to formulate coherent plans for the development of postwar armed forces. 'Defence of sea communications' was a priority in British defence policy, second only to 'Defence of the United Kingdom base'. In April 1947 a ten-year plan provided a time frame for the creation of forces ready for war. There was a 'small' risk of war over the next five years and a gradually increasing one for the five years after that. Yet the Admiralty's first plans were totally unrealistic: a peacetime active fleet of 128 major surface ships, including three battleships and four fleet carriers, 29 submarines and 500 front-line aircraft. The wartime fleet would comprise over 600 major units and over 1000 aircraft. A £3.3 billion programme was produced which would cost some £465 million annually by the mid-1950s. In the prevailing atmosphere of economic crisis, Alexander told the three services to budget on the total allocation of £600 million. The 1957 assumption became very close to being a five-year no-war rule, albeit one fixed not rolling, as the prewar ten-year rule had been. The Admiralty planners set about revising their plans downwards.

Lord Andrew Cunningham had been replaced as First Sea Lord in June 1946 by Admiral Sir John Cunningham, whose intelligence and less charismatic style suited the adverse times. The Government's reforms to the central organization of defence, which became operative at the start of 1947, set up a new post of Minister of Defence in the Cabinet act as a kind of referee between the three services. The latter kept their separate administrations under more junior political leadership. Alexander became the first of the new Defence Ministers, being replaced at the Admiralty by the former Colonial Secretary, Viscount Hall. Like the Ministers for War and Air, he only had access to the Cabinet on request.

By the end of 1947 the Royal Navy was in a parlous state indeed. The Home Fleet, with many of its units 'temporarily immobilized', was composed of a tiny operational cadre of a cruiser, a couple of large destroyers, half a dozen frigates and 20 submarines. The Mediterranean had the only 'fleet' worthy of the name, with one operational light fleet carrier with the new standard air group of 28 aircraft, a squadron of

Seafires and a squadron of Fireflies. (US aircraft had been discarded with the end of lend-lease as the dollar situation precluded acquiring spares.) Also in the Mediterranean were four cruisers, 20 destroyers and frigates and two submarines. The Pacific Fleet had temporarily lost its carrier and was down to three operational cruisers, four destroyers, four frigates and three submarines. A cruiser and two frigates were operational in the South Atlantic and a similar force was on the American and West Indies Station. Two cruisers and two frigates composed the East Indies Squadron at Trincomalee and a lone frigate kept the White Ensign flying in the Persian Gulf.

Many of the duties of the Royal Navy had a very familiar ring about them: maintaining freedom of access to international straits (the Corfu Channel incident of 1946), preventing illegal immigration to colonial territories (notably Palestine) while helping maintain order within them and even attempting to maintain British interests on Chinese rivers (despite the end of extraterritorial rights and the river gunboats). The Yangtze Incident of 1949, when the frigate (former sloop) *Amethyst* was damaged, trapped and eventually escaped after a spectacular but abortive attempt at rescue by the cruiser *London* and frigate *Black Swan*, demonstrated dramatically that opposition to the Royal Navy's attentions was growing. Meanwhile, the increasing polarization between East and West added a Cold War dimension to traditional imperial policing and extra incentives to maintaining a global presence.

Maintaining a sufficiently large fleet for peacetime Cold War duties became a major priority, as defence planners recovered from the low point of the winter of 1947–8. The deteriorating situation in Europe helped speed recovery, but not to the extent the Admiralty wished. Future defence expenditure, the Treasury hoped, would be limited to a marginal increase of £700 million per annum. At the end of 1948, at the request of the Chiefs of Staff, the Harwood Committee drew up a defence policy within this financial parameter, one which promised radical changes in British naval posture and organization: withdrawal to the Atlantic, abolition of the battleship and reductions in cruisers, a new emphasis on carriers, even transferring the Royal Marines to the Army, and abolishing once more the Women's Royal Naval Service. But these proposals were only made to demonstrate their impracticability. The Government was unwilling to contemplate a withdrawal from its world responsibilities, especially not from the dollar-producing territories of Southeast Asia. It was by no means clear who would take over from Britain if she decided on precipitate withdrawal.

The Naval Staff finally drew up a practical fleet plan in the middle of 1949. The 'Revised Restricted Fleet' was to be capable of carrying out the foreign and colonial policy of the Government in peacetime, and then to be able to meet the immediate requirements of a 1957 war, serving as a nucleus for expansion. It contained no battleship in full peacetime commission. HMS *Vanguard*, not completed until August 1946, would be retained in service for training and royal yacht duties; the four surviving King George V class would be added to the Reserve Fleet. Two fleet carriers and three light fleet carriers would be kept active, with one of each in addition for training. There would be 250 front-line carrier-based aircraft. Thirteen cruisers would be in peacetime commission, 38 destroyers, 32 frigates (the term now used to cover corvettes, escort destroyers and sloops as well as the old frigates proper) and 20 submarines. A large reserve of small minesweepers would be built up and over a hundred frigates would be kept in reserve. Some 50 fast patrol boats (as MTBs and MGBs were now known) would be kept for training and in reserve. Such a fleet could maintain British peacetime interests worldwide and, with the Americans, take half the wartime responsibility for the Atlantic and Mediterranean.

The Revised Restricted Fleet still emphasized 'hot war' priorities in new construction. The threat of mining, a type of warfare for which the Soviet Union had a known predilection, was reflected in the plans for large numbers of new construction coastal and inshore mine countermeasures (MCM) vessels. Other new construction investment was to go into frigates for convoy escort, over half of which were anti-submarine warfare (ASW) ships. Wartime fleet destroyers were to be converted into fast Type 15 and 16 ASW frigates to provide a readily available answer to the menace of the much faster modern submarine. The heavy backup to these smaller vessels would come from the two new fleet and four new light fleet carriers, supplemented by extensive modernization to some of the older fleet carriers. In the meantime, one fleet carrier, HMS *Implacable*, was returned to full commission with the Home Fleet. She had a special air group of twin-engined Sea Hornet fighters and Firebrand fighter-torpedo bombers.

The Admiralty had learned the lessons of the recent war. With large surface ships known to be under construction in the USSR it could not abandon the 'essential insurance' of battleships and other powerful surface warfare vessels; new large Daring-class destroyers that had survived the 1945 cuts were continued and a still larger 5000-ton cross between destroyer and cruiser planned. Nevertheless, the three-dimensional nature of naval warfare was clearly recognized. The new First Sea Lord, Lord Fraser of North Cape, who took up office in 1948, put the direct protection of shipping from underwater and air threats as the top wartime priority. As he said to naval airmen who were campaigning for a greater role for strike aircraft in 1949: 'Planning can only proceed on something we know we must do. Escort safely our convoys.'[5] With the entire strength of naval aviation currently below the level of that deemed necessary by the Americans for a successful strike (200 aircraft), there was little alternative. Fleet carriers would cover convoys in the Mediterranean with their fighters; light fleets would act as escort carriers with fighters and ASW aircraft in the Atlantic.

In the event, however, light fleet carriers operated primarily against land targets when limited war broke out in Korea in 1950. HMS *Triumph* operated her Seafires and Fireflies at the outset of the conflict and her sisters kept a Commonwealth carrier on station throughout the conflict, the Sea Fury replacing the Seafire. The Royal Navy played a significant role in this conflict, being responsible for the blockade of the western coast of the Peninsula. British cruisers played a major part in covering MacArthur's landing at Inchon and, together with destroyers and frigates, kept up a constant bombardment on the Chinese and North Koreans, firing over 170,000 rounds of ammunition to add to 23,000 carrier sorties. The war not only provided a useful demonstration of the Royal Navy in 'warm' war as well as 'cold', it also provided the context for the last postwar attempt to build up a fleet to fight an old-style war.

The Korean War launched Britain into a programme of rapid rearmament. The 1957 Planning Date was increasingly replaced by the North Atlantic Treaty Organization's date of 1954. The force goals set out in NATO's Medium-term Plan provided an ambitious target for a rapid naval build-up. Nevertheless, the 'Fraser Plan' of October 1950 showed only modest increases over the Revised Restricted Fleet, with an expanded frigate construction and conversion programme and even more mine countermeasures vessels. In December, however, after Attlee's talks with Truman in Washington, Britain began to rearm to the limit of her capability. An 'Accelerated Fraser Plan' was produced, with an emphasis on rapid results, even more MCM vessels, an accelerated frigate conversion programme and the rapid procurement of available types of aircraft. The new plan would cost £1610 million, over a third of the entire £4.7 billion revised rearmament plan.

Even this was not enough. In the summer of 1951 the Admiralty produced a third in-house expanded plan, more ambitious still. Although the emphasis remained on frigates and MCM vessels, a new fleet carrier was also requested to maintain the planned front line of six by 1956 with 300 aircraft. The financial assumptions upon which Exercise C was based were optimistic: an increased share of the existing £4.7 billion bonanza and continued expenditure at this high rate for succeeding years. It was clear, however, that Britain was not capable of spending even the money already allocated to naval rearmament. Given the reluctance of the Government to go over to a full war economy, the rearmament programme was beset by shortages of labour and materials. Work was seriously delayed by a shortage of drawing-office staff, both at the Admiralty's offices and the shipyards. Electricians, plumbers and fitters were also unavailable. Pipes, valves and electrical fittings were delivered late. Labour disputes caused further delay. Moreover, even if the resources now flowing into defence were allowing some of the ships left over from the war to be completed, the Navy's chronic manpower shortage, despite increased conscription and the recall of reservists, meant that older ships had to be decommissioned to man the newer ones.

Winston Churchill's new Conservative Government inherited these problems after its 1951 election victory and soon decided that Britain was arming beyond her means. Churchill's formidable Chancellor of the Exchequer, R. A. Butler, recognized the serious consequences to the balance of payments of diverting too high a proportion of

Britain's export-earning 'metal-using industries' into the defence sector. Before the end of the year the rearmament programme had been cut back, fatally delaying some projects including the second fleet carrier conversion. The priority remained on short-term projects (e.g. completing the Darings). For the longer term, the Government had something more radical in mind.

The year 1952 was to see Britain explode her first nuclear bomb. Moreover, intelligence assessments seemed to demonstrate that the Soviet Union might well be deterred from starting a war for quite some time. Rearmament to fight a war had to be replaced by an affordable deterrent posture for the long haul. The Chiefs of Staff were tasked with formulating a revised Global Strategy for the new conditions. When their first attempt proved unsatisfactory, the famous week-long meeting took place at the Royal Naval College Greenwich, when the Chiefs formulated a revised Defence Policy and Global Strategy paper, which was forwarded to the Prime Minister in June 1952 and adopted by the Cabinet's Defence Committee the following month.[6]

The main thrust of this paper was that nuclear weapons, especially those delivered by the increasingly powerful US Strategic Air Command, meant that any future war promised to be short and intense. The First Sea Lord, Admiral Sir Rhoderick McGrigor, fought as hard as possible to sustain the interests of his service. He argued successfully that the Soviet submarine, surface and mining threats to Britain's vital sea communications were as much a threat to Britain's survival in the opening phase of a war as nuclear bombing. Although McGrigor was not willing to abandon the long-war scenario completely – 'alternative loading and unloading facilities' were being investigated to replace the major ports – he agreed with his colleagues that 'the fact that it is economically impracticable to make the preparations necessary for a long war should be faced, and a guiding principle of a rearmament programme should be to ensure survival in the short opening phase'.[7] McGrigor accepted that the fleet 90 days after mobilization in 1955 would now be one battleship, five aircraft carriers (280 aircraft), 14 cruisers, 163 destroyers and frigates, 263 MCM vessels, 39 submarines and three fast minelayers. This was one carrier, four cruisers, 113 destroyers and frigates, 104 MCM vessels under the NATO commitment. The level of naval modernization would also be reduced.

Even the reduced force levels reluctantly agreed upon at Greenwich proved too extensive for Butler to accept. Throughout 1952 a struggle continued as the Chancellor fought for still further reductions in defence expenditure. A compromise, agreed at the end of the year, involved cuts in manpower that meant that many ships were only semi-operational. Appearances were, however, kept up. External observers were not to know that the impressive British cruiser on the port visit had only 30 per cent of her armament manned or that the magnificent HMS *Vanguard*, now returned to notional full commission as Home Fleet flagship, usually had unmanned turrets and magazines and normally no ammunition on board except starshell for her secondary battery. Such solutions maintained British prestige in the short term as demanded by the Foreign Office. *Vanguard*'s role was officially classified as a peacetime one – she was not required for war until some three months after mobilization.

In 1953 a more 'Radical' Review began to bring defence policy into line with Butler's Treasury resources. The key to this reassessment was an extension of the logic of Global Strategy. Only those forces that contributed to the United Kingdom's world-power status and which were relevant in the first six weeks of war were to be retained. In 1952 the Chiefs of Staff had emphasized the importance of an 'immediate attack at source against airfields, U-boat bases and mine depots' but the RAF and the Minister of Supply, Duncan Sandys, saw this as a role for the RAF's planned medium bombers and mounted a serious joint attack on the Admiralty's fleet carrier and aircraft plans.

The early 1950s saw the Royal Navy's main wartime rationale move steadily towards the carrier strike role. This reflected closer British involvement with the NATO Strike Fleet concept and also the belated appearance, to the Admiralty's relief, of a surface threat, the Sverdlov-class cruiser, which seemed to have much potential as a commerce raider. These were, however, only part of the story. Forced, very reluctantly, to accept a subordinate position in the new NATO Atlantic command structure (the C.-in-C. Home Fleet was NATO C.-in-C. Eastern Atlantic), the Admiralty was determined to wield as much influence over the Alliance's main fleet as possible. This implied the retention of a fleet carrier force equipped with high-performance fighters to cover US carriers and, eventually, strike aircraft to add their nuclear weight to the American carrier offensive. In June 1952 a requirement was issued for a high-performance carrier-based NA39 (Buccaneer) nuclear strike aircraft and it was hoped that in the meantime the next generation N113 (Scimitar) and DH110 (Sea Vixen) fighters would provide an interim nuclear capability. This was important, as the British contribution to the Strike Fleet might have to hold the ring in northern waters alone before the arrival of American ships.

The competition between the services, and between Sandys (who had charge of aircraft procurement) and the Admiralty, became acute. In 1953 the Naval Staff abandoned its plans for a new 53,000-ton carrier, although it was still planned to lay down a 35,000-ton ship in 1957.[8] In the shorter term it would be lucky to save the one modernization of a wartime carrier that had actually begun (HMS *Victorious*). The Minister of Defence, Lord Alexander of Tunis, suggested a compromise that would have completed *Ark Royal*, to join her already commissioned sister *Eagle*, but which would have kept only one ship in commission, equipped only with fighters and ASW aircraft for escort duties. In their opposition to these proposals, the Admiralty argued that abolishing the fleet carrier would decisively weaken British claims to NATO commands as well as generally diminish the UK's international status.

A compromise was offered to the RAF in which it was agreed that, while bombing shore targets was its primary responsibility, the carriers would be required to attack the Sverdlovs at sea. The utility of the carrier in Cold War functions also helped save the day for the Admiralty. In mid-1954 a revised Chiefs of Staff Appreciation in the light of the H-bomb made the Cold War relevance of forces the overriding factor in their retention in Britain's force posture. The Admiralty were willing to give up a light carrier from their proposed active force, reducing the latter to two fleets and two light fleets. This was in line with the decreed de-emphasizing of escort duties inherent in the revised strategic concept. The Admiralty seem to have convinced Lord Alexander, at least, of the strength of their case.

Not even the Radical Review's Defence Policy Committee was able to get the budget down to Butler's target of £1500 million for 1955. Viscount Swinton, the Commonwealth Secretary, was tasked with a further review. With Sandys closely associated with the enquiry, it was not surprising that the decision should go against the Admiralty on the carrier question. It concluded that:

The three Services are equal in status and honour and will remain so. But each must vary in size and character as changes take place in the science of war and the course of world events. In the new strategic conditions, the relative importance of sea power in our defences is evidently diminishing and there is no sign that the trend will be arrested. There is no question of having a larger navy than we need or can afford; and we must make the best use of existing material. It is natural that the Navy should wish to have their (sic) share in air power, which is growing in importance. The cost of the Fleet Air Arm, however, ... appears to impose a burden disproportionate to the results. Moreover, the role of the aircraft carrier is already restricted through the ever-increasing range of shore-based aircraft.[9]

The new review recommended that all four carriers should be manned and equipped as escort carriers only, with the primary role of protecting Atlantic shipping in the later stages of a future war. The Admiralty reacted with a strongly worded protest, signed by the First Lord. McGrigor led the argument in Cabinet, however, stressing the need to have a British contribution to the main Allied Striking Fleet. He reiterated the importance of the British ships before the Americans arrived and the protection of Norway from amphibious attack. Churchill, very reluctantly, accepted that alternative naval economies might be made and tasked Macmillan, his new Defence Minister, to continue negotiations with the Admiralty on alternative cuts.

These were successful, for when the Defence White Paper and Naval Estimates appeared in February 1955, the continued presence of the carriers as 'the fists of the fleet' and 'the strength upon which all naval activities depend' was strongly asserted. The Allied striking fleet's carriers, it was even argued, 'will add powerfully to our ability to hit the enemy either independently or in support of allied land forces and land-based air forces'.[10] It was apt that *Ark Royal* should now appear to join *Eagle* and the two light fleet carriers *Centaur* and *Albion* in the first-line carrier force. They were beginning to operate the first generation of jet aircraft, the Sea Hawk single-seat fighter and the Sea Venom two-seat all-weather fighter. Following the failure of the last variant of the Firefly in the anti-submarine role, American Avengers had filled the gap before the turboprop Gannet entered service. Wyverns, also turboprop-powered, provided the fleet carriers with strike capability while American-supplied Skyraiders introduced airborne early warning. Much, however, had been forfeited. The minesweeper programme was drastically reduced despite the Admiralty's protests that the smaller ports that had not suffered nuclear attack might still face a mining threat. Nonetheless, a large number of Ton-class coastal minesweepers, Ham-class inshore minesweepers and some Ley-class inshore minehunters were built. Those proved useful for fishery protection and patrol duties.

Frigate building plans were reduced also, the slower Type 41 anti-aircraft (AA) and Type 61 aircraft direction ships that were unsuitable for carrier escort duties suffering disproportionately. The cruiser fleet was to be cut and its modernization drastically curtailed as sophisticated anti-aircraft armaments were now deemed to be unnecessary against unsophisticated Cold War opposition. Expensive plans to convert the small Dido-class ships into effective 'hot war' fleet escorts had already been replaced in 1953 by the retention of the larger Colony-class ships as shore-bombardment vessels. *Vanguard* was to be refitted as a combatant Home Fleet flagship and super-Sverdlov killer (at a cost of two cruisers).

The Admiralty still planned to have a few cruisers equipped with modern AA systems, notably the three incomplete Tiger-class ships, upon which work began once more after a long sojourn in Scottish lochs. It also planned to build a totally new large missile cruiser equipped with the large Seaslug missile system, upon which work had been going on for a decade. New fleet escort vessels were planned and the Type 12 anti-submarine frigates had enough speed to be useful carrier task-force escorts. What specialized convoy escorts had been built, however, would still be useful to escort replenishment groups and act as gunboats. The curtailed programme of austere and highly specialized Type 14 second-rate ASW frigates would find peacetime roles in training and fishery protection. Nevertheless, the long review process had seen some notable casualties, among them the 5000-ton cruiser/destroyer, an east-coast gunboat to protect convoys from attack by coastal forces, an even more austere mass-production ASW frigate, and a new ocean minesweeper.

It could have been much worse for the Admiralty. Churchill had definitively lost interest in the Navy and his resignation in 1955 was something of an advantage for its interests. He had unsuccessfully opposed the appointment of the influential Lord Louis Mountbatten as First Sea Lord to replace McGrigor in April 1955. The old Prime Minister was quoted as saying he did not want a strong man in charge of it. Although McGrigor's achievement in saving the Navy from the first phase of the Conservatives' review, and reshaping it in a more modern image, should not be underestimated, the extraordinary skills of Mountbatten in committee and his enormous powers of persuasion in face-to-face discussion were badly needed to maintain the Navy's position against a renewed series of serious attacks that were rapidly approaching. Moreover, Mountbatten's social status and connections, which had sustained him through an equivocal record as a commander, now stood the service in excellent stead to weather the storms.

Mountbatten's arrival at the Admiralty more or less coincided with Anthony Eden's at Downing Street, and the First Sea Lord exerted as much influence as possible on the new Prime Minister. Eden was determined to emphasize cuts in general war forces in future defence reviews. Mountbatten's response to the challenge was twofold: first he supported a set of pre-emptive cuts making the maximum internal economies; second, an even greater emphasis was placed on the Navy's limited war and peacekeeping functions. A Way Ahead Committee was created as the instrument of the First Sea Lord's personal authority, to ram through radical administrative reforms. Rationalization of shore establishments began and the Reserve Fleet was drastically cut. *Vanguard* was quietly reduced to reserve after her refit; there were rather better uses for her scarce manpower. Reform also took place in the Navy's officer corps. Mountbatten had inherited a Committee on Officer Structure and Training that recommended the creation of General and Supplementary lists of officers of all specializations. The coloured rings that had previously distinguished officers such as engineers and supply officers from seamen were abolished. The committee also set 18 as the minimum entry age for officers, and Dartmouth (whose entry age had been increased to 16 by the Labour Government) was transformed into a Naval Academy.[11]

In 1956 Eden set up a Policy Review Committee to draw up plans for forces based on the assumption that the UK would be knocked out in a thermonuclear war. The Navy should be reduced to 'the minimum necessary for situations short of global war'.[12] The Admiralty rejected this logic, asserting the Soviet naval threat, but it was forced to accept that global war forces were the lowest priority and that its future was best safeguarded by an emphasis on cold and limited war. Indeed this would require additions to the active fleet, including a new 'commando carrier', a light fleet carrier converted to land Royal Marines by helicopter (plans for the new strike carrier were quietly dropped). The Admiralty accepted a reduction in strength from 120,000 men (almost 10 per cent conscripts) to 90,000 (all regulars) by the early 1960s.

In the second half of 1956 the weaknesses of Britain's existing limited war forces were being shown up dramatically. In July 1956 President Nasser nationalized the Suez Canal. Immediate action was impossible and when the attack eventually went in to recover the Canal and topple Nasser, the political context was all wrong and failure inevitable. Nevertheless, the operation allowed the Navy to make various useful points: the greater effectiveness of carrier air power for providing air support (*Eagle, Centaur* and *Bulwark* were engaged); the commando carrier concept (*Ocean* and *Theseus* used a joint ad hoc group of Whirlwinds and Sycamores), the continued importance of sealift and amphibious assault (even though the existing fleet proved to be inadequate); and the crucial importance of rapidly deployable forces which could act when the political context was right. Suez also implied that those forces need not be too large. The capitulation to American pressure demonstrated that the kinds of action that Britain would undertake alone would be relatively limited.

The departure of Eden after the humiliation of Suez led to the culmination of the long process of the Conservative Defence Review. The new Prime Minister, Macmillan, appointed the Navy's old enemy,

Duncan Sandys, as Minister of Defence, vested with far-reaching powers for root-and-branch reform, notably the abolition of conscription.

Sandys and Mountbatten fought out what the latter called a 'pretty good tussle' in the early months of 1957. The stakes were high – possibly a cut of half of the Navy's strength within a year – and every pro-Navy influence that could be mobilized was brought to bear. Much to the Defence Minister's surprise, complete Chiefs of Staff endorsement of the carrier was obtained. It was agreed that the Navy's role in general war was 'somewhat uncertain' but the White Paper confirmed the continued utility of naval forces as a 'means of bringing power rapidly to bear in peacetime emergencies or limited hostilities'.[13] Although the Royal Navy at home was to be reduced, forces East of Suez were to remain as a carrier-centred 'fire brigade' (in the homely metaphor of the Admiralty's own Statement on the Naval Estimates).[14] Investment in preparing for a general war that would be deterred from breaking out by nuclear weapons was still further reduced. The reserves, both volunteer and regular, were drastically cut and special austere Seamew anti-submarine aircraft, designed for use by unrefitted light fleet carriers or converted merchantmen in the convoy escort role, were finally abandoned.

The Admiralty also made the historic decision that traditional cruiser roles could be taken over by carriers and 6000-ton guided missile destroyers, the design of which was presented to the Board in March 1957. The following month it accepted the abandonment 'forthwith' of the 16,000-ton guided missile cruiser in which much work and publicity had been invested 'if the future of the GW destroyers and the four carriers were assured'.[15] The force of nine cruisers in commission and four in reserve was to be run down to the three Tigers, which were to be completed as 'a great deal of money has been invested in these ships, and apart from awkward criticism if they were again suspended or cancelled, their ultra modern gunnery systems will make them rather better than stop gaps till the GW destroyers come into service in adequate numbers'.[16] Modernization plans for other cruisers were finally abandoned.

Sandys still did not believe in the Striking Fleet concept. As the second phase of the Sandys Review went on in 1957, the Admiralty emphasized that the USA was committed to the Striking Fleet and that it would be better for Alliance relations if Britain continued to make a contribution, just as she did to NATO's forces in Europe. The Ministry of Defence was persuaded that, even if no provision was made for fighting a global thermonuclear war, the Navy had an important role in meeting Soviet challenges that might not necessarily bring the deterrent into play and should be sized accordingly. Naval forces also had a vital role in deterring limited war and fighting it if it occurred. It also had an 'unquestioned' role in 'imperial policing'.[17] On this basis Mountbatten won the argument on retaining a strength of 88,000 personnel; he considered he had got the Navy a 'reasonable deal – better than the Army and RAF'.[18]

He had to make a few compromises. He agreed that the two carriers west of Suez should have anti-submarine air groups, but even this concession was short-lived. Because of operational shortcomings it was decided to hasten the withdrawal of the existing ASW aircraft, the Fairey Gannet. It was replaced between 1958 and 1960 by the Whirlwind helicopter. By the time this was done Harold Watkinson was Minister of Defence and he allowed all four operational carriers to retain mixed, general-purpose air groups. From 1961 these included an improved Wessex ASW helicopter. The Gannet continued in a new form as an airborne early-warning aircraft carrying the radar formerly fitted to the Skyraiders.

A new Navy was taking shape. The battleships disappeared, HMS *Vanguard* finally going for scrap in 1960. The last of the Hermes-class light fleet carriers (*Hermes* herself) was completed in 1959 with a fully angled deck and steam catapults to operate the latest aircraft. *Victorious*, the only wartime carrier to receive a full rebuild, also finally joined the fleet, similarly equipped. Both also carried the latest 984 three-dimensional radar, combined with a pioneering Comprehensive Display System, analogue action information system. They carried high-performance swept-wing aircraft, the single-seat Scimitar and two-seat all-weather Sea Vixen for which Red Beard 15-kiloton nuclear weapons became available in 1961. The longer-ranged Buccaneer strike aircraft replaced the Scimitar from 1962.

The fleet carrier *Eagle* went into the yards for a massive reconstruction with a fully digital Action Data Automation system. While she was in rebuild, *Centaur* backed up *Ark Royal, Victorious* and *Hermes*. Planning for a totally new carrier also continued, with an ambitious programme of new ships to be begun in the mid-1960s. Two existing light fleet carriers were converted into commando ships with Whirlwind (later Wessex) transport helicopters, and two modern assault ships finally ordered (after a decade's wait, when other priorities had seemed more pressing). The Royal Marines were concentrated into an expanded commando force.

The first of ten planned County-class guided missile destroyers were begun, combining four 4.5-inch guns with Seaslug and Seacat anti-air missiles and a Wessex ASW helicopter. Unable to carry the 984 radar and retain general-purpose capability, they were fitted with pioneering digital data links to operate with the carriers. The programme was eventually cut back to eight, the second group of four carrying Seaslug Mk 2 and a digital combat data system of their own. A new general-purpose frigate programme also began to replace the ships designed for specialized convoy escort roles. These new ships, the first-rate Leanders and second-rate Tribals, were designed primarily as task-force ASW escorts and 'Gulf gunboats' respectively. They carried small Wasp helicopters, primarily for ASW weapons delivery.

Some rationalization took place East of Suez. The East Indies Squadron, no longer welcome at Ceylon, was combined with the existing Far East Fleet in a base at Singapore that grew into the Royal Navy's major operational centre. It was, however, in the Middle East, where a Rear Admiral at Bahrain now commanded the Gulf deployment, that the first major East of Suez emergency took place. The operation in support of Kuwait in 1961 allowed *Bulwark*, the first of the commando ships, to demonstrate its effectiveness. In the aftermath, the Chiefs of Staff carried out a study which placed even more emphasis on the importance of intervention to ensure the correct kind of successor regime as decolonization gathered strength.

The 1962 Naval Estimates revealed the almost total commitment to East of Suez and amphibious operations by identifying no other role of the Navy than the following scenario:

In peacetime the ships of the Royal Navy are stationed all over the world. But when danger threatens they can be quickly assembled to take their place with the Army and Royal Air Force in combined operations to meet the threat. Every ship has her part to play. The commando ships and assault ships put ashore the spearhead of the landing forces with their guns, tanks and vehicles. The aircraft carriers provide reconnaissance and tactical strike ahead of the landing; air defence for the seaborne force; and close support for the troops ashore – especially when this cannot be done, either adequately or at all, by land based aircraft. Cruisers and escorts reinforce the air and anti-submarine cover, direct our aircraft and give warning of the enemy's and use their guns for bombardment if required. Submarines provide additional protection against hostile submarines and carry out reconnaissance and minelaying. The minesweepers clear a way to the land.[19]

This document was also able to report the departure of the last one hundred conscripts. The Royal Navy, a little larger than intended in 1958 at 94,300 men and women, was entirely 'regular' by 1962.

Amphibious operations seemed much more natural to most naval officers than the new role that was somewhat reluctantly accepted at the end of 1962 – that of the deployment of the strategic nuclear deterrent in nuclear submarines. Submarines of a more conventional type had always been important in the postwar Navy. The need to operate close to a hostile Soviet coast and to exercise British surface ASW escorts led the operational force to rise to a peak of over 40 boats in the mid-1950s. Despite experiments with hydrogen peroxide, the more conventional fast-battery electric drive was chosen for postwar conversions and new construction, although the latter was delayed and the first completely new Porpoise-class fast-battery drive boat did not enter service until 1961.

By that time, a nuclear-powered submarine programme was well under way, helped by the strong advocacy of Mountbatten, to whose enthusiasm for technical novelty and innovation the idea appealed. Considerations of prestige were also important. The nuclear submarine was being referred to in some quarters as the new capital ship. A navy with Britain's traditions could not forego sharing in this vital new dimension of naval warfare. The help of the US Navy was enlisted. Mountbatten promised Admiral Rickover, head of the American nuclear propulsion programme, that he would be allowed to interview all British nuclear submariners as he did American. The First Sea

Lord knew he could not deliver but the ploy worked. After a complete propulsion system had been purchased from the United States, HMS *Dreadnought*, Britain's first nuclear-powered attack submarine (SSN), was at sea on her trials before the end of 1962. An all-British nuclear submarine, *Valiant*, was already under construction. The SSNs could even be fitted into the East of Suez context, given their long range and the delivery of large surface ships to potential enemies such as the Indonesians.

Expertise in nuclear submarines also meant that the option was there to put the British deterrent to sea, where it was less vulnerable to pre-emption. This appealed to Mountbatten, but both he and the service as a whole had reservations. Led by Mountbatten, the Royal Navy was at the forefront of the 'nuclear sufficiency' debate, arguing that, in a world of mutual nuclear deterrence, scarce defence resources should be spent on usable limited war forces rather than over-provision on thermonuclear striking forces.[20] A ballistic missile firing nuclear submarine (SSBN) programme would be a diversion for the Navy. It would also tread firmly on the toes of the RAF, a service the Navy wished to see as fully committed as possible to the role of strategic bombing – for the time being at least. If the junior service lost strategic bombing, its competition with the Navy for the role of providing Britain's limited war air resources would become more intense.

With a carrier replacement an increasingly pressing issue, the Navy wished to avoid such a conflict, especially as naval airmen were becoming the dominant faction in the East of Suez Navy. Mountbatten's successor as First Sea Lord, his old associate Sir Charles Lambe, although not himself an airman, was an ex-carrier captain and a strong supporter of naval air power. Lambe's successor (following his premature retirement through illness) was Sir Casper John, the first naval aviator to hold the post. New carriers would be needed in the 1970s and this was top priority.

When, to the relief of the Admiralty, the expensive Blue Streak intermediate-range ballistic missile was cancelled the Navy was happy to see it replaced by the Skybolt air-launched ballistic missile. Polaris, it was thought, would be a logical follow-on to the latter as a limited national contribution to the overall Western deterrent and some preliminary planning took place. However, the Naval Staff wished the carrier question to be settled first. Unfortunately for them, the Americans cancelled Skybolt. Polaris was the only realistic alternative and its procurement was agreed at a meeting between Prime Minister Macmillan and President Kennedy in Nassau in December.

The impact on the rest of the Navy was limited by the favourable terms of the Polaris sales agreement, the efficiency of the sophisticated Polaris management team and, not least, the internal budgetary formula, which shared some of the costs of the project across the three services. Nevertheless, the effect on the RAF was as predicted. With military aircraft more expensive than ever, the Air Staff doubted whether Britain could afford its own ambitious programme of new strike aircraft and fighters, and the air groups for a new carrier fleet. The RAF and the Royal Navy had become competitive suppliers of tactical air power. The RAF had no other role whereas the Royal Navy had others upon which it could fall back. The stakes for the former service in this struggle were thus rather higher.

In the early 1960s the Admiralty, fearing RAF opposition, had tried to develop the idea of a joint RAF/RN carrier-based air force for use East of Suez. The RAF, in return, began to formulate the 'Island Stance', a scheme of bases to provide a land-based alternative, supplemented perhaps by smaller carrier-type vessels to act as forward bases for the P1154 short take-off/vertical landing (STOVL) fighter. There was deadlock between the two services, but Watkinson, and his successor, Peter Thorneycroft, were favourable to the joint idea, especially by the Admiralty's apparent willingness to investigate the possibility of using the RAF's version of the P1154. Despite strong opposition from both the Air Ministry and the Treasury and after two full Cabinet meetings, approval was obtained on 30 July 1963 for one new 53,000-ton fleet carrier CVA01 to be built to replace *Victorious* and *Ark Royal*.[21]

The following year the context of British defence policy making changed fundamentally. Firstly, in April 1964 the three separate service ministries were combined into a unified Ministry of Defence and the Board of Admiralty ceased to exist. The latter was replaced within the new ministry by an 'Admiralty Board' subject to the overall Defence Council.[22] Six months later, Labour resumed office after

13 years in opposition, committed to a self-consciously reformist line. The new Government inherited a defence budget that was steadily rising but which, nevertheless, could not fully cover commitments. The Royal Navy was costing more than it had since 1947 in real terms and its personnel strength was growing, from 94,300 in 1962 to 98,600 in 1965.

The increased numbers were, however, insufficient to meet extended commitments. East of Suez was no mere presence. In 1964 the carrier *Centaur* put down army mutinies in newly independent East African states and an extended Confrontation had begun with Indonesia. Overworked sailors were leaving the service in significant numbers, creating manning difficulties and further compounding the problem of 'over-stretch', as the new Government called it. The Wilson administration and its strong-minded Defence Minister, Denis Healey, were determined to produce a healthier relationship of inputs to outputs in defence policy, while reducing the burden of defence on an unhealthy economy. The Government as a whole was most unwilling to withdraw from East of Suez; indeed, its commitment to a worldwide role was, if anything, greater than that of its Conservative predecessor. Nevertheless, it wished to fulfil its peacekeeping and limited war responsibilities in the most cost-effective manner possible.

As Healey's Defence Review began, the Royal Navy and RAF put their respective cases. The new bureaucratic structure picked out the weaknesses in the Navy's forensic skills. The centralized Defence Secretariat would no longer provide the committed pro-single service support the dedicated and experienced Admiralty civil servants had once done. The RAF trained its officers to sell the service in high places. The Royal Navy did not put as much stress on staff training and placed most emphasis on practical officership. It was to pay the price for this limitation. Healey was persuaded by the apparent strength of the RAF's case, and the Navy Minister could no longer, in the new MOD structure, put his service case directly before the Cabinet. The Island Stance was adopted and CVA01 (for which the name *Queen Elizabeth* had been chosen but not published) cancelled. Although *Ark Royal* was to be given a major refit to sustain a carrier force as long as possible, the RAF would provide the air support East of Suez when the carriers disappeared.

The blow stunned the Royal Navy. The First Sea Lord, Admiral Sir David Luce, and the Navy Minister, Christopher Mayhew, both resigned. Although the rest of the East of Suez Navy was to remain, including the commando carriers, the newly delivered assault ships and their impressive and modern escorts, the carriers were the essential feature of the Navy's self-image as a first-class fleet. Yet there were those within the service who had doubts about the overconcentration on carriers: some submariners and surface sailors had alternative priorities and those in charge of the Royal Navy's manpower recognized the burden that retention of a carrier force would put on service manpower.

The new First Sea Lord, Sir Varyl Begg, himself a gunner and therefore the archetypal 'surface' sailor, presided over a major reassessment of the Navy's future role, size and shape. In April 1966 a Future Fleet Working Party was set up under the chairmanship of Rear Admiral J. H. Adams. Adams was appointed the first Assistant Chief of Naval Staff (Policy), a post created as a direct counterpart to the Assistant Chief of Air Staff (Plans and Policy) who had led the anti-carrier campaign. The Working Party accepted the Government's commitment to Britain's economic health and a cap on defence expenditure. It recognized that Britain's interests East of Suez were fast diminishing. The Royal Navy's future role was shifting to seas closer to home, where the growing nuclear parity between East and West and improvements in Soviet naval capabilities promised greater scope for applications of naval force beneath the nuclear threshold.

The Working Party explored a number of studies, most notably an escort cruiser. Such a vessel, designed to carry anti-submarine helicopters and surface-to-air missiles, had been studied since 1960, either as a complement to carriers East of Suez, relieving them of the necessity to carry ASW aircraft, or as the largest ship required to fight submarines in the Atlantic. Various layouts and sizes were considered, a process which the Working Party continued. When its report was presented in August there were eight 'large ship' studies, most of which were also able to operate derivatives of the subsonic vertical/ short take-off and landing P1127 development aircraft (which underwent carrier trials). Adams's enthusiasm for this concept caused a serious clash between him and the First Sea Lord, who would not countenance any reopening of the carrier controversy. When the report was presented to the Board in October and November most opinion was against the P1127 and it was decided that the cruiser should be kept as small as possible, perhaps only a further enlargement of the Type 82 destroyer. This enlarged frigate was armed both with the Sea Dart anti-air and Ikara ASW missile and had been primarily designed to escort the carriers. A more austere Type 19 frigate would maintain hull numbers for constabulary duties. The programme was eight 82s and thirteen 19s in 1971–6, for a total frigate/destroyer force of 90.[23]

It was acknowledged that, as an escort, the Type 82 was too large and expensive and the programme was cut back to one ship, HMS *Bristol*. The Working Party explored a number of destroyer, frigate and patrol vessel studies of various sizes from 1200 tons to 4500.[24] Its report was briefed to Healey and a Board subcommittee appointed to consider its findings. By mid-1967 three new classes of ship were being planned: the cruiser, a smaller Sea Dart destroyer and a new Leander-successor frigate.

The Working Party had pointed out that the Government's planned budgetary allocations were insufficient to meet commitments both East and West of Suez. The old imperial economic order was breaking down. Britain's trade with Europe was increasing, as was the trade of other sterling-area nations with countries outside. There was no longer any certainty that money spent defending sterling-area countries East of Suez would automatically come back to Britain as it traditionally did. It might well be a loss in balance-of-payments terms. When anti-imperialist sentiment within the governing party aligned with an increasingly pro-European foreign policy stance, the Government was drawn inexorably towards withdrawal from East of Suez. With confrontation with Indonesia ending and withdrawal from Aden being advanced, the Eastern deployments seemed obvious ones from which to make the further savings required to restore faith in a failing pound. In 1967 it was decided first to halve expenditure East of Suez and then to withdraw by the mid-1970s, although a 'special capability', including perhaps naval and amphibious forces, would be retained for use in the area. This compromise lasted only a few months. The economic situation worsened rapidly in the second half of 1967 and, in the aftermath of devaluation in January 1968, it was decided to withdraw from East of Suez by 1971, and withdraw all the carriers in that year.

Given the salience of East of Suez to the Royal Navy's rationale for survival, these events posed a serious challenge, but a new First Sea Lord, Sir Michael Le Fanu, and Navy Minister, David Owen, provided dynamic and innovative leadership. A new role was soon asserted for amphibious forces on the northern flank of NATO and the expanded commando force suffered only marginal reductions. Anti-submarine warfare was given a new lease of life, along with the British contribution to the NATO Striking Fleet. In 1968 an 18,700-ton, nine-helicopter 'through deck' design was chosen for the ASW cruiser.

The British were also considering a return to the Mediterranean, where the permanent naval presence had been reduced to negligible proportions to sustain East of Suez. Only two destroyers and six minesweepers remained based at Malta by 1966, and even these were often deployed elsewhere. In 1967 the post of C.-in-C. Allied Forces Mediterranean, hard-fought for a decade and a half before, was abolished and a combined British Western Fleet command created. The growth of Soviet naval deployments in the area provided the rationale for periodic deployments of major units released by the East of Suez run-down – assault ships, commando carriers and fleet carriers. It was stated that the Mediterranean might become the primary deployment area for Britain's amphibious forces after 1971.

That there would still be more calls for British maritime forces even further afield was shown by the Royal Navy's involvement in continued peacekeeping operations in the Caribbean, in Hong Kong and in the Beira Patrol (necessitated by Rhodesia's unilateral declaration of independence). Indeed, naval forces were to form a major part of the general capability that would be retained for areas outside NATO. Nevertheless, the major role of the Royal Navy would be significantly recast. This had been spelt out in March 1968:

our withdrawal from overseas will enable us to increase the number of ships at immediate readiness for NATO's shield forces, and so enable us to continue to play a leading part among the European navies in the NATO maritime alliance ... The growth of Soviet maritime strength ... has underlined the importance of the shield forces especially in relation to the flanks of Europe, Scandinavia and the Mediterranean, where the increase in the Soviet naval presence has been most evident. Such shield forces were not, it was argued, intended to fight a full-scale battle of the Atlantic, but they would 'identify aggression when it occurred' and prevent it developing into a more serious conflict.[25]

Despite the election of a new Conservative Government in 1970, pledged to reverse the military withdrawal to Europe, the even greater commitment of that Government to Britain's economic and political integration with Europe mitigated against a reassertion of the East of Suez policy. The withdrawal duly went ahead in 1971 and the following year the deployment of operational major surface combatants and amphibious ships looked very different from what it had been eight years before. In 1964 there had been 28 assets in European waters, 35 East of Suez, two in the South Atlantic at Simonstown and two in the West Indies. In 1972 there were 51 in European waters, six East of Suez and three in the West Indies (the South Atlantic Station had been abolished in 1967). There had been only a 10 per cent reduction in total strength.[26]

The Heath administration decided to retain the recently rebuilt HMS *Ark Royal*, which operated Buccaneers and American-built Phantoms for most of the rest of the 1970s, but *Eagle* was decommissioned and *Hermes* converted to a commando carrier to replace *Albion*. The two rebuilt cruisers, *Blake* and *Tiger*, effectively replaced the two carriers as interim ASW helicopter cruisers.

The withdrawal from East of Suez allowed the entire British fleet to be brought under a single command. Under the Commander-in-Chief Fleet (CINCFLEET) were three subordinate seagoing flag officers, Flag Officer First and Second Flotillas (FOF1 and FOF2) and Flag Officer Carriers and Amphibious Ships (FOCAS). The two flotillas were composed of cruisers and guided missile destroyers, together with frigate squadrons, divided up on a geographical basis (Portsmouth and Chatham ships First Flotilla; Devonport ships Second Flotilla). As an official source put it, they were 'designed to provide a clear and positive chain of command for operational and support purposes and to provide the maximum possible association of each flotilla with its flag officer with benefits to fighting efficiency, training and administration'.[27] It was recognized, however, that a Flotilla Flag Officer, when in command of an operational task force, would exercise tactical command over any available ship, regardless of which notional flotilla it belonged to. FOCAS was the administrative commander of the Royal Navy's big ships and designated commander of Carrier Group 2 of the NATO Strike Fleet. The retention of *Ark Royal* allowed FOCAS to continue his old title, but when she finally disappeared (to be replaced by new cruiser/carriers), FOCAS became FOF3 and Carrier Group 2 became Anti-Submarine Group 2.

These three officers were the Royal Navy's senior seagoing commanders. CINCFLEET himself was firmly ashore at HMS *Warrior* at Northwood. During the 1950s the then Home Fleet Commander (and NATO Commander-in-Chief Eastern Atlantic) had flown his flag at sea in HMS *Vanguard*, and his enlarged staff had to be accommodated in the apartments fitted for royal tours and the empty magazine spaces. The requirements for space eventually outran a combatant warship's capacity and submarine depot ships were used until 1960, when the C.-in-C. moved permanently to Northwood, which had already been utilized for some years as a shore headquarters for the NATO staff and as an operational headquarters for exercises. In 1966 the NATO Channel Command was also concentrated at Northwood. This had previously been a NATO 'hat' for Commander-in-Chief Portsmouth, who, together with the other local Commanders-in-Chief, had their posts unified into a Naval Home Command under a single C.-in-C. (CINCNAVHOME) in 1967.

The Royal Navy's manpower had been reduced to 78,000 by January 1972, a reduction of 18 per cent over the 1965 peak. Of this total, some 25,000 were serving in surface ships. Both the submarine service and the Fleet Air Arm utilized 2000 men each, the latter not just serving in commando carriers and *Ark Royal*, but virtually every ship of the fleet, as the helicopter became the main ASW delivery system of the Royal Navy's escort fleet. Almost all new ships carried helicopters and some older frigates were modified to carry them. After the sinking of the Israeli destroyer *Eilath* in 1967 by Soviet-supplied anti-ship missiles, the Wasp helicopters of escorts were fitted with wire-guided AS12 anti-surface missiles to deal with the threat of missile-armed fast attack craft. The Polaris force, operational from 1968, required 3000 men, a significant extra burden; the 8000 Royal Marines represented over 10 per cent of total naval manpower. Some 38,000 naval personnel, just over half, were serving ashore in headquarters, bases and training establishments; 3500 women of the Women's Royal Naval Service (WRNS) and the Queen Alexandra's Royal Naval Nursing Service (QUARNNS) made up the balance of total naval personnel strength.

During the 1970s a new fleet began to take shape to replace the old. The gun-armed destroyers finally disappeared from service and the Type 42 Sea Dart destroyers that had emerged from the Future Fleet Working Party began to be delivered to replace them. Their all-gas turbine propulsion had been validated by trials in the converted Type 14 *Exmouth*. Two new frigate programmes were eventually adopted. In an attempt to produce a cheaper frigate based on export models, Vosper Thornycroft designed the rakish 3100-ton Type 21 Amazon class. These replaced the diesel Type 41s and 61s. The definitive replacement for the Leander was the more expensive, 4000-ton Type 22. Laying down the first, *Broadsword*, was delayed until 1975 by problems with its advanced Sea Wolf short-range anti-missile missile and two extra Type 21s were built instead, bringing total numbers to eight. Delivery of Leanders ended in 1973 but the class began to be modernized with Ikara ASW or Exocet surface-to-surface missiles. The latter were procured to make up for the limited anti-surface strike potential of the post carrier Navy; they were also fitted to the four later Counties and the new frigates. The SSN programme also went steadily ahead after the hiatus caused by the construction of the Polaris force. A boat of improved design was developed to supplement the five Valiant class. The first of six, *Swiftsure*, was commissioned in 1973 and the last, *Splendid*, in 1981, in which year was launched the first of the next class of seven, *Trafalgar*, having been ordered in 1977.

It was large surface ships, however, which seemed to provide a more obvious index of naval capability. There was much rejoicing, therefore, when the first of the through-deck command cruisers, HMS *Invincible*, was ordered in 1973. At that time it was still not entirely clear whether this class would operate the Harrier V/STOL fighter, the decision being delayed by the Government's political and economic problems, which culminated in its premature fall. The returning Labour administration, however, finally ordered a special Sea Harrier for *Invincible* and two extra ships of the class that were also laid down. In the meantime, the commando carriers were given an ASW role to fill the gap between the withdrawal of *Ark Royal* and the delivery of the Invincibles. Despite much rhetoric of Defence Review and cuts in expenditure, expenditure on the Navy increased under Wilson and his traditionally pro-Navy successor, James Callaghan. In 1978–9 as much was being spent on Naval General Purpose Forces in real terms as in 1966–7.

Withdrawals, however, continued. The Labour Defence Review of 1975 officially liquidated naval commitments outside the Eastern Atlantic and Channel areas. The last British warship finally sailed from Malta in 1979, although Hong Kong and the West Indies remained significant commitments outside European waters, as did the Falkland Islands with its ice patrol vessel, the retention of which was insisted on by the Foreign Office. Group deployments also continued to go on world cruises to demonstrate the global dimension of the residual general capability.

Increased budgets also reflected the increased costs of new construction, such vessels as the Type 22 frigates being over four times more expensive than the Leanders. The programme might have been curtailed at four ships rather than the originally planned 12 but the Americans offered the advanced Classic Outboard electronic warfare system that ensured the construction of a lengthened Batch 2 design, the first pair of which were ordered in April 1979.[28]

Even a rising naval budget was not sufficient to sustain naval strength without signs of obvious strain. The Wilson and Callaghan administrations were able to maintain operational strength and much of the building programme, but only at the cost of an increasingly dissatisfied service. The pay of naval personnel was limited, along with other Government servants, and conditions of service suffered by the deliberate cuts in 'tail' rather than 'teeth'. The Royal Navy, buffeted by decades of apparent cuts, was in no mood to take rational stock of the situation and recognize its continued and sustained level of capability. The Government, struggling to maintain solvency, could not increase the budget enough to maintain both fleet strength and morale. By 1979 the efflux of men and women from the service was reaching crisis proportions, forcing the withdrawal of units from the active fleet in significant quantities.

This was but part of a more general perception of crisis that was taking hold of Britain as the 1970s came to an end. The old postwar consensus was breaking down. The Conservative opposition was developing radical new economic ideas that it had a chance to put into effect when the Callaghan Government staggered to its fall in 1979 and Mrs Thatcher won the ensuing election. The postwar era was coming to an end. A new way forward was about to be mapped out, although it turned out less to the Royal Navy's liking than most of its personnel expected.

9 The Falklands and After

The Thatcher administration claimed to be pro-defence and able to solve the manpower problem by increasing service pay, but that only exacerbated the problem of funding the other aspects of the Royal Navy and the defence programme in general. After signs that the defence budget could not be controlled as well as the Prime Minister would have liked, a new economy-minded Defence Minister, John Nott, was appointed to sort out the situation. Nott recognized that the planned programmes of the services were still too large to be fitted within expected defence budgets. The Callaghan Government had signed up to a 3 per cent increase in real terms. This had been endorsed by Thatcher but, as Nott put it in his memoirs, 'no-one in the government when I joined the MOD had suggested that the 3 % annual growth target might last beyond 1983–4, yet public commitments to the equipment programme were being given on the assumption that 3 per cent volume growth would continue until 1989–90. This would have bankrupted the exchequer'.[1] As Nott carried out a root-and-branch examination of the defence programme as a whole, the Naval Staff, led by the First Sea Lord, Admiral Sir Henry Leach, found themselves very much on the defensive. Nott was not anti-Navy, as they suspected, but felt constrained to put the Navy's major commitment, the contribution to NATO's defences in the Eastern Atlantic (Eastlant), last in his list of priorities after the strategic deterrent, defence of the home base, and the land and air contribution to mainland Europe.

It was not that the Royal Navy as an institution had no role to play in the revised Nott strategy. Indeed, it provided the top priority defence commitment; the strategic deterrent that the Government had announced in 1980 would take the form of the American submarine-launched Trident ballistic-missile system. This would replace Polaris, which had been modified in a highly expensive Chevaline programme (a pair of hardened warheads, one mounted, together with decoys, on a manoeuvring space vehicle) that went into service in 1982. John Nott now insisted that Trident's costs should in future come more directly out of the naval budget.

The Royal Navy also had a vital part to play in Nott's second priority, defence of the home base, on which the Minister put an emphasis some felt was overdue. In the decade before 1981, the increasing enclosure of the ocean and the wider dispersion of the technologies of maritime mineral extraction had transformed the utilization of sea resources. Although British fishermen were edged steadily out of their traditional northern fishing areas, despite a dogged rearguard action fought by British warships against purpose-built Icelandic coastguard vessels, the opening up of the North Sea oilfields and the declaration of a 200-mile fishing zone around the waters of the British Isles meant that the old established constabulary role of the Navy became much more important. Nine offshore patrol vessels, the Isles and Castle classes, had been launched between 1976 and 1981, to help police the 'offshore tapestry', along with the coastal MCM vessels traditionally used in the role. Nott's increased emphasis on home defence, coupled with a greater perception of the mining threat to the strategic deterrent, meant significant resources would be devoted to relatively unspectacular small craft. The programme of highly expensive Hunt-class hunter/sweepers continued to a total of 13 units and the programme for a dozen reservist manned minesweepers with 'Extra Deep Armed Team Sweeps' was continued unchanged.

The relegation of the flourishing Eastlant navy to fourth place at the bottom of the priority list, below the Continental Commitment, alarmed the regular Navy deeply, especially as it was coupled with a change in how the Eastlant task was to be fulfilled. The Secretary of State, perplexed to find that the US Navy was talking about a rather different kind of Atlantic battle from that described by Leach and his colleagues, was unimpressed by the Naval Staff's arguments for their existing fleet. Nott looked to others who, like Sir Ronald Mason, his Chief Scientific Adviser, found the defence of shipping convoys a somewhat 'fragile' scenario.[2] Submariners also gave Nott unofficial briefings on the utility of their platforms. The Secretary of State thus chose to meet the future Eastlant commitment primarily with submarines, both conventional and nuclear, together with RAF shore-based aircraft and a new generation of cheaper Type 23 frigates with long-range towed array sonars.

Nott regarded the surface fleet as primarily intended to fulfil a reasserted limited intervention role out of the NATO area. His supplementary White Paper 'The Way Forward' (Cmnd. 8288) stated that the Royal Navy had a 'particularly valuable role' in such 'efforts' for which British 'needs, outlooks and interests gave [her] a special role and special duty'. Nott planned 'to resume from 1982 onwards the practice of sending a substantial naval task group on long detachment for visits and exercises in the South Atlantic, Caribbean, Indian Ocean and further east. We intend to make particular use of the new carriers with Sea Harriers and helicopters in "out of area" deployment'.[3] Nevertheless this required fewer ships than previously planned and Chatham Dockyard was to close. The active frigate/destroyer force would come down to 42 with eight in reserve. A planned Type 44 destroyer with Sea Dart Mk. 2 was cancelled along with the improved missile, and the modernization programme to convert Leanders into ships with capabilities akin to the Type 22 frigate was abandoned. Most controversially, the carrier *Invincible* was to be sold to the Australians, leaving only her two sisters, *Illustrious* and *Ark Royal*, with the Royal Navy. It was also intended to decommission the two assault ships, *Fearless* and *Intrepid*, over the next two years, but the decision to go to Trident D5 rather than C4 allowed a rearrangement of the programme releasing funds for their retention. The Americans had also raised anxieties about their disappearance.

The Nott process was a bruising one with lasting effects on the higher political direction of the Royal Navy. Between 1964 and 1967 the Navy had been represented in the unified ministry by a relatively senior Minister of Defence (Royal Navy). In 1967 the ministers at this level became 'functional' rather than single-service and the latter representation was reduced to Under Secretary of State level. The last Labour Parliamentary Under Secretary (Navy) had been the sympathetic former Fleet Air Arm officer Dr Patrick Duffy, who was succeeded in 1979 by another former naval person, Keith Speed.

Speed loyally and publicly backed Leach in his anti-Nott campaign and was subsequently sacked by Mrs Thatcher, who also abolished the post. Speed was thus the last ever Navy Minister. Nott wanted Speed transferred rather than dismissed, but was overruled. He was, however, able to defend Leach from dismissal for his contacts with opponents of the review (including former Prime Minister, Callaghan). Another change shortly afterwards was making the Chief of Defence Staff the independent senior defence adviser to the Government. Leach opposed but could not prevent this.[4]

The controversy over the 1981 Defence Review had not died down when Leach received a magnificent opportunity to demonstrate the continued utility of his forces. The Argentinian invasion of the Falkland Islands was prompted by the withdrawal of the ice patrol ship *Endurance* and a misplaced perception of a British loss of both capability and nerve. With little thought for the risks, but with a great deal of expectation of positive pro-Navy results if success was achieved, two Task Forces, one of carriers and amphibious forces (Task Force 317) and one of submarines (Task Force 324), were sent to the South Atlantic. The flagship of TF 317's carrier group was *Hermes*, refitted to operate Sea Harriers after a few years in the 1970s as a commando ship. She provided twice the air capability of HMS *Invincible*, which accompanied her. The amphibious ships built for East of Suez, *Fearless* and *Intrepid* and the RFA manned landing ships logistic (LSLs), reinforced by ships taken up from trade (STUFT), carried land forces to recover the Islands. The screen was provided by a mix of the latest Type 42s, 21s and 22s plus older Counties, Leanders and Type 12s. Even the SSN force was able to make a convincing display of its capabilities by despatching the old gun-armed cruiser *General Belgrano* rapidly and efficiently.

The cost was significant. At the outset of the conflict the Type 42 HMS *Sheffield* was hit and sunk by an Argentine Exocet missile launched from an Etendard aircraft. *Sheffield*'s operations-room team, not yet attuned to the dynamics of a war zone, failed to cope adequately with the engagement. Two Exocets also sank the transport *Atlantic Conveyor*, after being decoyed onto the merchant ship by the chaff countermeasures of the escorts, and a land-based Exocet damaged the destroyer *Glamorgan*. The Type 21 frigate HMS *Avenger*, with the support of the missiles of HMS *Exeter*, was, however, able to fight off a combined Etendard and Skyhawk strike. The main threat came from bombers, especially the Argentine Naval Skyhawks with their retarded bombs that, together with Air Force Daggers, sank HMS *Ardent*. The Argentine aircraft were forced by TF 317's defences to fly too low for their conventionally fused bombs to explode. Several ships were hit by unexploded bombs and had lucky escapes but the bomb in the Type 21 *Antelope* exploded while being dismantled and the ship was lost. The tactics of operating Sea Wolf-equipped Type 22s in 'combos' with Sea Dart-equipped 42s proved problematical. *Glasgow* had a lucky escape when a bomb went through her without exploding. *Coventry* was less lucky, being bombed and sunk after her partner *Broadsword* had had her attention distracted by missile malfunction and an unexploded but still damaging bomb hit. Most tragically of all, the inexperience of the troops being landed at Bluff Cove led to the loss of *Sir Galahad*, with heavy loss of life. In all, 84 Royal Navy personnel were killed in the Falklands campaign, a remarkably low loss rate considering the losses of ships. The helicopter and survival suit had transformed the chances of living through a sinking.

The achievement outweighed the losses. The carriers and their Sea Harrier fighters, armed with the latest AIM-9L Sidewinder missiles, had been particularly successful. RAF Harrier GR3s, which concentrated on the ground attack role, later supplemented them. Using these aircraft, *Hermes* and *Invincible* accounted for 33 enemy aircraft in the air and on the ground for the loss of no aircraft in air-to-air combat. Six Sea Harriers and four RAF Harriers had been lost to ground fire and operational accidents.[5]

There is a commonly held view that the Falklands War led to a major reappraisal of John Nott's policies. In fact, there is a good case to be made that, although the war did have some marginal effects, the basic direction mapped out in 1981 was not greatly altered by the war and that policy remained much as Nott had planned. The Secretary of State made plain that this would be the case in a loose Foreword inserted into the Statement on the Defence Estimates published in June 1982. The fact that the pre-Falklands Statement should be published unamended was itself indicative of the stress on continuity. 'The events of recent weeks,' Nott argued, should not 'obscure the fact that the main threat to the security of the United Kingdom is from the nuclear and conventional forces of the Soviet Union and her Warsaw pact allies.' It was, however, 'right that we should consider whether any adjustments or changes of emphasis are now required'.[6] The paper reiterated the emphasis on the threats out of area where it was 'our intention to sustain and where appropriate expand our activities', including maintaining a capacity for 'intervention for deterrent or defensive purposes'.[7]

In his supporting remarks in the House of Commons, Nott announced that Falklands losses in naval aircraft would be replaced and that reserves would be increased. To cover the four ships lost in the Falklands, a ninth Type 22 frigate would be ordered (a new HMS *Sheffield*), while three older destroyers slated for early disposal would be retained, *Fife, Glamorgan* and *Bristol*. The definitive replacement of the four lost ships was still under consideration. The Type 23 frigate was upgraded into a general-purpose frigate with a gun for shore bombardment and a helicopter. It was later announced that, in order to maintain two carriers in commission at all times, *Invincible* would be maintained in RN hands.

The supplementary White Paper, 'The Falklands Campaign: The Lessons' (Cmnd. 8758), was published at the end of 1982. This insisted that the Government had not changed its mind as to where the major threat lay. 'The remorseless growth in the size and sophistication of the Soviet armed forces, and the disposition of Soviet leaders to exploit their military power for political purposes – directly or indirectly – continue unabated. It is still in Europe that we and our allies face the greatest concentration of Warsaw Pact forces.' Cmnd. 8758 confirmed Cmnd. 8288's four main roles for the armed forces, which remained 'the priority of our defence effort – and the enhancement and modernization of the forces devoted to these tasks must still have first call on our resources'.

Cmnd. 8758 then went on to 'Out-of-Area' commitments. It reminded readers how 8288 had drawn 'attention to the significance of threats posed to Western interests outside the NATO area', and how the maintenance of a 'capability to intervene unilaterally or with Allies either to protect our national interests or in response to a request for help from our friends [had] just been demonstrated so effectively in the Falklands Campaign'. The policy of successive governments had been that operations out-of-area should be carried out by forces whose primary role was NATO-assigned. The war had demonstrated that these forces had 'the basic characters of flexibility which make them well suited to respond to unforeseen challenges arising outside Europe'. Accordingly there was a renewed emphasis on the amphibious capability of 3 Commando Brigade which 'would give us a greatly improved ability to respond to the unforeseen in a flexible and rapid way'. The retention of the two LPDs was confirmed. In a very John Nott-like way, Cmnd. 8758 concluded this section by saying that 'we should have liked to have done more in this area but there has been little margin within the defence programme for additions of this kind in recent years'.

This statement put the planned 'adjustments' to the defence programme firmly in the context of 'the success of last year's review of the defence programme in matching resources to our revised forward plans'. The defence budget was to be increased beyond the planned 3 per cent real-terms increase to 1985–6, to pay for the costs of replacements and the necessary Falklands garrison. This allowed 'significant force enhancements'. In addition to a last Batch 2 Type 22 frigate, HMS *Coventry*, to be laid down with the new *Sheffield* in 1984, four more Type 22s to a Batch 3 design, with a 4.5-inch gun – *Cornwall, Cumberland, Campbeltown* and *Chatham* – were the definitive Falklands replacements; they were laid down annually from 1983. A replacement for the Landing Ship Logistic, *Sir Galahad*, was also ordered. The withdrawal of HMS *Endurance*, whose proposed withdrawal had done much to encourage the Argentine invasion, was cancelled.

The frigate/destroyer fleet was not to be rapidly cut to 50 ships, as planned under Cmnd. 8288 (of which eight would be in reserve in the Standby Squadron). Instead, to April 1984 numbers would be retained at about 55. In addition to the destroyers already announced for retention, three unmodernized Leander-class frigates, three Ikara Leanders and a Type 12 frigate were reprieved. Improved point defences would be fitted to all the carriers, the LPDs, the DLG Bristol and the Type 42 destroyers. Airborne early-warning Sea Kings were to be provided for the carriers and ammunition stocks were to be increased.

The 1982–3 defence budget of £14.1 billion maintained the 3 per cent real-terms increase, increased by Falklands costs to £14.4 billion. In 1983 the re-elected Prime Minister resisted Treasury pressure and reconfirmed the Falklands cash windfall for equipment replacements. She also extended the annual 3 per cent growth rate up to 1986, together with more realistic allowances for defence-cost inflation.[8] In 1983–4 the defence budget totalled almost £16 billion, of which over £600 million was to meet Falklands costs. The budget was pushed up to over £17 billion in 1984–5 and there were hopes of further real-terms increases into 1986–7, but the 1985 Defence Statement made it clear that 1985–6 would indeed be the last year of the 3 per cent increase. From 1986–7, when the costs of defending the Falklands were taken into account, the planned increases in defence expenditure were barely ahead of the inflation rate.

This was not enough to maintain the strength of the Royal Navy in either personnel or ships. Personnel numbers, which had peaked at over 74,000 in 1981, were reduced to less than 70,000 in 1985. The 55 frigates and destroyers of 1983 were reduced to 52 front-line ships in 1984, the year in which it was announced that the total force would be Nott's 50 units, albeit all in commission. The following year, front-line numbers had dropped to 46 and in 1986 the words 'about 50' were being used to describe the frigate/destroyer force level that dropped to 41 in 1988, smaller than the proposed Nott active fleet. Claims that the Falklands somehow saved the surface fleet need revision.

The main gain was the extra carrier, but the impact even of that was mitigated by the maintenance of only two air groups. *Hermes* was taken out of service in April 1984, over a year and a half before *Ark Royal* was commissioned. The third carrier would always be at considerable notice when in reserve or extended refit. The Royal Navy's future ambitions were also running into the wall. Announced plans for a much more enhanced third-generation OPV 3 offshore patrol vessel, to be ordered from 1986 to supplement the new Type 23s and maintain surface combatant numbers, were shelved. A major debate also went on over the replacement of specialist amphibious shipping. A 'firm decision' to keep the amphibious assault role was eventually announced in 1986, but little was done in the short term to put this into effect.

The case for these ships was helped by the renewed emphasis on Northern Flank operations with the US Forward Maritime Strategy, adopted by NATO. The year 1982 saw the first moves to conflate US fleet war planning into an overall strategy. The result was an unprecedentedly coherent doctrine of forward operations. Allied nuclear-powered attack submarines would penetrate the defended bastions where the Soviet ballistic-missile-firing boats lurked, and tie down Soviet assets in their defence. The advance of the NATO carrier Striking Fleet would be led by an RN-commanded Anti-Submarine Striking Force (as Anti-Submarine Group 2 was redesignated in 1985) of towed array surface assets centred around a British ASW carrier. The Strike Fleet would cover amphibious landings in Norway and so threaten the Soviet Northern Fleet that its main assets, both submarines and land-based missile aircraft, would be drawn out and destroyed. During the mid-1980s this concept was tested and developed in NATO exercises.[9] The Striking Fleet also began to exploit the Norwegian fiords as bastions from which to take on the Soviet forces.

Despite all this, the UK defence establishment remained very continentally orientated. Naval spokespeople might make the case that the Falklands campaign had greatly strengthened the argument for the out-of-area role. As the Vice Chief of Naval Staff, Sir Peter Stanford, put it in autumn 1983 at a conference in London: 'Did not the Falklands Campaign teach you something about the need to react to the contingent circumstances of an uncertain and violent world, outside the institutionalised Euro-Atlantic situation, in areas where conflict is endemic?'[10] The usual answer in Whitehall to this was 'Not much.' As one insider has put it, 'Consensus within the Whitehall marketplace remained firmly in favour of the continental commitment and the belief that this was as much as the Defence budget could accommodate. The Nott policy of placing maritime defence last amongst the four major components of British strategy remained in vogue, although the Falklands naval losses were to be replaced using money specially voted for the purpose from outside the Defence vote.'[11]

In 1983 the Chiefs of Staff had begun work on studies that emphasized the greater likelihood of operations outside rather than inside the NATO area. This thinking became known as the 'Fifth Pillar' of British defence policy, added to the existing four as prioritized in Cmnd. 8288. This fitted in well with the announced developments in capability mentioned in contemporary policy documents but it never became official policy. The reason was that Secretary of State Heseltine had other fish to fry, notably a reorganization of the Ministry of Defence to save resources and further the cause of functionalism and centralization rather than single-service policy making. Much of the Naval Staff was transferred to a new combined Defence Staff. It looked for a time that it might disappear entirely but the First Sea Lord, Admiral Sir John Fieldhouse, and his two colleagues persuaded the Prime Minister in person that it was necessary that they should, as continuing heads of the services, have sufficient staffs to allow them to formulate a single-service strategic view and give the Secretary of State alternative views in defence policy. Thus the First Sea Lord was left with a small (four department) staff, Naval Warfare, Operations and Training, Staff Duties and a civilian Secretariat, all under a single ACNS.

Heseltine stormed out of Mrs Thatcher's Cabinet at the beginning of 1986, to be replaced by George Younger. A new set of Chiefs of Staff had just been created. Sir William Stavely became First Sea Lord and Sir John Fieldhouse was the new Chief of Defence Staff. Mrs Thatcher wished her trusted Falklands Admiral to take office out of normal service turn. Fieldhouse had championed the out-of-area role as First Sea Lord, making 'numerous statements that emphasized operations outside the NATO area as a major reason why Britain possessed a balanced fleet'. Indeed, he even went so far as to say that Britain's worldwide role had 'increased many fold'.[12] He continued to do this as CDS, given his Falklands experience and 'his deeply held conviction that greater emphasis on a maritime out-of-area strategy was good for the Navy and ipso facto good for the country'. As he said to the Staff Colleges in 1986: 'you may confidently expect only the unexpected. The most serious threat against which we must be prepared is at the same time the least likely actually to require us to take action'.[13] There was, however, a serious problem. 'We will not be able to devote substantially greater resources directly to our out-of-area capability than we do today. We must therefore ensure that what we do is best tailored to our needs, and that we engineer flexibility and mobility into our NATO forces wherever possible so that double earmarking makes sense.'[14]

There were elements of Falklands experience in this, but the diminished threat from Gorbachev's USSR was making the overwhelming preoccupation with the Soviet and Warsaw Pact threat look misplaced. Out-of-area exercises were beginning to take more prominence, notably 'Saif Sareea' in and off Oman in 1986, supported by the aircraft carrier *Illustrious* and the Global 86 Task Group, the first RN Task Group to circumnavigate the globe for a decade. The year 1987 saw 'Purple Warrior', held in and off Scotland, designed to test operations against a fictitious island group 1500 miles from the UK. Purple Warrior involved some 20,000 personnel and 37 ships and was among the largest amphibious exercises carried out by Britain since the end of the Second World War.

A more maritime strategic emphasis for the United Kingdom was therefore stirring even before the Berlin Wall came down in 1989 and the Soviet Union collapsed at the end of 1991. Margaret Thatcher also resigned in 1990, to be replaced as Conservative Prime Minister by John Major. Despite these changes the power of the residual Continentalists in the defence establishment remained strong. Even when the post-Thatcher and post-Cold War 'Options for Change' review began, there was considerable reluctance to put too much emphasis on out-of-area. The Fifth Pillar put in a belated public appearance as Defence Role 3, 'to contribute to promoting the United Kingdom's wider security interests through the maintenance of international peace and security', but it was only to be carried out by forces procured for DR1, ensuring the security of the UK and dependent territories, and DR2, insuring against a major external threat to the UK and allies. Although the main force of Options naturally fell on the Continental commitment of ground and air forces, the Royal Navy was forced to take its share of the post-Cold War cuts. It shed all ten of its remaining relatively recently modernized Oberon-class conventional submarines, only leaving the four new conventional Upholders to accompany a dozen S and T-class SSNs (*Swiftsure* being decommissioned). The frigate and destroyer force was reduced officially to 'about 40'.[15]

The year 1991 showed that out-of-area conflict might be quite large scale. The war between Iran and Iraq had led to the deployment of the Armilla Patrol in the Gulf as early as 1980. The first ship was the ill-fated Type 42, HMS *Coventry*. Four destroyers and frigates were deployed East of Suez in 1981 to provide a continuous presence, but this was reduced to a pair of ships at the end of the year.[16] The patrols went on for the rest of the decade as the threat to British shipping increased. In 1985 a standby 'Armilla Accomplice' mine countermeasures flotilla was created at home as a contingency force. In March 1987, with increased attacks on merchant ships, the Armilla Patrol was increased to three units and in July, with a growing mine threat, the standby MCM force was activated as Operation Cimnel. Four Hunt-class minehunters, supported by the support ship *Abdiel* and repair ship *Diligence*, were deployed to the Gulf, arriving in September. *Diligence* was transferred to support the Armilla ships in November and the survey ship *Herald* replaced *Abdiel* as Cimnel support vessel in February1988. Shortly afterwards, the MCM force was reduced to three vessels which, in the middle of the year became, with Belgian and Dutch vessels, part of the Western European Union Operation Calendar II. Following the cease-fire in August, Calendar vessels joined with US, Italian and French units in Operation Team Sweep, a general mine clear-up operation.

The Armilla ships remained when Calendar assets returned to Britain in February 1989 and were still there in the shape of the Type 42 destroyer *York*, modernized Leander *Jupiter* and Type 22 frigate *Battleaxe* when Iraq invaded Kuwait in August 1990. Operation Granby was activated and absorbed both the Armilla patrol, reinforced by HMS *Gloucester*, and a flotilla of three Hunts – *Cattistock, Hurworth* and *Atherstone* – which left Rosyth, supported by HMS *Herald* from Devonport. *Diligence* was redeployed from the Falklands. The composition of the force changed in October, when the previous three Armilla ships were replaced by *Brazen, London* and *Cardiff*. The RN ships helped impose sanctions on Iraq, carrying out over 3000 challenges by April 1991. Two more minehunters arrived in January, *Dulverton* and *Ledbury*, and the next scheduled Armilla patrol *Manchester. Exeter, Brave* and *Brilliant* were sent into the Gulf. Under the command of Senior Officer Middle East, Commodore Chris Craig, the whole Granby force, along with RFAs in various roles, played a leading role in the maritime dimension of Desert Storm, the liberation of Kuwait, which began in January.[17]

The Lynx helicopters of the frigates and destroyers used their Sea Skua missiles to destroy or disable about a quarter of Iraq's naval strength and helped open the way for minehunting to begin. The Hunts cleared the way for the American battleships *Missouri* and *Wisconsin* to support the forces ashore. The British Type 42s also provided 40 per cent of the forward air cover to the US carriers and surface ships carrying out the air campaign. On 25 February *Gloucester*, covering USS *Missouri*, brought down a Silkworm anti-ship missile. After the war the MCM flotilla continued to play an important role in the international clear-up operations.

HMS *Ark Royal* was deployed to the Mediterranean in January 1991, with two escorts, and there was some pressure from the Americans to send her forward, but this was resisted in London and the UK Task Group 323.2 had to content itself with the important but secondary task of maintaining communications through the Mediterranean. This seemed to reflect prejudices within the Ministry of Defence not to give the Royal Navy too prominent a role in Granby.

That the Continentalists were still putting up a major rearguard action in Whitehall was shown by the struggle over the 1993 Long-term Costings, a kind of mini-Nott review with continued investment on the European mainland (in the new form of NATO's Allied Rapid Reaction Corps) set against deployable maritime capability. The planned new amphibious helicopter carrier, the LPH (an addition to amphibious capability to allow a two-company helicopter lift and for which tenders had been submitted in 1989 but been allowed to lapse) only escaped cancellation by the skin of its teeth. The Royal Navy had, however, to sacrifice all its conventional submarines and accept 'about 35' frigates and destroyers. The LPH herself, HMS *Ocean*, was laid down in 1994.

Financial pressure continued to increase. The Treasury revised downwards its annual planned defence provision, to little over £22 million for the mid-1990s. As the 1994 White Paper made clear, this represented reductions of £260 million for 1994–5 and £520 million for 1995–6 compared to the 1992 Public Expenditure

Survey. The budget for 1996–7 was reduced by £420 million. As the First Sea Lord, Admiral Sir Benjamin Bathurst, put it in retrospect:

The scale of the challenge we faced was considerable. The Chancellor's unified budget last year had removed a considerable sum from the defence programme and the immediate prospect for each of the Services' fighting capabilities was far from encouraging...either the front line could be replaced by finding savings elsewhere, or the challenge could be ducked, with the result that fighting capabilities would be diminished. The decision to place the front line first was entirely the right one, and it was the course of action that accorded exactly with long held Navy Board practices.[18]

There had indeed already been considerable change in the Royal Navy's shore organization, with an emphasis on rationalization. It was announced in 1991 that the bases at Portsmouth, Devonport, Rosyth and Faslane would continue but Portland was to be run down. Rosyth's Type 42 Squadron was transferred to Portsmouth to concentrate the type there, and various other closures, mainly of depots, took place. C.-in-C. Fleet's responsibilities changed. He took over command of the Royal Fleet Auxiliary, a sign of its ever-greater integration into the fighting capability of the Royal Navy. In 1994 CINCFLEET, Admiral Sir Hugo White, ceased to be NATO Commander-in-Chief Channel. Instead, he became, under Supreme Allied Commander Europe, Commander Allied Naval Forces North Western Europe. With the shrinking fleet size, a single Flag Officer Surface Flotilla had by now taken over the previous three flotilla commands, including FOF3's command of the Striking Fleet Anti-Submarine Striking Force. This was passed on to a new UK Task Group command in 1991. Another major change was the merging of the posts of Commander-in-Chief Naval Home Command with Second Sea Lord, the first incumbent of the combined post being Admiral Sir Michael Layard. His staff was housed in a new Victory Building at Portsmouth Naval Base. Another development at Portsmouth was the recommissioning in 1994 of the old HMS *Excellent* on Whale Island, which was reopened as a successor to several smaller training establishments. Not so lucky was the old HMS *Vernon* site at the Gunwharf, which was sold.

The Defence Costs Study (DCS) established at the beginning of December 1993 to meet the budgetary shortfall found only limited scope within the Royal Navy for more cuts in support. It was, however, found possible to make significant savings by closing down Rosyth as a naval base (moving the minor war vessels to Faslane and Portsmouth), the Royal Naval Air Station at Portland, three more stores/victualling depots and the Royal Marines School of Music at Deal. 'Jointery', the close co-operation of the three services, was the major theme of the DCS and an important feature was the announcement of the setting up of a Permanent Joint Headquarters at Northwood. Parts of CINCFLEET's administrative staff were transferred to Portsmouth. As 'sweeteners', various plans to enhance the front line were announced simultaneously with the Study, notably abandonment of plans to place a surface ship and a submarine in reserve, an examination of the arming of SSNs with cruise missiles and the completion of the Sandown-class single-role minehunter programme. Five of these cheaper MCM vessels had been completed before the Ministry had cancelled tenders in 1991. Now all the last seven projected assets were to be ordered to bring the total number of MCM vessels up to the planned total of 25.

'Front Line First' inevitably enhanced the major reduction in the personnel strength of the Royal Navy that marked the 1990s. Total naval personnel (including the Royal Marines and nurses) had fallen from 65,500 in 1988 to 62,100 in 1991–2 and 55,800 in 1994.[19] The trend was still rapidly downwards, as recruitment virtually stopped as a cost-cutting measure. The strength of the Royal Navy and Royal Marines was only 48,258 at the beginning of 1996 and 45,233 at the beginning of 1997.[20] In these circumstances it was more important than ever to replace older ships by more manpower-intensive assets. By the end of 1996 there were 11 Type 23 Duke frigates in service, each requiring only 174 officers and men, compared to about 250 or more in a Type 22 or Type 42. The six remaining Type 21s were sold to Pakistan in 1993–4 and the first batch of four Type 22s soon followed them out of service, being sold to Brazil in November 1994. The last Leander, the modernized HMS *Scylla*, was decommissioned in 1993.

In such a personnel climate there was no question of retaining gender discrimination in the service. Members of the WRNS (subject to the full rigours of the Naval Discipline Act since the late 1970s) began to serve at sea in surface combatants in 1990 and on 1 November 1993 the service was formally integrated into the Royal Navy. There were some initial problems in ships, but these were soon overcome.

Another important development in the mid-1990s was the replacement of the Polaris submarines by the new Trident vessels. The impressive 16,000-ton HMS *Vanguard* began her first operational patrol, with 16 Trident D-5 missiles, at the end of 1994. The arrival of *Victorious* in 1995 allowed the withdrawal of the last Resolution-class Polaris SSBN, HMS *Repulse*, the following year (the class had begun paying off in 1992). The Royal Navy had lost its free-fall multi-purpose WE177 nuclear bombs at the beginning of the decade as a result of agreement between the Americans and Russians to abolish tactical nuclear weapons at sea, but the accuracy and flexibility of Trident allowed the Vanguards to take over the 'sub-strategic' as well as strategic nuclear role.

The Government's financial problems delayed the replacement of the two LPDs. The decision to build the ships was taken in 1991, but project definition was not completed until 1994. An attempt at competitive tendering proved abortive and the contract was awarded in mid-1996. *Fearless* and *Intrepid* soldiered on, the last steam-powered Royal Navy major surface combatants. The latter was kept at 30 days' notice in reserve.

During this period the break-up of Yugoslavia allowed the Royal Navy to demonstrate its key roles in the new world order. From late 1991 a surface combatant was deployed in the Adriatic. As the crisis escalated in 1992, RN ships contributed both to Western European Union and NATO surveillance and, later, embargo operations, which were eventually combined. As peacekeeping forces were deployed ashore, a carrier with its Sea Harriers was kept on station from the beginning of 1993 to provide a national contingency capability to support the British contribution. The Government regarded its presence as a condition for the presence of a British component in UNPROFOR. *Ark Royal* and *Invincible* served turn and turn about in 1994. Their Sea Harriers operated over Bosnia as part of the NATO 'Deny Flight' operations.[21]

Despite its declining size, strategically things were moving the Royal Navy's way in the 1990s. In a context where potential enemies were unknown in terms of location and identity, the flexibility inherent in maritime forces were at a premium. This was stressed in the first public expression of 'The Fundamentals of British Maritime Doctrine' which appeared in 1995. Never before had the Royal Navy been allowed to lay out the potential and utility of maritime power with such clarity.[22] When joint British Defence Doctrine was subsequently drafted, the naval document had disproportionate impact.

In 1997 the era of Conservative government finally ended with the defeat of John Major and the election of a 'New Labour' Government under Tony Blair. George Robertson was Secretary of State for Defence; he immediately embarked on the Strategic Defence Review (SDR) promised in Labour's opposition days. The review process was unprecedentedly open and the result was a necessary departure from the incrementalism of the Major years. Published in 1998, it was a triumph for the Royal Navy. As Robertson put it baldly in the introduction to the review: 'In the post Cold War World, we must be prepared to go to the crisis, rather than have it come to us. So we plan to build two new larger aircraft carriers to project power more flexibly around the world.'[23]

Recent experience in the Gulf was quoted. There, as a result of Saddam Hussein's non-compliance with the post-1991 armistice agreement, HM *Invincible* was deployed in early 1998 from off the eastern seaboard of the United States to the Mediterranean. Her squadron of Sea Harrier FA2 fighters (the new electronic and weapons-enhanced variants in service since the mid-1990s) were reinforced by RAF Harrier GR7s. She was then sent into the Gulf, together with the frigate *Coventry* and destroyer *Nottingham*, to operate with the US carrier battle groups threatening Iraq. Carriers were particularly important in this situation, as host-nation support for Anglo-American operations was difficult to obtain. The British carrier operated up-threat of the Americans, who were impressed by the number of aircraft she could keep in the air. Exploiting the Deny Flight regime to penetrate southern Iraq, packages of 30 aircraft were flown over southern Iraq, to which *Invincible* contributed Harrier GR7s, in the laser-guided bombing role, and FA2 fighters. The crisis was defused in February before *Illustrious* arrived to relieve her sister but Operation Bolton provided a timely reminder of the utility of carrier basing in the power-projection role just as the SDR was being drawn up.

The joint air group was a symbol of an operation that had been jointly controlled from the new PJHQ. It also presaged the announcement in the SDR of Joint Force 2000, a grouping of Naval Sea Harriers and RAF Harriers. The RN's transport helicopters were to go to a Joint Helicopter command but large ASW helicopters and ships' Lynx flights would remain purely Naval.

Improved efficiency, it was hoped, would contribute to reducing defence expenditure. The SDR announced that defence expenditure by 2001–2 would be just below £23 billion, almost a billion lower in real terms than the 1998–9 figure. Britain would be spending only 4 per cent of its GDP on defence. The RN would do best out of the revised force posture, although there would be marginal reductions: the submarine force by two to ten, the destroyers and frigates by three to 32 (16 Type 23s, 5 Type 22s and 11 Type 42s) and the mine warfare vessels to 22 (two Brecons and one of the first of the Sandowns were to be sold). The SDR also confirmed the importance of the amphibious ships. The month before it appeared, in June 1998, the first of the new LPDs, *Albion*, was finally laid down at Barrow and her her sister *Bulwark* followed in 2000. With the coming into full service of *Ocean* in 1999, the opportunity was taken to put *Intrepid* for disposal, leaving *Fearless* to soldier on until the two new ships appeared. The Government was, however, committed to an amphibious squadron of eight ships, including five LSLs.

The submarine service regarded ten boats as too small a force to meet commitments, but it could console itself that it was obtaining a real power-projection role. The previous Government had decided to go for Tomahawk in some units but the SDR announced that it would be fitted in all SSNs. The first with Tomahawk, HMS *Splendid*, fired its missiles in October 1998. *Spartan* was fitted in 1999 and the first two T-class boats to get Tomahawk were fitted in 2000. The 1997 contract to build three new larger SSNs with more weapons capacity was continued, first steel being cut in 1999.

The Royal Navy now clearly saw power projection as its basic role, with the major platforms, carriers, amphibious ships and SSNs 'enabled' by the frigate/destroyer force and the MCMs. Even before the SDR, the Royal Navy had been developing the key concept of the Maritime Contribution to Joint Operations (MCJO) first conceived in 1997. MCJO soon emerged as the Navy's core operational doctrine.[24] It was intended 'to improve the meshing of the attributes of maritime forces with other elements of UK capability, both military and non military'.[25] ACNS, Rear Admiral Jonathan Band, explained in 1998:

The majority of the world's population lives and works within 200 miles of a coastline and demographically, politically and militarily, the chance of crises arising in this area, the littoral, is greater than elsewhere. It follows therefore that the strategy of a maritime nation should focus on this area for the early, swift and measured application of force for crisis resolution. In recognition of this our posture has moved away from the Cold War continental focus on the north German plain and the north Atlantic to a doctrine of integrated expeditionary operations within which the maritime contribution is crucial. Forces will be integrated in a Joint (i.e. national) and/or Combined (with allies under a coalition of the willing under unified command). They are Expeditionary in that they will be formed and tailored for crises as they occur. Of course, a maritime expeditionary force is not the fastest way to reach a crisis, nor can it necessarily deliver the heaviest punch. But a maritime force is the most rapid means of delivering a logistically sustainable, tactically coherent force package with application across the spectrum of operations, capable of early action, and without the need for geographic host nation support.[26]

MCJO allowed the service to produce a 'theory, rooted in traditional virtues yet highly relevant to, and congruent with modern needs, operational and tactical doctrine and providing as much strategic choice and operational flexibility as is likely to be possible'.[27] It certainly stood the Royal Navy in good stead for ambitious plans. By 2000 the future carrier programme was well under way, with two competing contractors and a target date for the first ship of 2012. The aircraft it would carry would be a version of the planned American Joint Strike Fighter, a major increase in capability over the Sea Harrier. The plan to replace the Type 42 destroyers with a common French/Italian/ UK Project, Horizon, came to an end in 1999 and was replaced by a programme for a national Type 45; the contract for the first batch of these was placed at the end of 2000 for delivery in 2007–9. These 7200-ton ships were to be armed with the highly advanced PAAMS antiair missile system, which remained a trinational project. They were also to be able to carry a helicopter and a Royal Marine landing party. The cruiser was being reborn.

As 2000 ended, the strength of the Royal Navy and Royal Marines was still over 42,000 men and women, but the trend was downwards and it remained to be seen how far the Government would sustain their strength both in personnel and equipment. The auguries were, however, good. The Blair administration seemed securely in office and its willingness to use force, with or without a UN mandate, had been demonstrated in Operation Allied Force against Serbia in 1999. HMS *Splendid* was able to make a significant contribution with her Tomahawks to the air campaign, resupplying from US missile stocks in theatre.[28]

The year 2000 saw operations that combined tradition with all the latest developments of joint operations. Chaos in Sierra Leone, which had already called for the presence of frigates, led to an urgent requirement for evacuation. The Amphibious Ready Group (ARG) was diverted from exercises for Operation Palliser, controlled from the new Joint Headquarters. *Ocean*, operating a joint helicopter group and landing Royal Marines, the frigate *Chatham*, two LSLs and RFA Fort Austin, were joined by the carrier *Illustrious* with a joint Harrier air group and RFA Fort George.[29] Support was also provided to forces ashore, with *Chatham* sailing up the Sierra Leone river to offer gunfire support. The frigate *Argyll* remained after the main force withdrew but the ARG was back in November to support the Sierra Leone government.

Sierra Leone was considered to be a major 'validation and demonstration' of MCJO.[30] It was also considered to be a 'key pillar achievement' of the Naval Strategic Plan, first published in October 1999. The 'key pillar objectives' looked forward to the 'secure introduction' of the planned new assets, LPDs, SSNs, Type 45s and carriers, as well as bringing strength and requirements into balance by 2002. This was related to the Future Navy Paper produced in November 2000. As ACNS, now Rear Admiral James Burnell-Nugent, put it, the essence of this future Navy was 'versatility'. This was seen in current equipment such as the Invincible-class carrier or Type 23 frigate, both of which were performing far beyond their original design parameters. For the future, versatility would be built in from the start 'so that across our capabilities we can more easily be responsive to change'. The future 'versatile maritime force' would be optimized for power projection, have global reach, sustainability and endurance and be configured for all planned scales of effort. It would be fully interoperable with other services and be able to change effectively between different levels of readiness. If this could 'be achieved by design rather than by improvisation we will have a truly future-proof naval service'.[31]

The Blair Government's interventionist impulse, for which maritime capabilities were essential, could not but help propel the Royal Navy to a near to medium future that looked in 2000 as least as bright, if not brighter, than any it had had at any time in the previous half-century. Its material strength in relation to its rivals was actually on the way up and its expertise in naval operations was still unrivalled. It remained to be seen if this promise would be fulfilled in the new century.

Notes

1 The Coming of Steam

1 A. Lambert, *The Last Sailing Battlefleet* (London, 1991) p. 1.
2 W. L. Clowes, *The Royal Navy: A History*, vol. VI (London, 1997) p. 190.
3 2448: see M. Lewis, *The Navy in Transition* (London, 1965) p. 69.
4 Total ships available, including those 'in ordinary', i.e. reserve, were almost 1000 in 1814 and less than 500 in 1820 (ibid., p. 66).
5 Lambert, op. cit., p. 16.
6 From 20.2 per cent in 1814–15 to 9.2 per cent in 1822–3. J. F. Beeler, *British Naval Policy in the Gladstone–Disraeli Era* (Stanford, CT, 1997) p. 58.
7 Lambert, op. cit., p. 5.
8 Ibid., pp. 19–21.
9 For differing views see N. A. M. Rodger, *The Admiralty* (Lavenham, 1979) and Lambert, op. cit.
10 Figure from table in E. H. H. Archibald, *The Fighting Ship in the Royal Navy* (London, 1984).
11 Archibald, ibid.; D. Lyon, *The Sailing Navy List* (London, 1993).
12 Built to the lines of a 1782 French capture. Nine were launched during the war. See Lyon, ibid., pp. 119–20.
13 See B. Greenhill and A. Giffard, *Steam Politics and Patronage: The Transformation of the Royal Navy, 1815–54* (London, 1994), p. 37.
14 Ibid., pp. 33–8.
15 Clowes, op. cit., p. 227.
16 A. Lambert, 'The Shield of Empire', in J. R. Hill, *The Oxford Illustrated History of the Royal Navy* (1995) p. 167.
17 Greenhill and Giffard, op. cit., p. 34.
18 J. C. Daly, *Russian Sea Power and the 'Eastern Question', 1827–41* (Annapolis, 1991), p. 6.
19 Codrington, quoted in ibid.

20 See figures as reported by the French in Lady Bourchier (ed.), *Memoir of the Life of Admiral Sir Edward Codrington* (London, 1875) p. 304.

21 Codrington to Turkish Admiral, 19 September 1827, ibid., p. 207.

22 Bourchier, op. cit., pp. 355–6.

23 See Daly, op. cit., p. 210 for structure of Muslim fleet. Numbers vary in different sources but these seem the most reliable.

24 Quoted Daly, op. cit., p. 15.

25 Clowes, op. cit., p. 190.

26 Lambert, *The Last Sailing Battlefleet*, p. 26.

27 Ibid., p. 27.

28 Rodger, op. cit., p. 98.

29 Compared to almost 11 per cent in 1830. Beeler, op. cit., p. 58.

30 Clowes, op. cit., p. 191.

31 Lewis, op. cit., tables in Chapter 5. There were 982 Flag Officers, Captains, Commanders and Lieutenants employed at the beginning of 1832.

32 C. J. Bartlett, *Great Britain and Sea Power* (Oxford, 1963), Appendix III.

33 Ibid., pp. 74–7.

34 Ibid., p. 95.

35 Ibid., p. 87.

36 Clowes, op. cit., p. 271.

37 Bartlett, op. cit., p. 91.

38 Ibid., pp. 92–5.

39 Lambert, *Last Sailing Battlefleet*, p. 34.

40 Clowes, op. cit., p.191.

41 Lambert, *Last Sailing Battlefleet*, p. 35.

42 Treasury to Admiralty 25/7/37, ADM1/4311, quoted by Lambert, *Last Sailing Battlefleet*, p. 35.

43 Quoted in Bartlett, op. cit., pp. 93–4.

44 Lambert, *Last Sailing Battlefleet*, p. 35.

45 D. K. Brown, *Paddle Warships* (London, 1994), pp. 12–13, 19.

46 Ibid., p. 16.

47 Ibid., pp. 82–7.

48 Lambert, *Last Sailing Battlefleet*, p. 102.

49 Ibid., pp. 105–7.

50 Bartlett, op. cit., pp. 116–22.

51 Beeler, op. cit., p. 58.

52 Clowes, op. cit., p. 191.

53 Lewis, op. cit., pp. 179–82.

54 Bartlett, op. cit., App. II.

55 Ibid., p. 129.

56   Ibid., pp. 140–1.
57   Clowes, op. cit., p. 319.
58   A. Lambert, 'Stopford, Acre 1840', in E. J. Grove, *Great Battles of the Royal Navy* (London, 1994), p. 158.
59   Quoted Clowes, op. cit., p. 322.
60   Quoted Lambert, 'Stopford, Acre 1840', p. 160.
61   Greenhill and Giffard, op. cit., p. 117.

2   The Steam Battlefleet

 1   J. F. Beeler, *British Naval Policy in the Gladstone–Disraeli Era* (Stanford, CT, 1997), p. 58.
 2   W. L. Clowes, *The Royal Navy: A History*, vol. VI (London, 1997), p. 191.
 3   Quoted by C. J. Bartlett, *Great Britain and Sea Power* (Oxford, 1963), p. 171.
 4   A. Lambert, *The Last Sailing Battlefleet* (London, 1991), p. 39.
 5   See C. Lloyd, *The Royal Navy and the Slave Trade* (London, 1968) for the classic account.
 6   Ibid., p. 28.
 7   Clowes, op. cit., p. 275.
 8   Lloyd, op. cit., App. A.
 9   Clowes, op. cit., p. 277.
10   See note 8.
11   Bartlett, op. cit., p. 153.
12   D. K. Brown, *Paddle Warships* (London, 1994), p. 30.
13   Ibid., pp. 35–6.
14   M. Lewis, *The Navy in Transition* (London, 1965), pp. 199–200.
15   Brown, op. cit., pp. 46–50.
16   D. K. Brown, *Before the Ironclad* (London, 1990), p. 79.
17   Clowes, op. cit., p. 344.
18   Brown, *Before the Ironclad*, pp. 100–1.
19   A. Lambert, 'The Screw Propeller Warship', in R. Gardner (ed.), *Steam, Steel and Shellfire* (London, 1992), pp. 32–3.
20   Ibid. p. 35; Brown, *Before the Ironclad*, pp. 10–12.
21   Brown, ibid., pp. 118–19.
22   Lambert, *The Last Sailing Battlefleet*, pp. 41–2.
23   Brown, *Before the Ironclad*, p. 122.
24   Quoted, ibid., p. 50.
25   Clowes, op. cit., p. 191.
26   Lambert, *The Last Sailing Battlefleet*, p. 54.
27   Ibid., pp. 56–7.

28 A. Lambert, *Battleships in Transition: The Creation of the Steam Battle Fleet, 1815–1860* (London, 1984), pp. 31–2.

29 Clowes, op. cit., p. 191.

30 Beeler, op. cit., p. 58.

31 Clowes, op. cit., p. 183.

32 Lewis, op. cit., pp. 185–6.

33 Lambert, *The Last Sailing Battlefleet*, p. 38.

34 A. Lambert, *The Crimean War* (Manchester, 1990), p. 33.

35 Clowes, op. cit., pp. 400–1.

36 See B. Greenhill and A. Giffard, *Steam Politics and Patronage: The Transformation of the Royal Navy, 1815–54* (London, 1994), for a full account of this event.

37 Lambert, *The Crimean War*, pp. 90–3.

38 Lambert, *The Last Sailing Battlefleet*, p. 11.

39 Clowes, op. cit., p. 440.

40 Lambert, *The Crimean War*, pp. 73–7.

41 Quoted Clowes, op. cit., pp. 414–15.

42 Lambert, *The Crimean War*, p. 160.

43 Clowes, op. cit., p. 419.

44 Mate had been a substantive rank between Midshipman and Lieutenant since 1840. It became Sub-Lieutenant in 1861.

45 Lambert, *The Crimean War*, pp. 171–2.

46 Quoted Clowes, op. cit., p. 420.

47 There is a picture of this event on p. 140 of Brown, *Before the Ironclad*.

48 Lambert, *The Crimean War*, p. 207.

49 A. Preston and J. Major, *Send a Gunboat* (London, 1967) p. 13.

50 See Brown, *Before the Ironclad*, and Lambert, *Battleships in Transition* for details of these ships.

51 Lambert, *The Crimean War*, pp. 211–12.

52 Ibid., p. 255.

53 Ibid., p. 270.

54 Ibid. p. 271.

55 Ibid., pp. 284–8.

3   The Ironclad Age

1 Quoted D. K. Brown, *Before the Ironclad* (London, 1990), p. 174.

2 A. Lambert, 'Iron Hulls and Armour Plate', in R. Gardner (ed.), *Steel, Steam and Shellfire* (London, 1992), p. 56. See also Lambert's *Warrior:*

The World's First Ironclad (London, 1987) for the best technical and strategic appreciation.

3 Quoted by O. Parkes, *British Battleships* (London, 1990), p. 50.

4 Ibid., p. 45.

5 Ibid., p. 115.

6 A. Lambert, 'The Shield of Empire', in J. R. Hill, *The Oxford Illustrated History of the Royal Navy* (Oxford, 1995), p. 184.

7 W. L. Clowes, *The Royal Navy: A History*, vol. VI (London, 1901), pp. 123–31, gives a full account of this action.

8 British chargé d'affaires to the Prince of Satsuma, quoted in Clowes, *The Royal Navy*, vol. VII, p. 196, which also see for an account of the action.

9 Clowes, ibid.

10 Parkes, op. cit., p. 34.

11 Clowes, op. cit., vol. III, pp. 202–9.

12 A. Lambert, *Battleships in Transition* (London, 1984), pp. 84–5.

13 Clowes, op. cit., vol. VII, p. 12.

14 M. J. Winton, 'Life and Education in a Technically Evolving Navy', in J. R. Hill, *The Oxford Illustrated History of the Royal Navy* (1995), p. 263.

15 M. Lewis, *The Navy in Transition* (London, 1965), pp. 187–8.

16 Ibid., pp. 255–6.

17 Lewis, ibid., p. 191.

18 Winton, op. cit., p. 263.

19 J. F. Beeler, *British Naval Policy in the Gladstone–Disradi Era* (Stanford, CT, 1997), pp. 69–70.

20 Lambert, *Battleships in Transition*, pp. 83–5.

21 D. K. Brown, *Warrior to Dreadnought* (London, 1997), p. 45.

22 Ibid., p. 47.

23 Ibid., p. 22.

24 See N. A. M. Rodger, *The Admiralty* (Lavenham, 1979), p. 109.

25 Op. cit., chapters 5 and 6.

26 See Beeler, op. cit., pp. 113–14.

27 Ibid., pp. 114–15.

28 Ibid., pp. 57–8.

29 Quoted by J. Beeler, *Birth of the Battleship* (London, 2001), pp. 93–5.

30 Beeler, *British Naval Policy*, pp. 136–9.

31 Quoted by Beeler, *Birth of the Battleship*, p. 90.

32 Beeler, *British Naval Policy*, pp. 57–8.

33 Quoted Beeler, *Birth of the Battleship*, p. 108.

34 Ibid., p. 69.
35 Brown, *Warrior to Dreadnought*, p. 82.
36 A. Cowpe, 'The Royal Navy and the Whitehead Torpedo', in B. Ranft, *Technical Change and British Naval Policy* (London, 1977).
37 Quoted by A. Preston and J. Major, *Send a Gunboat* (London, 1967), p. 35.
38 Beeler, *British Naval Policy*, pp. 28–9.
39 Ibid., pp. 30–1.
40 Preston and Major, op. cit., p. 69.
41 Clowes, op. cit., vol. VII, pp. 243–6.
42 Ibid., pp. 247–62.
43 Lambert, *Battleships in Transition*, p. 124.
44 Parkes, op. cit., p. 250.
45 Beeler, *British Naval Policy*, pp. 57–8.
46 Ibid., p. 151.
47 Rodger, op. cit., p. 112.
48 Quoted ibid., p. 153.
49 Ibid., pp. 160–1.
50 Ibid., pp. 57, 161–3.
51 Ibid., p. 164.
52 Parkes, op. cit., pp. 258–9. See also Beeler, *Birth of the Battleship*, chapter 7.
53 See report: *Naval Force for the China Station*, 2 February 1882, held in the Naval Historical Branch, Portsmouth.
54 Beeler, *Birth of the Battleship*, p. 140.
55 Ibid., p. 143.
56 For strength see Beeler, *British Naval Policy*, table 1.
57 Clowes, op. cit., vol. VII, p. 263.
58 Ibid., p. 264.
59 Clowes, op. cit., vol. VII, pp. 275–7.
60 Ibid., pp. 285–9.
61 Ibid., pp. 291–2.
62 Ibid., p. 300.
63 Parkes, op. cit., p. 285.
64 Beeler, *Birth of the Battleship*, p. 149.
65 Beeler, *British Naval Policy*, p. 185.
66 Beeler, *Birth of the Battleship*, pp. 72–3.
67 Ibid., p. 79.
68 Beeler, *British Naval Policy*, p. 186.
69 Clowes, op. cit., vol. VII, p. 12, and Beeler, *British Naval Policy*, p. 578.
70 Quoted by Beeler, *Birth of the Battleship*, p. 167.
71 Clowes, op. cit., p. 321.

72   Ibid., pp. 321–31; Parkes, op. cit., pp. 314–15; Beeler, *Birth of the Battleship*, pp. 77–8.

73   Clowes, op. cit., p. 334.

74   Parkes, op. cit., p. 325.

4   The Two-power Standard

1   Quoted in B. Ranft, 'The Protection of British Seaborne Trade and the Development of Systematic Planning for War 1860–1906', in B. Ranft, *Technical Change and British Naval Policy* (London, 1977), p. 3.

2   W. L. Clowes, *The Royal Navy: A History*, vol. VI (London, 1901), p. 10. See also O. Parkes, *British Battleships* (London, 1990), pp. 324–5.

3   See letter: Cooper Key to Phipps Hornby, quoted by Parkes, op. cit., p. 328.

4   Quoted by Parkes, ibid., p. 325.

5   Clowes, op. cit., p. 12 and J. F. Beeler, *British Naval Policy*, p. 58.

6   Parkes, op. cit., p. 329; see also J. F. Beeler, *Birth of the Battleship* (London, 2001).

7   Quoted Parkes, op. cit., p. 342.

8   See *A List of Her Majesty's Ships in Commission* (London: HMSO, 1897); copy in the Naval Historical Branch, Portsmouth.

9   See A. Marder, *British Naval Policy, 1880–1905: The Anatomy of British Sea Power* (London, 1941), p. 130.

10   Parkes, op. cit., p. 350.

11   Clowes, op. cit., p. 12 and Beeler, *British Naval Policy*, p. 58.

12   Marder, op. cit., p. 123.

13   Quoted, ibid.

14   Clowes, op. cit., p. 12.

15   D. K. Brown, *Warrior to Dreadnought* (London, 1997), p. 125.

16   Parkes, op. cit., p. 351.

17   J. Sumida, *In Defence of Naval Supremacy* (London, 1989), p. 12.

18   Parkes, op. cit., p. 352.

19   Ibid.

20   Sumida, op. cit., p. 15.

21   Ibid., p. 14.

22   Quoted, ibid., p. 15.

23   Clowes, op. cit., p. 329.

24   Sumida, op. cit., pp. 16–17.

25   A. Cowpe, 'The Royal Navy and the Whitehead Jorpedo', in Ranft, op. cit., p. 32.

26 Ibid.
27 D. Lyon, *The First Destroyers* (London, 1996).
28 Clowes, op. cit., p. 12, and Beeler, *British Naval Policy*, p. 58.
29 Marder, op. cit., pp. 175–6.
30 Ibid.
31 Ibid.
32 Ibid., pp. 194–5.
33 See G. A. Gordon, *The Rules of the Game* (London, 1996) for the best modern account of this episode.
34 For details see Brown, op. cit., p. 151.
35 Clowes, op. cit., p. 84; Marder, op. cit., p. 281.
36 Beeler, *British Naval Policy*, p. 58.
37 Figures from Parkes, op. cit.
38 Marder, op. cit., p. 285.
39 Sumida, op. cit., tables 9 and 3.
40 Clowes, op. cit., p. 12.
41 Beeler, *British Naval Policy*, table 1.
42 Clowes, op. cit., pp. 437–9.
43 N. Lambert, *Sir John Fisher's Naval Revolution* (Columbia, 1999), p. 46.
44 Quoted Sumida, op. cit., p. 23.
45 Ibid., p. 22.
46 Quoted ibid., p. 23.
47 Ibid., p. 20.
48 Ibid., pp. 23–4.
49 Ibid., tables; Beeler, *British Naval Policy*, p. 58.
50 Sumida, op. cit., p. 25.
51 The best biography of Fisher is R. F. Mackay, *Fisher of Kilverstone* (Oxford, 1973) but it must be read together with Nicholas Lambert's work.
52 See J. M. Kenworthy (Lord Strabolgi), *Sailors, Statesmen and Others: An Autobiography* (London, 1933).
53 Lambert, op. cit., p. 132.
54 Ibid., pp. 100–1.
55 A. Preston and J. Major, *Send a Gunboat* (London, 1967), pp. 169–70.
56 Lambert, op. cit., pp. 38–50.
57 Ibid., pp. 121–2.
58 See, for example, quotations in Sumida, op. cit., p. 52.
59 Fisher in the Report of the Naval Estimates Committee 16/11/05, quoted by Sumida, op. cit., pp. 58–9.
60 Quoted Sumida, op. cit., p. 60.

61 Ibid., table 3.
62 Beeler, *British Naval Policy*, p. 58.
63 Lambert, op. cit., p. 132.
64 Ibid., pp. 157–64.
65 Battenberg later recollection, see ibid.
66 Parkes, op. cit., p. 694.
67 Ibid., pp. 139–40.
68 Mackay, op. cit., p. 387.
69 Sumida, op. cit., is the main source for this controversy, although some of his conclusions have been challenged by John Brooks in his soon-to-be-published thesis.
70 Lambert, op. cit., provides a convincing case for this.
71 W. S. Churchill, *The World Crisis*. vol. 1 (London, 1923), p. 37.
72 Sumida, op. cit., p. 189.
73 Beeler, op. cit., p. 88.
74 Quoted in N. Lambert, 'Economy or Empire?', in K. Neilson and G. Kennedy, *Far Flung Lines* (London, 1997).
75 See Sumida, op. cit., pp. 256–7 and Lambert, 'Economy or Empire', pp. 62–3.
76 Quoted Lambert, ibid., p. 67.
77 Ibid., p. 188.
78 Ibid., p. 190.
79 Quoted, Mackay, op. cit., p. 416.
80 Lambert, *Sir John Fisher's Naval Revolution*, p. 202.
81 A. Marder, *From Dreadnought to Scapa Flow* (Oxford, 1961–70), vol. 1, p. 243.
82 Lambert, *Sir John Fisher's Naval Revolution*, pp. 204–5.
83 Ibid., p. 252.
84 See R. D. Layman, *Before the Aircraft Carrier* (London, 1989), p. 45.
85 See S. Roskill, *The Naval Air Service* (London: Navy Records Society, 1969), pp. 156–62.
86 See Sumida, op. cit., and Brooks, op. cit.
87 J. Sumida, 'A Matter of Timing: The Royal Navy and the Tactics of Decisive Battle', *Journal of Military History*, vol. 67 (2003), pp. 85–137.
88 See S. Roskill, *Churchill and the Admirals* (London, 1977); the quotation comes from Marder, op. cit., vol. 1, pp. 260–1.
89 Marder, ibid., p. 262.
90 Ibid., p. 259.
91 Nicholas Lambert, op. cit., p. 276; Sumida, *In Defence of Naval Supremacy*, table 3.
92 Lambert, ibid., p. 280.

93 Ibid., pp. 300–3.
94 Lambert, 'Fleet Unit and Collective Security', p. 75.
95 'Financial Limitation and Strategic Revolution', *Journal of Modern History*, vol. 67, no. 3 (1995), pp. 599–626.
96 Parkes, op. cit., p. 594.

5 The First World War

1 P. G. Halpern, *A Naval History of World War One* (London and Annapolis, 1994), pp. 24–5. See also A. Marder, *From Dreadnought to Scapa Flow* (Oxford, 1961–70), vol. 2 (1965), pp. 51–4. The fullest account of the opening moves in the North Sea is J. Goldrick, *The King's Ships Were At Sea* (Annapolis, 1984).
2 Goldrick, ibid., pp. 64–8.
3 Halpern, op. cit., pp. 30–1. See Goldrick, op. cit., chapter 5 for the best account.
4 Halpern, op. cit., p. 33. For *Aboukir, Hogue* and *Cressy* see also Marder, op. cit., pp. 56–9.
5 Ibid., pp. 188–90.
6 See Sir Edward Ashmore's memoirs, *The Battle and the Breeze* (Thrupp, 1997). Ashmore's father eventually left the submarine service as a result.
7 G. Miller, *Superior Force* (Hull, 1996), pp. 25–31.
8 Ibid., pp. 99–112.
9 Ibid., pp. 285–98; Marder, op. cit., pp. 31–41.
10 See Marder, op. cit., pp. 85–9.
11 The words are from W. S. Churchill, *World Crisis*, quoted by Marder, op. cit., vol. 2, p. 105.
12 Ibid., pp. 110–11.
13 Marder, op. cit., pp. 113–17.
14 Ibid., pp. 122–3.
15 For the designation see Fisher's list of new construction quoted in R. F. Mackay, *Fisher of Kilverstone* (Oxford, 1973), p. 494.
16 Ibid.
17 Goldrick, op. cit., p. 215.
18 Quoted by Halpern, op. cit., p. 46. See also Goldrick, chapter 11.
19 Quoted by Mackay, op. cit., p. 498. See also his excellent account of the end of Fisher's final period of office, pp. 493–505.
20 Halpern, op. cit., pp. 294.
21 Marder, op. cit., vol. 2, p. 344.

22   Cdr. K. Edwards, quoted in ibid.

23   P. G. Cooksley, *The RFC/RNAS Handbook* (Thrupp, 2000).

24   See R. D. Layman, *The Cuxhaven Raid* (London, 1985), p. 126.

25   Marder, op. cit., p. 297.

26   Hankey, quoted ibid., p. 301.

27   V. E. Tarrant, *The U-Boat Offensive, 1914–1945* (London, 1989), p. 21.

28   See Marder, vol. 2, pp. 362–3 and ADM 167/57, p. 24.

29   Marder, vol. 2, p. 313.

30   ADM 167/57, p. 14.

31   The rest of this account is based largely on my *Fleet to Fleet Encounters* (London, 1991). Other important sources are Marder, op. cit., vols 2 and 3; Halpern, op. cit.; and G. A. Gordon, *The Rules of the Game* (London, 2000).

32   Gordon is particularly important on this 'Conflict of Styles'.

33   See Marder, vol. 3, pp. 279–80.

34   Quoted ibid., p. 292, which gives an excellent account.

35   Letter in the Jellicoe papers, quoted ibid., p. 302.

36   See also Halpern, op. cit., pp. 331–2.

37   H. Popham, *Into Wind: A History at British Naval Flying* (London, 1969), pp. 260–1.

38   S. Roskill, *The Naval Air Service* (London, 1969), pp. 225–6.

39   R. D. Layman, *Before the Aircraft Carrier* (London, 1989), p. 50.

40   Ibid., and R. Sturtivant and G. Page, *Royal Navy Aircraft Serials and Units, 1911 to 1919* (Tonbridge, 1992).

41   See Marder, vol. 3, pp. 314–20.

42   Ibid., pp. 320–9.

43   Quoted ibid., p. 330.

44   Ibid.

45   Marder, vol. 4, pp. 119–20.

46   See my paper in S. Palmer and G. Williams (eds), *Charted and Uncharted Waters: Proceedings of a Conference on the Study of British Maritime History* (National Maritime Museum, 1982).

47   Quoted Marder, op. cit., vol. 4, pp. 159–60.

48   Ibid., p. 189.

49   Ibid., p. 258.

50   Ibid., p. 260.

51   Tarrant, op. cit., p. 56.

52   See W. S. Sims, *The Victory at Sea* (London, 1920). See also Marder, op. cit., vol. 4, pp. 265–7.

53   Marder, op. cit., vol. 4, p. 275.

54 Halpern, op. cit., pp. 366–8.
55 Marder, op. cit., vol. 4, p. 311.
56 See Roskill, *The Naval Air Service*, for the correspondence.
57 Marder, vol. 5, pp. 5–6.
58 Ibid., p. 9.
59 Ibid., p. 78.
60 See the figures of Commander W. Waters quoted by Marder, vol. 5, p. 103.
61 See notably the work of Captain Christopher Page.
62 National Archives ADM 167/57.
63 Ibid.
64 Ibid.

6   The Interwar Period

1 ADM 116/1774 quoted in S. Roskill, *Naval Policy Between the Wars* (London, 1968–76), vol.1, p. 214; and C. M. Bell, *The Royal Navy, Seapower and Strategy Between the Wars* (London, 2000), p. 9.
2 Cab. 27/72, quoted by Bell, op. cit., p. 9.
3 Quoted ibid., p. 10.
4 Ibid.
5 Ibid., p. 50.
6 See the Plan Red records in the US Naval War College Archives at Newport, Rhode Island.
7 Roskill, op. cit., vol. 1, pp. 125–6.
8 G. Franklin, *Britain's Anti-Submarine Capability, 1919–1939* (London 2003), pp. 57–8. The origin of the term seems to come from the initials ASD of the Anti Submarine Division of the naval staff. See also W. Hackmann, *Seek and Strike: Sonar, Antisubmarine Warfare and the Royal Navy, 1914–54* (London, 1984).
9 Quoted Roskill, op. cit., vol. 1, p. 346.
10 Ibid., p. 144. The account of the intervention is based primarily on Chapter III of this work and the unfinished Staff History of the interwar period, held in Naval Historical Branch.
11 Roskill, op. cit., p. 169.
12 Quoted in the unfinished interwar Staff History, chapter 5.
13 Roskill, op. cit., vol. 1, p. 21.
14 Lord Stamfordham, quoted in Roskill, op. cit., vol. 1, p. 34.
15 Personal letter of 22 November 1919, quoted Roskill, op. cit., vol. 1, p. 255.
16 Quoted ibid., p. 256.

17 Quoted ibid., pp. 365–6.
18 Bell, op. cit., p. 23.
19 See E. Chatfield, *It Might Happen Again* (London, 1947).
20 J. Ferris, 'The Last Decade of British Maritime Supremacy, 1919–29', in K. Neilson and G. Kennedy, *Far Flung Lines* (London, 1997).
21 Roskill, op. cit., pp. 47–8.
22 Ibid., p. 125.
23 Chatfield Papers, National Maritime Museum CHT2/1.
24 See Chatfield, op. cit. For an excellent study of lower deck problems in this period see A. Carew, *The Lower Deck of the Royal 1900–39: The Invergordon Mutiny in Perspective* (Manchester, 1981)
25 Quoted Bell, op. cit., p. 27.
26 Ibid., p. 29.
27 J. A. Maiolo, *The Royal Navy and Nazi Germany, 1933–39* (London, 1998), p. 31.
28 Chatfield Papers, letter to Dreyer, CHT4/4.
29 See Bell, op. cit., pp. 30–1.
30 Chatfield, op. cit.
31 G. Till, *Air Power and the Royal Navy, 1914–45* (London, 1979), p. 10.
32 Quoted by Till, op. cit., p. 103.
33 Quoted Roskill, op. cit., vol. 2, p. 203.
34 See Naval Aviation Staff History, vol. 1.
35 Ibid.
36 See Till, op. cit., pp. 75–7.
37 G. A. Gordon, *British Sea Power and Procurement between the Wars* (London, 1988), p. 173.
38 Quoted in J. Neidpath, *The Singapore Naval Base and the Defence of Britain's Eastern Empire, 1919–41* (Oxford, 1981), p. 148.
39 See M. Murfett, 'Admiral Sir Roger Roland Backhouse', in M. Murfett (ed.), *The First Sea Lords: From Fisher to Mountbatten* (Westport, CT and London, 1995) pp. 173–89.
40 Neidpath, op. cit., p. 149.
41 Ibid., p. 150.
42 For a study of this affair see Sir James Cable, *The Royal Navy and the Siege of Bilbao* (Cambridge, 1979).
43 Franklin, op. cit. This important new work has altered the conventional view on British preparedness for anti-submarine warfare.
44 Quoted by Franklin, ibid., p. 94.
45 J. Moretz, *The Royal Navy and the Capital Ship in the Interwar Period* (London, 2002).

7   The Second World War

1   This account of the Second World War is largely based on the official history, S. W. Roskill, *The War at Sea* vols 1–4 (London, 1954–61) and C. Barnett, *Engage the Enemy More Closely* (London, 1991).

2   For a modern account of this action see the author's *The Price of Disobedience* (Thrupp, 2000).

3   For alternative views see S. W. Roskill, *Churchill and the Admirals* (London, 1977) and Robin Brodhurst's sympathetic biography of Pound, *Churchill's Anchor* (London, 2000).

4   See S. Roskill, *Naval Policy Between the Wars* (London, 1968–76) and Barnett, op. cit. The counter view is from interviews with Admiralty scientists concerned with fire-control experiments.

5   'Pink Lists', Naval Historical Branch, Ministry of Defence.

6   M. Van Creveld, *Supplying War* (London, 1977).

7   I am grateful to David Hobbs of the Fleet Air Museum for this last important perspective.

8   M. Middlebrook and P. Mahoney, *Battleship* (London and New York, 1979) is still perhaps the best account of this action.

9   For an excellent and fair assessment of the role of special intelligence in the Battle of the Atlantic, see W. J. R. Gardner, *Decoding History: The Battle of the Atlantic and Ultra* (London, 1999).

10 This is clear from new German work revealed at RUSI in July 2003.

11 R. Sturtivant, *The Squadrons of the Fleet Air Arm* (Tonbridge, 1984), pp. 474–5.

12 For the standard work on British carriers, see N. Friedman, *British Carrier Aviation* (London, 1988).

13 P. C. Smith, *Task Force 57* (London, 1994), pp. 165–6.

14 For how these greatly enhanced numbers were trained see B. Lavery, *Hostilities Only: Training in the Wartime Royal Navy* (London, 2004).

8   The Postwar Navy

1   *The Atomic Bomb: Its Influence on Naval Warfare and Policy* (National Archives ADM1/17259).

2   For descriptions of these operations, further discussion of the rest of this chapter and full sources see E. J. Grove, *Vanguard to Trident: British Naval Policy since World War II* (Annapolis and London, 1987).

3   Minutes of the 6th and 11th Meetings of the Defence Committee (Operations), National Archives, CAB69/7.

4   DO(46)97, CAB131/3.

5   First Sea Lord's papers, ADM205/69.

6   It can be found as COS(52)361 at DEFE5/40.

7   Ibid.

8   D. K. Brown and G. Moore, *Rebuilding the Royal Navy* (London, 2003), p. 56.

9   National Archives C(54)250.

10 Statement on Naval Estimates 1955. Cmnd. 9396, para.12.

11 The term used in the committee's first report setting up the so-called COST system.

12 Quoted by M. S. Navias, *Nuclear Weapons and British Strategic Planning, 1955–58* (Oxford, 1991), p. 75.

13 Defence, Outline of Future Policy, Cmnd. 124.

14 Cmnd. 151.

15 National Archives, ADM 167/150.

16 Ibid.

17 Ministry of Defence Role of the Navy Paper, 27/9/57, DEFE7/1669.

18 P. Zeigler, *Mountbatten* (London, 1985), pp. 553–4.

19 Cmnd. 1629, para. 2.

20 See Richard Moore, *The Royal Navy and Nuclear Weapons* (London, 2001).

21 See my 'Partnership Spurned: The Royal Navy's Search for a Joint Maritime–Air Strategy East of Suez, 1961–63', in N. A. M. Rodger, *Naval Power in the Twentieth Century* (London, 1996).

22 Although a very different constitutional animal, the new Board's papers are filed in the National Archives with the Board of Admiralty's at ADM 167.

23 Brown and Moore, op. cit., pp. 61–8.

24 Ibid., pp. 90–3.

25 House of Commons debate, 11 March 1968, cols. 1008–9.

26 Deployment figures from *Navy International*, March 1964 and February 1972.

27 L. Philips, 'HMS Warrior; the Flagship in Upper Suburbia', *Navy International*, January 1972.

28 See Sir Edward Ashmore (ed. E. J. Grove), *The Battle and the Breeze* (Thrupp, 1997), p. 223.

9   The Falklands and After

1   John Nott, *Here Today Gone Tomorrow* (London, 2002), p. 108.

2   Quoted in my *Vanguard to Trident: British Naval Policy since World War II* (Annapolis and London, 1987), p. 351.

3 'The Way Forward', Cmnd. 8288, paras 32 and 34.

4 Nott, op. cit.

5 This account is based on a number of sources. British Aviation Study Group, *The Falklands Air War* (Twickenham, 1986) is still by far the fullest reference work on the forces engaged in the sea/air war and a remarkable work of reference. Denys Blakeway, *The Falklands War* (London, 1999) is an excellent modern short account that benefits from the latest research. J. D. Brown, *The Royal Navy and the Falklands War* (London, 1987) is the nearest thing to an official history of the Royal Navy's role in the war. J. Ethell and Alfred Price, *Air War South Atlantic* (London, 1983) was the first detailed operational study of the air/sea war and is still useful. L. Freedman and V. Gamba-Stonehouse, *Signals of War* (London, 1990) is the most comprehensive politico-military account of the war, seen from both sides. Cdr. 'Sharkey' Ward, *Sea Harrier Over the Falklands* (London, 1992) is a delightfully provocative account from the Fleet Air Arm perspective. Admiral Sandy Woodward (with Patrick Robinson), *One Hundred Days: The Memoirs of the Falklands Battle Group Commander* (London, 1992) is an irreplaceable source, as it gives access to Woodward's diaries that he used as a decision-making aid. It must, however, be read in conjunction with M. Clapp and E. Southby Tailtour, *Amphibious Assault Falklands* (London, 1996).

6 Statement on the Defence Estimates, 1982, Cmnd. 8529, loose Foreword.

7 Ibid.

8 Bill Jackson and Owen Bramall, *The Chiefs: The Story of the United Kingdom's Chiefs of Staff* (London, 1992) p. 283.

9 See the author's *Battle for the Fiords* (London, 1991).

10 In G. Till (ed.), *The Future of British Sea Power* (London, 1984), p. 29.

11 Sir William Jackson, *Britain's Defence Dilemma: An Inside View* (London, 1990), p. 169.

12 Quoted *Vanguard to Trident*, p. 387.

13 Quoted Jackson and Bramall, op. cit., p. 389.

14 Ibid.

15 Statement on the Defence Estimates 1992, Cmnd. 1981, p. 9.

16 *The Royal Navy in the Post War Years: N and RM Operational Deployments 1964–96*, produced by the Naval Historical Branch in 1997. Subsequent operational details come from this document.

17 See Commodore Craig's interesting account, *Call for Fire* (London, 1995). This also contains material on the Falklands.

18 *Broadsheet*. RN Annual Publication 1994–5, p. 2.

19   UK Defence Statistics, 1994 edition, table 2.7.
20   Figures from contemporary *Jane's Fighting Ships*.
21   Personal experience. See the author's book *Ark Royal* published in 2002.
22   The book, *The Fundamentals of British Maritime Doctrine*, BR 1806, was drafted by the author and Cdr. Mike Codner RN. A second edition, redrafted by Cdr. S. Haynes, appeared in 1999.
23   *The Strategic Defence Review*, Cm. 3999, p. 2.
24   *The Future Navy*, Admiralty Board Paper 2/00, paragraph 13.
25   Quoted in: *The Future Navy Operational Concept*, paper NAVB/P(01)13.
26   *Broadsheet*, 1998/9, p. 4.
27   *British Maritime Doctrine*, 2nd edn (1999), p. 171.
28   L. Willett, 'The Royal Navy TLAM and British Strategic Planning', in G. Till (ed.), *Seapower in the New Millennium* (Thrupp, 2001).
29   *Broadsheet*, 2000–2001, p. 13.
30   Ibid., p. 4.
31   Ibid., p. 3.

Bibliography

Archibald, E. H. H., *The Fighting Ship in the Royal Navy*. Poole: Blandford Press, 1984.

Ashmore, Sir Edward (ed. E. J. Grove), *The Battle and the Breeze*. Thrupp: Sutton, 1997.

Barnett, Correlli, *Engage the Enemy More Closely*. London: Hodder & Stoughton, 1991.

Bartlett, C. J., *Great Britain and Sea Power, 1815–1853*. Oxford: Oxford University Press, 1963.

Beeler, F. J., *British Naval Policy in the Gladstone–Disraeli Era, 1866–1880*. Stanford, CA: Stanford University Press, 1997.

Beeler, F. J., *The Birth of the Battleship*. London: Chatham, 2001.

Bell, C. M., *The Royal Navy, Sea Power and Strategy between the Wars*. London: Macmillan, 2000.

Brodhurst, Robin, *Churchill's Anchor*. London: Pen and Sword, 2001.

Brown, D. K., *Paddle Warships*. London: Conway, 1994.

Brown, D. K., *Before the Ironclad: The Development of Ship Design, Propulsion and Armament in the Royal Navy, 1815–1860*. London: Chatham, 1990.

Brown, D. K., *Warrior to Dreadnought: Warship Development, 1860–1995*. London: Chatham, 1997.

Brown, D. K., *The Grand Fleet: Warship Design and Development, 1906–1922*. London: Chatham, 1999.

Brown, D. K., *Nelson to Vanguard: Warship Design and Development, 1923–1945*. London: Chatham, 2000.

Brown, D. K. and Moore, George, *Rebuilding the Royal Navy: Warship Design since 1945*. London: Chatham, 2003.

Brown, J. D., *The Royal Navy and the Falklands War*. London: Leo Cooper, 1987.

Cable, Sir James, *The Royal Navy and the Siege of Bilbao*. Cambridge: Cambridge University Press, 1979.

Carew, A., *The Lower Deck of the Royal Navy, 1900–39: The Invergordon Mutiny in Perspective*. Manchester: Manchester University Press, 1981.

Chatfield, Lord, Admiral of the Fleet, *The Navy and Defence*. London: William Heinemann, 1942.

Chatfield, Lord, Admiral of the Fleet, *It Might Happen Again*. London: William Heinemann, 1947.

Clapp, M. and Tailyour, E. Southby, *Amphibious Assault Falklands*. London: Leo Cooper, 1996.

Clowes, W. L., *The Royal Navy: A History from the Earliest Times to 1900*, vols VI and VII. London: Chatham, 1997 (rev. edn).

Edmonds, Martin, *100 Years of the Trade: Royal Navy Submarines Past, Present and Future*. Lancaster: Centre for Defence and International Security Studies, 2001.

Edwards, K., *The Grey Diplomatists*. London: Rich and Cowan, 1938.

Franklin, G., *Britain's Anti-submarine Capability, 1919–1939*. London: Frank Cass, 2003.

Friedman, Norman, *British Carrier Aviation: The Evolution of the Ships and Their Aircraft*. London: Conway, 1988.

Gardner, W. J. R., *Decoding History: The Battle of the Atlantic and Ultra*. Basingstoke: Macmillan, 1999.

Goldrick, James, *The King's Ships were at Sea: The War in the North Sea, August 1914–February 1915*. Annapolis, MA: Naval Institute Press, 1984.

Gordon, G. A. H., *British Sea Power and Procurement between the Wars*. Basingstoke: Macmillan Press, 1988.

Gordon, G. A. H., *The Rules of the Game*. London: John Murray, 1996.

Graham, G. S., *The Politics of Naval Supremacy*. Cambridge: Cambridge University Press, 1965.

Greenhill, Basil and Giffard, A., *Steam Politics and Patronage*. London: Conway, 1994.

Grove, E. J., *Vanguard to Trident*. Annapolis, MA: Naval Institute Press, 1987.

Grove, E. J. (ed.), *Great Battles of the Royal Navy*. London: Cassell, 1994.

Grove, E. J., *The Defeat of the Enemy Attack on Shipping, 1939–1945*. Aldershot: Ashgate for the Navy Records Society, 1997.

Hackmann, W., *Seek and Strike: Anti-Submarine Warfare and the Royal Navy, 1914–54* London: HMSO, 1984.

Halpern, Paul G., *A Naval History of World War I*. Annapolis, MA: Naval Institute Press, 1994.

Hill, J. R. (ed.), *The Oxford Illustrated History of the Royal Navy*. Oxford: Oxford University Press, 1995.

Howse, Derek, *Radar at Sea: The Royal Navy in World War 2*. Basingstoke: Macmillan, 1993.

Lambert, Andrew, *Battleships in Transition: The Creation of the Steam Battle Fleet, 1815–1860*. London: Conway, 1984.

Lambert, Andrew, *The Crimean War: British Grand Strategy against Russia, 1853–1856*. Manchester: Manchester University Press, 1991.

Lambert, Andrew, *The Last Sailing Battle Fleet: Maintaining Naval Mastery, 1815–1850*. London: Conway, 1991.

Lambert, Nicholas A., *Sir John Fisher's Naval Revolution*. Columbia, SC: University of South Carolina Press, 1999.

Lambert, Nicholas A., *The Submarine Service, 1900–1918*. Aldershot: Ashgate for the Navy Records Society, 2001.

Lavery, Brian, *Hostilities Only: Training in the Wartime Royal Navy*. London: National Maritime Museum, 2004.

Layman, R. D., *Before the Aircraft Carrier: The Development of Aviation Vessels, 1849–1922*. London: Conway, 1989.

Layman, R. D., *The Cuxhaven Raid*. London: Conway, 1985.

Levy, James P., *The Royal Navy's Home Fleet in World War II*. Basingstoke: Palgrave Macmillan, 2003.

Lewis, M., *The Navy in Transition: A Social History, 1814–1864*. London: Hodder & Stoughton, 1965.

Lloyd, Christopher, *The Navy and the Slave Trade*. London: Frank Cass, 1968.

Lyon, David, *The Sailing Navy List: All the Ships of the Royal Navy Built, Purchased and Captured, 1688–1860*. London: Conway, 1993.

Lyon, David, *The First Destroyers*. London: Chatham, 1996.

Mackay, R. F., *Fisher of Kilverstone*. Oxford: Oxford University Press, 1973.

Maiolo, J. A., *The Royal Navy and Nazi Germany, 1933–39*. Basingstoke: Palgrave Macmillan, 1998.

Marder, Arthur, *British Naval Policy, 1880–1903: The Anatomy of British Sea Power*. London: Putnam, 1941.

Marder, Arthur, *From the Dreadnought to Scapa Flow: The Royal Navy in the Fisher Era, 1904–1919* (5 volumes). Oxford: Oxford University Press, 1961–70.

Moore, Richard, *The Royal Navy and Nuclear Weapons*. London: Frank Cass, 2001.

Moretz, J., *The Royal Navy and the Capital Ships in the Interwar Period: An Operational Perspective*. London: Frank Cass, 2002.

Morriss, Roger, *Cockburn and the British Navy in Transition*. Exeter: Exeter University Press, 1997.

Murfett, Malcolm (ed.), *The First Sea Lords: From Fisher to Mountbatten*. Westport, CT, and London: Praeger, 1995.

Neidpath, J., *The Singapore Naval Base and the Defence of Britain's Eastern Empire*. Oxford: Oxford University Press, 1981.

Neilson, K. and Kennedy, G., *Far Flung Lines: Studies in Imperial Defence in Honour of Donald Mackenzie Schurman*. London: Frank Cass, 1997.

Parkes, O., *British Battleships: A History of Design Construction and Armament*. London: Leo Cooper, 1990.

Penn, Geoffrey, *Fisher, Churchill and the Dardanelles*. Yorkshire: Leo Cooper, 1999.

Popham, H., *Into Wind: A History of British Naval Flying*. London: Hamish Hamilton, 1969.

Preston, A. and Major, J., *Send a Gunboat*. London: Conway Maritime Press, 1967; new. edn 2003.

Ranft, Brian (ed.), *Technical Change and British Naval Policy*. London: Hodder & Stoughton, 1977.

Rodger, N. A. M., *The Admiralty*. Lavenham: Terrence Dalton, 1979.

Rodger, N. A. M. (ed.), *Naval Power in the 20th Century*. Basingstoke: Macmillan, 1996.

Roskill, Stephen, *Churchill and the Admirals*. London: Collins, 1977.

Roskill, Stephen, *The Naval Air Service, vol. 1: 1908–1918*. London: Spottiswoode, Ballantyne for the Navy Records Society, 1969.

Roskill, Stephen, *Naval Policy between the Wars*, 2 vols. London: Collins, 1968–76.

Roskill, Stephen, *The War at Sea*, 3 vols (vol. 3 in two parts). London: HMSO, 1954–61.

Smith, P. C., *Task Force 57: The British Pacific Fleet, 1944–1945*. London: Crecy, 1994.

Speller, Ian, *The Role of Amphibious Warfare in British Naval Policy, 1945–56*. Basingstoke: Palgrave Macmillan, 2001.

Sumida, Jon T., *In Defence of Naval Supremacy: Finance, Technology and British Naval Policy, 1889–1914*. London: Unwin Hyman, 1989.

Tarrant, V. E., *The U-boat Offensive, 1914–1945*. London: Arms and Armour, 1989.

Till, Geoffrey, *Air Power and the Royal Navy, 1914–45: A Historical Survey*. London: Jane's, 1979.

Woodward, Admiral Sandy and Robinson, P., *One Hundred Days: The Memoirs of the Falklands Battle Group Commander*. London: HarperCollins, 1992.

General Index

Index of Ships

RN ships

Abdiel (support ship), 254
Aboukir (battleship), 84, 109
Achates (destroyer), 205
Achilles (ironclad), 40, 62, 67; (light cruiser), 184
Active (corvette), 60
Adventure (cruiser minelayer), 154, 164
Afridi (Tribal class destroyer), 187
Agamemnon (steam ship of the line), 26, 29, 31, 35, 36; (ironclad), 59, 64; (battleship), 88
Agincourt (ironclad), 41, 62, 67, 71; (battlecruiser), 106; (battleship), 110
Aigle (wooden corvette), 54
Ajax (blockship), 25; (ironclad turret ship), 59, 64; (light cruiser), 152, 184
Alacrity (despatch vessel), 86
Alban (paddle steamer), 33
Albion (ship of the line), 6; (Hermes-class carrier), 214, 225, 238; (LPD), 260
Alecto (wooden paddle sloop), 23, 24
Alexandra (centre battery ironclad), 53, 59, 62, 66, 67
Algerine (sloop), 86
Algiers (two decker), 27, 35
Amazon (destroyer), 155
Ambuscade (destroyer), 155
Amethyst (corvette), 60; (frigate), 217

Amphion (screw frigate), 33; (cruiser), 108
Anson (barbette ship), 65; (battleship), 72
Antelope (Type 21 frigate), 247
Arabic (passenger liner), 119
Ardent (destroyer), 126; (Type 21 frigate), 247
Archimedes (screw demonstrator), 24
Arethusa (sailing frigate), 31
Argonaut (Dido class light cruiser), 210
Argus (converted liner), 140; (carrier), 200
Argyll (frigate), 261
Ariadne (cruiser), 97
Arial (gunboat), 60
Ark Royal (seaplane carrier), 104, 120, 152; (carrier), 176, 183, 188, 193, 194, 195; (armoured hanger carrier), 214, 223, 224–5, 230, 233, 234; (rebuilt carrier), 238, 239, 240; (Invincible class carrier), 245, 250, 255, 258
Arrow (merchantman), 43
Asia (two-decker), 6, 7
Athenia (liner), 183
Atherstone (Hunt class), 254
Atlantic Conveyor (transport ship), 246
Attacker (escort carrier), 203

Shore establishments

U-boats and other submarines

Non-British aircraft